Praise for Jeff Goulding's Books

Red Odyssey: Liverpool FC 1892–2017

'This eminently readable and beguiling addition to the Liverpool FC story should adorn every Red's bookshelf.'

Racing Post

'Celebrates the club's incredible journey, recounting tales and memories that tell of friendships, rivalries and of course trophies. He brings to life this pre-war era using his extensive knowledge of the club's history tallied with reports in local media and club folklore. Provides a complete picture of Liverpool's colourful history. Here's looking forward to *Red Odyssey* part two.'

It's Round and It's White

'A history of Liverpool, but one written in an affectionate way, and from a personal perspective. Particularly informative on the pre-Bill Shankly years, which are much less well documented than the subsequent decades.'

Backpass Magazine

We Conquered All of Europe: Red Odyssey II

'*We Conquered All of Europe* brings things back to life. Although you know the ending you will still get that funny feeling as you go through this account of what was a wonderful season and how the past four years under Jürgen and company have seen Liverpool Football Club rise again.'

Red All Over the Land

'Excellent as always. I'd highly recommend it.'

Dave Usher, The Liverpool Way

'*We Conquered All of Europe* provides a unique first-hand view from around the stands, from not only Jeff but a plethora of supporters who you discover each find varying degrees of significance in moments which have transpired over the last four years. It's a journey from the stands, grounded in emotion – with a touch of humour – which is then delicately intertwined with statements from the media and Klopp at the time, with views from former players Jamie Carragher, Jimmy Case and John Barnes also adding another valuable perspective. And as a result, I found myself transported into the exact moment of time each chapter homed in on; whether that be stood in Anfield for the spine-tingling rendition of "You'll Never Walk Alone" against Borussia Dortmund or the ferocious Anfield atmosphere that awaited Man City in Europe.'

This is Anfield

Stanley Park Story: Life, Love and the Merseyside Derby

'Crossing football fact with the fictional is an art form, which few authors can pull off. A genre popularised by Nick Hornby's iconic *Fever Pitch* and continued adeptly by *Mr Shankly's Photograph, The Damned United* and *Red or Dead*, Jeff Goulding's brilliant Stanley Park Story is the modern benchmark and successor to the football faction greats.'

These Football Times Lob Podcast

'The author's storytelling is simply brilliant. A wonderful knack of informing the reader whilst entertaining them at the same time. A respected expert in the knowledge of the history of Liverpool FC and the social dynamics of the city, Goulding is well versed to tell this football story of sporting rivalry.'

Fields of Anfield Road

'An insight into the social and cultural history that created one of the game's most passionate rivalries, the book offers perspective from both those who sit on the Kop and those who frequent the Gwladys Street.'

Official Liverpool FC Magazine

'Jeff Goulding makes it the real thing as he brings to life a genuine rivalry which exists in households and families throughout Liverpool. Captures the humour of the best of times and the darker mood of the not so good social times and of life in general. Encapsulates life on Merseyside in the way only few have previously done.'

Red All Over the Land

'*Stanley Park Story* is a history lesson with a heart; a generational saga set against the backdrop of 50 years of Merseyside footballing rivalry telling the story of lives that all of us from the area will find familiar. Highly recommended.'

Ian Salmon, playwright, and author

'Brilliant.'

This Is Anfield

'Full-on Merseyside football.'

David Maddock, *Daily Mirror*

'A rich tapestry. Evocative and always entertaining. A hugely engaging novel, it is also a documentary of the times in which the story takes place. So rich is the setting that on finishing the book, I almost wished it had an index. Highly recommended.'

Public Reading Rooms

'Jeff Goulding has achieved something unexpected and remarkable with both the style and content of this book, which more than deserves its place among the pantheon of great books about football in Liverpool.'

Mike Morris, co-director, Writing on the Wall

Champions

Under Lockdown

Champions

Under Lockdown

Red Odyssey III
Jürgen and the Holy Grail

JEFF GOULDING

pitch

First published by Pitch Publishing, 2020

Pitch Publishing
A2 Yeoman Gate
Yeoman Way
Worthing
Sussex
BN13 3QZ
www.pitchpublishing.co.uk
info@pitchpublishing.co.uk

A CIP catalogue record is available for this book from the British Library.

ISBN 978 1 78531 718 7

Typesetting and origination by Pitch Publishing

Printed and bound by TJ International, Padstow, UK

Contents

Dedication

I dedicate this book to all the essential workers who have helped us through the coronavirus crisis in 2020. To the cleaners, the delivery drivers, the bin collectors, the postal workers, the shop workers, the carers, the nurses, the doctors, paramedics and all who labour in healthcare and elsewhere to keep us safe.

But I must also pay tribute to the eternally maligned football supporter. Singled out so often as not to be trusted and forced to fight to have their voices heard, they have nonetheless been a beacon of community solidarity and social responsibility both before and during this crisis. I know they will continue to do so long after it is over. Therefore, this book is also dedicated to the magnificent people at Fans Supporting Foodbanks.

You'll Never Walk Alone.

Acknowledgements

AS EVER, I would like to acknowledge the contributions of many people who have helped bring this book to life. It is their unique viewpoints that illuminate the social history of our club and provide the context behind each of the stories that made up this remarkable season.

Thanks must go to the many Liverpool supporters who shared their views and experiences of this most remarkable season: Peter Carney; the Wadsworth family; Bill, Jacqueline, Susan, David, Jamie, Ty and Catherine Dunne; Lee Tracy; Andy 'Toggsy' James; George Scott; John Whitehead; Ricky Olivares; Ian Salmon; Keith Salmon; Mari Lewis; Marie Eakins; John Thompson; Tony Zeverona; Ricky Olivares; Stephen Lawrence; Tracey Murray; Jayne Rodgers; Cal Maloney; Graeme James Strain; Gary Stanford; Victor Gill; Karen Elizabeth Gill; David King; Dermot and Fionn Nolan; Ray Carrick; Val Westbury Birchall; Helen Littlejohn; Justin Shanahan; Christopher Wood; Kieran Smith; Joe Goulding; Sean MacGregor; Kevin Cowdall; Ruth Rule-Mullen; Chet Murarji; Dhriti Bania; Moushumi Bora; David Goulding; Fahd Basheer; Louise Lacey; Matthieu Pierre and Nassos Siotropos. Your contributions are very much appreciated.

To the many groups, businesses, organisations, officials and representatives who were generous with their time and their views: Liverpool FC; Brighton and Hove Albion FC; Amanda

Ellem of LFC New South Wales Official Supporters' Club; Andy Beijer of Liverpool FC Swedish Branch; the voice of Anfield – George Sephton; Deputy Chief Constable Mark Roberts of South Yorkshire Police; Assistant Chief Constable Rob Carden of Merseyside Police; Ian Maloney of Love Follow Conquer; City of Liverpool FC's Peter Furmedge; Ian Byrne MP; the folk at Hat Scarf or a Badge and Transalpino; Fans Supporting Foodbanks; Spirit of Shankly; Jay McKenna of the North West TUC; Councillor Harry Doyle; I say a heartfelt thank you.

Appreciation also goes to the many writers, broadcasters and journalists whose insights have been invaluable: *These Football Times*'s Gary Thacker and Will Sharp; Copa 90's Ben Webb; This is Anfield's Joanna Durkan; Henry Jackson and Jack Lusby; the *Morning Star*'s James Nalton; Redmen TV's Chris Pajak and Ross Chandley; The Liverpool Way's Dave Usher; *Red All Over the Land*'s John Pearman; Across the Park's Phil Roberts; BBC Radio Merseyside Sport's Paul Salt; Football writer and historian Peter Kenny Jones; Liverpool FC Museum curator Stephen Done; Steven Kelly of the *Irish Examiner*; the *Daily Mirror*'s David Maddock; the *Liverpool Echo*'s Dan Kay; Steven Scragg of This is Anfield and These Football Times; Aaron Cutler of The Anfield Wrap, Reds legend and Sky Sports pundit, Jamie Carragher and This is Anfield; Bundesliga journalist Chris Williams.

Finally, to the many supporters of other clubs, who agreed to speak to me and provide their viewpoints, including: Derek King; Chris Rule-Mullen; Ian Pierce Hayes; Alex Dutton; Robert Daniels; Aidan Williams and Richard Dooler; Gary Judge and Dave Kelly; I'd like to say a big thank you.

Foreword

THIS BOOK is the third in the *Red Odyssey* series. When I finished the first in 2018, which marked the 125th anniversary of the birth of Liverpool FC, I didn't anticipate adding another chapter until the 130th milestone had been reached. However, since then the club I love has achieved so much, there have been so many new stories written, so much history made and enough new heroes to fill not just one, but two new volumes.

So rich is the story of this football club that I am compelled to keep writing. As I delve into each experience, I am often transported back to those instances in time, reminded of what I was feeling and how the world looked in those moments. I relive each of them, and they lift me. I hope you, the reader, will feel some of that too, as you wind your way through the pages.

Now more than ever, as we contend with a global pandemic and the agony of loss and lockdown, we need the joy that these memories bring. That's the power of football for so many of us. That's the power of Liverpool FC for me.

This instalment is the story of a generational quest. For 30 years we have waited for its conclusion and for the prize to be delivered. Three long decades punctuated with painful near-misses have eaten away at the souls of countless Liverpool supporters. Prior to the arrival of Jürgen Klopp in the winter of 2015, many of us had come to believe we may never see another league title in our lifetime. It had become a millstone around our necks. A burden that not even a slurry of domestic and European silverware could alleviate.

Since I stood on the Kop, and watched the Reds crowned champions for the 18th time, in 1990, I have raised four children. My eldest is a regular of home and European away-days. He was born in 1995, and though his eyes have seen wondrous things while following Liverpool, he had not seen them crowned champions of England. I had wanted that for him for so long.

He had seen Liverpool win two European Cups, a UEFA Cup, two FA Cups, four League Cups, and an assortment of Community Shields and UEFA Super Cups. However, there had always been a gaping hole lurking at the heart of the club's trophy room. One that left an ache in the bellies of every Liverpool supporter, and weighed heavily on the shoulders of every player.

At the end of a career most could only dream of, Steven Gerrard, writing the opening pages of his autobiography, would focus not on his many cup final goals, or the trophies he had lifted at venues like Cardiff, Wembley and Istanbul, but on the pain of *that* slip at Anfield. The surrender of the league title in the fag end of the 2013/14 season had overshadowed the glittering career of a one-club man who had single-handedly elevated his team above their station.

Gerrard, carved from the streets of Huyton and thrust into a red shirt, knew what every Liverpool supporter knows. The league title means more than all the rest because it means domestic domination and winning it pushes the mute button once and for all, silencing our critics and restoring the Reds to their 'fucking perch'.

This was the legacy inherited by Klopp. In 2015 he knew that no matter how many trophies the club won under his stewardship, one above all others was craved by generations of Liverpool fans. For all Europe holds a special place in the hearts of Reds everywhere, all of us wanted to win that 19th league title. If Jürgen could deliver that holy grail, statues would one day be erected in his honour. He would join the pantheon of legends at the club and become immortal.

So, as the 2019/2020 season got under way, in the afterglow of that remarkable Champions League trophy parade, he had just one mission. He had conquered all of Europe, but there remained an island outlier. And he would not rest until Liverpool were the undisputed kings of England too.

He would achieve that of course, but he would also conquer the world. In doing so, Liverpool would become the first club ever to simultaneously hold the Champions League, UEFA Super Cup, Club World Cup and Premier League. He had delivered the holy grail and much more.

For all the magnificence of his achievement, there are those who have said that Liverpool's 19th league title is not a real one; that it is tainted or in some way inferior. The suspension of football in March 2020, and the need to play behind closed doors upon its resumption handed ammunition to Liverpool's detractors and allowed them to question the validity of the season. Some have called for an asterisk to be placed next to the title, as if that could devalue it.

An asterisk could only elevate Liverpool's triumphs, and illustrate just how remarkable this season has been. A title won under lockdown, against all odds and added to the world and European crowns, in the most one-sided race in the history of the game, yes, that does deserve an asterisk. For this is no ordinary team. It may be the greatest in Liverpool's history.

However, while it is true to say that there were voices who attempted to undermine Liverpool's achievement during this incredible season, even to the point of calling for the campaign to be declared 'null and void', I don't wish to amplify these or give them more prominence than they deserve. I've come to realise the dangers of living in social media bubbles, where, if we're not careful, we can get a warped view of the world and of each other.

I can of course see that for every keyboard warrior tapping away about conspiracy theories and tainted titles, there is an army of football fans, whose allegiances lie with other clubs but who think fairly and critically about the game. Now, more than ever, I see the value in seeking out the things we have in common and not resorting to stereotypes.

So, if some future historian is reading this book – I should be so lucky – then I want them to understand how tribalism and rivalry coloured the views of many towards Liverpool's title charge. However, they should also know that those voices, though vocal and loud, didn't represent the majority. The records should also reflect the esteem in which this team and its achievements were held.

Clearly though, this season is as remarkable for the context in which it was played out, as it is for the football itself. The impact of the global coronavirus pandemic on the sport, society and people cannot be ignored and is woven into each chapter. The disease has been crippling in many ways, But, it has also taught us the value of community, solidarity, kindness and how much this game matters to us all.

Prior to the outbreak, Conservative politicians publicly talked about 'low-value people', questioned the benefits of immigration, and sought to judge a person's worth according to their income or the job they do. Three months into this public health crisis, we now understand more than they ever could, that society cannot function without the shop workers, the delivery drivers, the bin men and the cleaners, the nurses, the doctors and all the other healthcare workers who toil so hard and risk so much to keep us safe.

Indeed, the health service would not be able to keep us safe without the army of immigrants who staff it, alongside those who by accident of birth have been born on these shores. As Bill Shankly once said, 'Everyone working for each other, everyone sharing the rewards. It's the way I see football. It's the way I see life.'

During the health crisis of 2020 we have surely been taught the enduring value of these words. We have also seen the ability of football to unite people and bring about real change.

One day, the pandemic will be over, we will return to football stadiums in our thousands, and Liverpool supporters will revel in the glory of the 2019/20 season for years to come. But the fans of all clubs will feel a sense of joy at its return also. We all share that common bond.

The children and grandchildren of my generation now have their own stories to tell. They will doubtlessly bore their own grandkids with tales of how Liverpool's young guns humiliated the Blues of Everton, of how not one team in any of Europe's top five leagues could match Klopp's heroes, how they conquered the bloody world and how not even a global pandemic could prevent them from being crowned masters of all they surveyed.

The relief and the joy at ending 30 years of pain can never be dulled though, and the achievement can never be undermined. In this volume you will read first-hand accounts of the feelings of supporters, determined to revel in the glory of our *Champions Under Lockdown* regardless of the wishes of their detractors. It's been a long time coming, but now it's here. In these pages, I give you the whole story, as seen through the eyes of those who lived it.

Until we meet again my friends, you'll never walk alone.

Introduction

IN THE summer of 2019, Liverpool Football Club was arguably in rude health. It was advancing in all spheres. The holy trinity of manager, players and supporters was stronger than at any time since the days of Bill Shankly. Doubters were now undeniably devout believers. Off the field, the new Main Stand was three years old and pouring cash into the club coffers, helping to propel Liverpool up the money leagues.

On the playing side, Klopp had at last delivered silverware. As trophies go, he had won arguably the biggest prize of them all, wiping the slate clean after the misery of Basel and Kiev and enshrining Madrid as yet another glorious chapter in a history already littered with heroic deeds. The dark days of ownership debacles were a distant memory and Liverpool once more were kings of Europe.

The celebrations witnessed on the banks of the mighty Mersey were without parallel and as the street sweepers brushed away the ticker tape, and we all wandered off home, we dreamed of greater glory to come. There was a Community Shield at Wembley and a UEFA Super Cup in Istanbul to win. If they could triumph once more on the Bosphrus, then the Reds would again become the most decorated club in English football history, taking back their crown from Manchester United. Beyond that lay the FIFA Club World Cup in Qatar and the chance to become champions of the world.

Yet, despite all of that, a deep yearning that had burned in the bellies of Kopites for 30 years was slowly morphing into a sense of destiny. At long last Liverpool supporters felt they had a team capable of competing and winning over 38 gruelling games.

Winning the league is seen as the true test of a football team, a demonstration of fighting spirit, consistency and class. Liverpool had come agonisingly close at the end of 2019, amassing 97 points, and yet still falling short to Pep Guardiola's Manchester City. If they could go one better in 2019/20, we all knew that the celebrations would dwarf even the magnificence of the parade we had just witnessed.

Ahead lay nothing but optimism, summer holidays and dreams of future conquest. Klopp had assembled a squad that needed only minor adjustment and a few tactical tweaks. He would add a splash of youth in Harvey Elliott and Sepp van den Berg and goalkeeping cover in the form of Andy Lonergan and Adrián San Miguel. Takumi Minamino would join later, in January. There were no stellar signings, and nobody moaned. What could possibly go wrong?

Liverpool would go on to rewrite footballing history during a run that spanned 29 games, before football and indeed the world was put on lockdown due to the COVID-19 pandemic. They would win 27 of those games, before the course of world history intervened. Their football was nearly always sublime and when it couldn't be, grit and determination took over.

Faced with Liverpool's seemingly unstoppable march to a 19th league title, some rivals and pundits would variously drool or attempt to downplay the club's achievements. While some would graciously acknowledge the brilliance of Klopp's charges, detractors – and of those there were many – strained to find reasons to undermine what felt like an inevitable coronation in May 2020.

After spending most of the previous season claiming Liverpool would suffer with the introduction of the Video Assistant Referee

(VAR), a sizeable chunk of rival supporters took to social media to now claim that the club had only progressed because they were being given a leg-up by the FA, UEFA, the Premier League and Stockley Park. The phrase 'tainted title' became the rallying cry of the desperate and perhaps served as a perverse form of flattery, confirming that despite no league title for 30 years, the Reds remained the biggest show in town.

Earlier in the campaign, some Liverpool supporters had mused that the only thing that could stop this team would be a world war. When Donald Trump seemed intent on starting one with Iran, we began to worry. However, it would be the emergence of an invisible enemy that would prove to be the greatest threat to Jürgen Klopp's ambitions.

Liverpool would prove to be so good that only the cancellation of football itself could deny them their crown. Social media bubbles aside, Klopp and his players had earned tremendous admiration during a campaign that tore up the record books on a weekly basis.

Many would recognise that to strike these achievements from the record books would have been criminally unjust, both from a Liverpool-centric perspective and a footballing one too. They recognised that the call to declare such a season 'null and void' was a cry born out of jealousy and tribalism, and one that would have robbed the game of one of the greatest football teams of all time.

Rather than being decried for their achievements, Liverpool became a beacon for others. If nothing else, the 2019/20 season showed that a team could win without the riches of an oligarch or the funds of an entire state. That sound man-management, charisma and sheer force of personality could transform players who were merely great into world beaters. It proved that desire and persistence could overcome all obstacles and propel a team to a historic 25-point lead at the top of the table. To declare that all of that should be stricken from the records would have robbed football of one of its greatest stories.

As the Reds entered the new year at the summit of the table, having been crowned champions of the world and seemingly invincible on the home front, news of a deadly new virus was occupying our thoughts and creeping into conversations. Within months it would sweep the planet, causing tragedy and misery wherever it went, threatening to crash economies and bringing sport to a halt.

Football could never be more important than life and death and the eventual suspension of the Premier League, in March 2020, was right and proper. Large gatherings of supporters in close quarters was the perfect breeding ground for a virus that had already killed thousands. Indeed, many of us felt that the cessation of sport came one game too late.

The decision to allow thousands of Spanish supporters to enter Liverpool and Anfield, at the height of that country's pandemic, will be discussed later in this book. It will forever be a blot on the records of those who allowed it to happen.

Jürgen Klopp, quoting Italian coach Arrigo Sacchi, would later say, 'Football is the most important of the least important things.' It is clearly not as important as life and health. As such, Liverpool supporters accepted that their title dream had to be put on hold.

The decision to suspend football, initially until April but then extended until 17 June, taken on 13 March, was therefore correct. However, its timing meant that Liverpool were just two wins and six points from glory. The finishing line was so close we could see it. Now all we could do was wait and hope.

Eventually though, football would return under the guise of 'Project Restart'. That would ensure a remarkable and historic conclusion to the Premier League campaign. Football and life would never be the same again, but Liverpool would at last reach for and grasp hold of their holy grail. The celebrations would be unique also. With the parade on hold, supporters would find their own ways to mark the achievement and the triumph would taste just as sweet.

After 30 long and painful years, Liverpool Football Club had climbed back upon their perch and their nearest rivals were a distant second. The achievement would mark the end of a quite incredible campaign, one without parallel and perhaps even worthy of that asterisk so many had claimed should be placed next to it.

When Klopp arrived in 2015, he said, 'I am not the one to come in and say we're going to conquer the world.' However, by the end of the 2019/20 season, that is exactly what Liverpool had done.

They achieved that against all the odds. There could not be a more deserving group of champions. This is their story, it is ours too, woven together in the rich tapestry that is the history of this football club. It is our Red Odyssey.

PRELUDE TO BATTLE

Liverpool FC: June 2019–August 2019

The Phoney War: A Mixed Bag of 'Friendlies' but a 'Little Diamond' Sparkles

Our moods could not have been better. We bombarded social media with memes, variously showing Jürgen Klopp counting to six on his fingers, while perched precariously on the top deck of an open-topped bus, or of a gleaming European Cup with the number six next to it, on top of it or under it. The number six featured heavily in our conversations with everyone to be fair.

Many of us celebrated one-day, one-week, and one-month anniversaries. We were, as predicted, unbearable. Why shouldn't we be. Liverpool were champions of Europe; we had missed out on the Premier League by the slimmest of margins and we were convinced we could go one better in the forthcoming season. But, if we didn't, we could always just remind everyone that we won it six times, in Madrid.

This was the phoney war. A period of basking in past glory and rubbing your rivals' noses in it. At times like this, it's best to make the most of it. After all, who knows what's round the corner. And, to be fair, there are few better at milking success than Liverpool fans. We have proudly earned our 'unbearable' tag.

Throughout June and July, the sun shone, Britain was experiencing a heatwave with temperatures eventually reaching a record 38.7°C. TV audiences in their millions watched the Women's World Cup, with almost 12 million taking in England's 2-1 defeat to the USA in the semi-final. Meanwhile, Brexit rumbled on, and we all discovered that 'proroguing parliament' was a thing governments did when they didn't fancy being scrutinised.

There was also tension in the Middle East as Iran seized a British tanker, while Jeremy Hunt warned of 'severe consequences', and Boris Johnson became prime minister by winning the Conservative Party's leadership contest. The close-season simply flew by.

Before we knew it, pre-season games were upon us. Liverpool were scheduled to kick-off their preparations for 2019/20 with a visit to Tranmere Rovers. Liverpool dispensed with them with ease, winning 6-0. Then came a trip to Valley Parade and a 3-1 victory over Bradford City.

These were comfortable run-outs as players shook off the rust of the summer and youngsters like Rhian Brewster, Curtis Jones and Bobby Duncan did their best to convince Klopp and everyone else that they could break into one of the greatest Liverpool sides in the club's history. This too was something of a phoney war, and we all knew bigger challenges lay ahead.

A few days after the routing of Tranmere and Bradford, Liverpool would fly out to America and a three-game tour in which they would face much sterner tests. Lying in wait were Borussia Dortmund, Sevilla and Sporting Lisbon.

The Reds faced Klopp's old side, Dortmund, on 19 July at the Notre Dame Stadium. The ground holds some 81,000 spectators, but a mixture of ticket prices and perhaps the continuing second-class status of 'soccer' in the United States meant it would only be half full.

Liverpool were missing several players, including striker Mo Salah. Virgil van Dijk and Jordan Henderson didn't appear until the hour mark and once more the youngsters were given a run. The sun was shining, and it was only pre-season after all. Nobody reads too much into pre-season, do they?

Well Klopp did. The boss wasn't too keen on the pitch. He told the waiting media at a routine press call after the game, 'You want to talk to me about the pitch? What do you think? Difficult because it's not a soccer pitch. They put grass on it. Everybody tries his best, but in the end you saw these two teams can play much better football. It's difficult when the ball is not rolling. That's an important part of the game – that the ball rolls.'

Liverpool had lost 3-2. That didn't stop the supporters making the most of their chance to see the Reds up close and personal though.

The Indy, a supplement of *America Today*, observed, 'Pageantry in the red-bathed stands was on display as a heavily pro-Liverpool crowd sang along to the club's traditional "You'll Never Walk Alone" and "Allez, Allez, Allez" from the outset.'

Next up was a game against Sevilla. The game against the Spaniards was hardly an ideal outing either, with Liverpool going down to another defeat.

In truth, all Jürgen cared about was fitness, organisation, and tactics. This was a time to bond the group together and work on plans for a gruelling 38-game season, if the squad could come through it without any setbacks in terms of injury, then it will have been time well spent. Ahead of the tour, he played down expectation and told the media, 'Hopefully, we can go through this period without injuries. That would be very, very important. It would be cool.

'The boys are a year older; the boys are a year further in their career. They're more experienced in different situations. That's what we have to use – try to use – and then let's play football again, against a lot of very, very strong teams. The others don't sleep. They develop as well, so we have to be ready.'

The final game of the US tour was played against Sporting Lisbon at Yankee Stadium. It finished 2-2, and the Reds' preparations had so far failed to set the world alight. But this was only pre-season, right? Nobody cares about pre-season, do they?

The truth is, although we say we don't, we do. It wasn't always this way. There was a time, when I was a kid, when I didn't even know we were playing friendly games. What a glorious time that must have been for the club's coaching staff. Imagine watching the portly shapes of Liverpool players dragging their arses, which were on average 5lb bigger than they had been a matter of weeks earlier, around the world's stadiums. Thankfully there was no 24-hour sports coverage back then, or we would have doubtlessly entered every season fearing the worst, instead of the unbridled optimism that usually drove those eventually slimmed-down and toned-up players to glory.

There were now just two games remaining before Liverpool took on Manchester City at Wembley in the Community Shield. Now there's another 'pre-season friendly' that's taken on even greater significance in recent years. More of that later.

If Liverpool were to satisfy the army of experts who pour over these arguably meaningless fixtures, then they would need to up their performances significantly. Jürgen had it covered, but they worry about these things.

The Reds travelled to Edinburgh to play Napoli at Murrayfield and were beaten 3-0. They then faced Olympique Lyonnais and won 3-1. Who knows what would have happened had they also lost to the French side?

Not surprisingly, Goal.com saw problems for Liverpool. After watching the Reds limp through pre-season without capturing the heights of the previous campaign, the website suggested Klopp's men were still a little sluggish. The implication was that City may have a little too much for the Reds at Wembley.

'Liverpool must find an extra gear against Manchester City in Sunday's Community Shield despite ending their pre-season slump,' read its post-Lyon match report.

For the local media, the focus was on the Reds securing the services of a prodigious talent. Youngster Harvey Elliott had arrived at the Liverpool Academy from Fulham a year earlier and was about to sign his first professional contract in the summer of 2019. The *Liverpool Echo* drooled, 'Whether it's leaving opponents in his wake with a piece of trickery or progressing through the Academy ranks, the youngster has made the most of every second since arriving at Anfield last summer.

'From the moment Elliott first stepped on to the field for the closing moments of the pre-season friendly against Napoli at Murrayfield back in July, Liverpool supporters have been impressed.

'More importantly, so too have Jürgen Klopp and his backroom staff, both at Melwood and the Academy.'

He had been described as a 'little diamond' by those charged with guiding his development, and though he would find only a few opportunities to sparkle in the forthcoming season, his future at Liverpool was clearly bright. Although he wouldn't be the only Academy gem to shine.

In truth, nothing that happened on the field could dull the lustre of Klopp's Liverpool. Securing the Champions League crown at Madrid, the resultant parade and swashbuckling style with which Jürgen's men had fought for the Premier League had bought the club a lot of goodwill. Surely, they would do nothing to squander that, would they? Turns out, in the phoney war of pre-season, anything is possible.

A Spectacular Own Goal as Reds Attempt to Trademark the Word 'Liverpool'

In the summer of 2019, Liverpool Football Club sat on top of the world. Off the field, scepticism surrounding the club's American owners was beginning to dissipate, with opposition far less vocal. Fenway Sports Group (FSG), almost a decade into their stewardship of the club, were beginning to deliver in the footballing and business sense.

Talk of an expansion of the Anfield Road end was on the agenda and a new £50m training base in Kirkby was being built. Meanwhile the balance sheet made very good reading. What could possibly go wrong?

Towards the end of July, and with the team and supporters gearing up for another campaign, brimming with optimism, the club made an application to claim the word 'Liverpool' as its intellectual property when used in a football context. It would cause a great deal of controversy and threaten to overshadow the Anfield feelgood factor. Such was the reaction to the news that CEO Peter Moore took to the airwaves on BBC Radio Merseyside to explain the club's position.

Mr Moore was keen to point out that Liverpool FC were not seeking to penalise local vendors, but rather prevent those who would seek to mislead customers with fake products purporting to be official merchandise. However, he had to concede that even a T-shirt which simply contained the word 'Liverpool' on it, surrounded by images of footballs, could be in breach should the application be successful.

While some supporters suggested that the club was perfectly within its rights to protect its products from cheap counterfeits, pointing out that the sale of these damaged the reputation of Liverpool FC and deprive it of potential income, others were deeply troubled. They argued that the club was seeking to monopolise something that does not belong to it, the name of the city itself. A spokesperson for Liverpool Football Club told me, 'We are applying to register "Liverpool" as a trademark but only in the context of football products and services. We are not and wouldn't ever, seek to register "Liverpool" across the board. This application is strictly to protect the club and supporters from those benefiting from inauthentic products. The benefits to the club to have this protection in place are to ensure all revenues from official products and services are channelled back into the club and this is reinvested into the team and supporting infrastructure.'

He was also keen to make clear that only if the club felt an organisation was benefiting from inauthentic products or services, which were being sold to supporters, would it consider acting.

The club already held the intellectual property rights to several other words, phrases, and symbols. For example, they had trademarked 'This is Anfield', and 'YNWA'. They had an initial attempt to gain ownership of the Liver Bird image, in the context of football, refused. However, a subsequent appeal to the EU would prove successful.

Many supporters and traders argued that the club had already done enough to protect its interests, and that attempting to trademark the name of the city is a step too far. Ian Maloney, the Liverpool-born founder of Love Follow Conquer, an independent clothing label, suggested that if the club was successful in its application, it would lead to the right to police who is allowed to produce football-related clothing with the word 'Liverpool' on it.

He pointed out that the club's application included reference to classes ranging from apparel to podcasts, broadcasting, education, and catering. He argued, 'If LFC are successful in their application trademark law states the holder of a trademark must enforce their trademark. They won't be able to pick and choose when to enforce it otherwise the trademark could be challenged by others.'

This potentially contradicted the argument put forward by the club, that it would be able to pick and choose which independent producers it pursued. I don't possess the legal expertise to comment on the above, but a cursory internet search would suggest that an organisation is at risk of losing its trademark if it fails to use it after it is granted.

However, for Ian, there was a deeper issue at stake. And his concern is one shared by many of the people who responded to my original post – an objection to the club attempting to have ownership and control of something they didn't create or invent in the word 'Liverpool'. For many of us, it was simply unfathomable as to why trademarking 'Liverpool FC' wouldn't be enough to protect the club's brand. Why seek monopoly over the name of a city?

Ian felt the move threatened to drive a wedge between the club's owners, the city and its supporters, arguing, 'The city of

Liverpool is a community and has been a cultural centre for over 800 years. Liverpool FC wants to be part of that community and because of this it can't own the community it wants to belong to. Liverpool FC shouldn't have the right to trademark the word "Liverpool" in the same way any other business shouldn't. The word "Liverpool" belongs to the people of Liverpool, not to any corporate business.'

Liverpool City Councillor and future West Derby MP Ian Byrne, who was also a leading figure in the Fans Supporting Foodbanks charity, felt that the move jeopardised the futures of independent traders, and added his voice to calls for the club to withdraw its application, saying, 'The importance of the independents who do so much to add to our fan culture cannot be overestimated. They are fundamental to our current success on and off the pitch, and the club have previously embraced their role. This plan will place them in danger. FSG should cease with the trademark idea, which also endangers the huge bank of goodwill and optimism built up last season.'

Of course, the independent producers and traders weren't the only stakeholders concerned by the potential trademark. A few local amateur football teams, such as AFC Liverpool and City of Liverpool FC (COLFC) also use the name of the city. One of the directors of COLFC, Peter Furmedge, told me, 'City of Liverpool FC has a number of concerns about this trademark application, particularly as it would give LFC effective ownership over the word "Liverpool" in every conceivable football-related context.'

Peter explained that his club is committed to the principles of common ownership and community wealth building. Central to this is the fact that 'Liverpool' is part of a shared identity, an identity that represents significant social capital that has been built up over many generations. He continued, 'Such a shared asset, and the social capital it has accrued, belongs to all of us within the Liverpool community. We contribute to its value daily, just as previous generations have done, and future generations will do. A shared community asset, like "Liverpool", should never be appropriated into private ownership. At "fair value", nobody could ever afford to buy it!'

To Peter, the value of the name 'Liverpool' had been created by the activities, efforts and sacrifices of countless generations. All of us, as citizens of the city, continue to contribute to this 'social capital' daily. Liverpool FC are just one component of that community, as are Tranmere, Everton, and others. Sure, they have also contributed, quite considerably in fact, but does that entitle them to monopolise it in any context?

While there was no suggestion on the part of COLFC that Peter Moore was acting in bad faith, when he states that the club would never seek to act against City of Liverpool FC or others, the club objected strenuously to the suggestion that they should be placed in a subordinate position to the club, if the trademark is granted. The concern was that organisations, like COLFC, would be required to 'get the nod' from Liverpool FC to continue to use their own name.

In addition, others argued that, even if they accept the club's assurances, there is no guarantee that FSG's intentions wouldn't change in the future. And, there was a real fear that potential future owners could use the power of the trademark to shut down all competition. As Peter pointed out:

'This is something that could occur in any number of realistic scenarios. For whatever reason, future owners of the club may not be willing to accept the presence of other football-related activity taking place with the word "Liverpool" involved. Liverpool supporters will remember the antics of Hicks and Gillett, and the infamous "sons of strikers" dossier on supporter activists. Imagine that lot, and Christian Purslow, with these trademark rights to play with!

'Unfortunately, rogue football club owners and executives are not uncommon. In my 30 years' involvement in the football supporters' movement, I have met many supporters' groups at clubs with ownership regimes that would not hesitate to use the trademark rights that Liverpool has applied for as a weapon against perceived local rivals.

'Regardless of the expressed best intentions of the current ownership, they cannot guarantee that somewhere down the line the club will not have owners that will use these trademark rights in ways that the owners currently assure us they won't, but the wording of the trademark application clearly allows.

'A further concern of ours is that Liverpool FC may sell, or transfer, the trademark rights to a third party, such as a commercial partner. They have previously done this, when the Moores and Parry regime transferred rights to Adidas. That severely restricted their ability to develop its own brand. As things stand, if the trademark is granted, there is nothing to prevent a third party from using the rights as leverage in raising their brand awareness – this being the whole point of commercial partnerships after all.'

Another independent trader shared his concerns. Hat Scarf or a Badge has been producing Liverpool FC-related apparel close to Anfield for many years. Its products have been worn by supporters and ex-players alike. Indeed, its designs are inspired by and continue to inspire supporter culture. I contacted the company for comment, and found they share many of the concerns raised by others. A spokesperson told me, 'We are concerned about how these trademark rights may be used by future owners.'

Transalpino, which takes its name from the epic trans-Alpine trek taken by Liverpool supporters on their way to Rome in 1977 harboured similar concerns. A spokesperson told me, 'The main concern is that "Liverpool" belongs to the city. I totally get that they are a business and they have to protect their brand. I can accept them trademarking "Liverpool FC".

'Peter Moore said on BBC Radio 5 Live that it wasn't the small local vendors they were after, but he then went on to say that a red shirt with "Liverpool" on surrounded by footballs would be viewed as alluding to be official merchandise.

'The club will do what they want once they have the trademark. They're a US multinational who want to take ownership of the name of our city; what happens once they sell to unscrupulous owners?

'When I learned of this, in protest, I made an application to trademark "Manchester" in a couple of classes, I will be monitoring it to see if we succeed. I will make a big song and dance about it if we lose, especially if Liverpool win.'

Another group of creators and innovators who could have been potentially affected by this move, are the various fanzines, websites, podcasts, and other online content producers. It has often been via these mediums that fan culture is propagated.

Indeed, something of a symbiotic relationship has been at work between Liverpool FC and these outlets for many years. By that I mean the club latches on to supporter content and uses it for marketing purposes and vice-versa. There may be nothing wrong with this, in fact it may well be desirable. However, the attempt by one partner in the relationship to monopolise words associated with the club dangerously shifts the balance of power in the direction of the club.

I discussed this with Dave Usher, founder and editor of The Liverpool Way, a popular fanzine and website, and Chris Pajak, co-founder and presenter of The Redmen TV, a supporter-generated show that broadcasts daily on YouTube. Both were concerned about the club's attempts to trademark the city's name.

Dave told me that, while he felt the club would eventually back away from the idea, he has been angered by the move. He was even more irritated though, by supporters who he believed were supportive of the club's application. He said, 'Frankly, it's appalling that some suit in a marketing department thinks they have the right to monopolise the word. But what bothers me even more than that are the fans who are attempting to justify it.

'The same thing happened when they wanted to put the ticket prices up. There were fans out there saying it's okay because it means more money in the transfer kitty. I mean, really? The hundreds of millions they get from sponsorship deals and the unprecedented revenue from TV isn't enough?

'Worse than that, though, are those fans who can't seem to differentiate between FSG and the club. As far as owners go, we could do a lot worse, but let's not forget who they are and why they got into this. They are a group of rich American fellas who made a shrewd overseas investment.

'They aren't "the club". They just currently own it. Yet some think it's okay for them to prevent anyone else from using the word "Liverpool" in a football context? It baffles me, to be honest. It's actually scary how some people see the world.'

Meanwhile, Chris Pajak doubted whether anyone, anywhere in the world, who purchases unofficial merchandise, outside of an official club store, does so believing it to be the real deal. He explained, 'It's a bit of a stretch to say they are protecting people from buying inauthentic products. To me, it looks like a land grab. Liverpool FC want all the money that's spent on Liverpool FC. With no unofficial merch [sic] on offer, then revenues go up. Simple as.

'As far as independent retailers go, I can see it affecting their livelihoods. Ninety per cent of the scarves sold outside the ground will have the word Liverpool on them. What does the club expect them to say – Merseyside Reds? Give over. The word Liverpool does not belong to a football club, it belongs to the people. And that's that.

'This is a foot through the door and, once they own it, there's no going back. If they own it, they'll want to protect it. Otherwise why do it in the first place. Even if FSG's intentions are pure, who's to say the next owners will feel the same. This needs to end before it reaches a point of no return.'

In my conversations with many of the stakeholders affected by this move, it is clear to me that the club's reassurances did little to assuage anxieties. Irrespective of the legalities many were sceptical of the club's intentions, and even those who are willing to believe they are acting in good faith, fear the repercussions under future ownership structures, if this trademark is granted.

With all of that, it felt astonishing that Liverpool FC had chosen to embark on this path. Especially as it risked such reputational damage and might have even undone much of the goodwill earned in the previous few years.

However, it appeared there was hope that the club were listening and may even compromise or even withdraw the application. Both City of Liverpool FC and Spirit of Shankly, the Liverpool FC supporters' union, told me that despite their opposition to the plan, they were encouraged by continuing dialogue between the club and interested parties. Peter Moore would describe those discussions as 'congenial and intelligent'. Peter Furmedge described them as 'friendly and constructive'.

COLFC's Furmedge also held out an olive branch, suggesting that he had sympathy for what the club was trying to achieve and was keen to meet with them to find an amicable solution. Fortunately, for all concerned, the application would ultimately fail, and the club indicated that it would not appeal on this occasion. Peter Moore would hail the decision and declare 'common sense had prevailed', even praising those who had objected for their intelligent and constructive engagement.

Today this feels like a pattern at the club. We will return to it later, in discussing another controversy that engulfed the club. Liverpool's ownership and leadership have not been immune to controversy and decisions that put them at odds with their followers; however, they have repeatedly shown a willingness to listen and step away, rather than dig in their corporate heels.

Reds Fans Take Aim at Establishment but City Edge Closely Fought Battle at Wembley

We begin our journey in London. It's 4 August and the city of Liverpool has once more dispatched a small army to the capital for the Community Shield. The opponents were last season's Premier League and FA Cup winners, Manchester City. They had sent a much smaller contingent, as is their style. Liverpool had earned their place by virtue of finishing second in the league, despite losing just one game all season and amassing 97 points.

The warm glow of our victory in Madrid still lingered, which was just as well given that the weather had forgotten it was summer and persisted in randomly dousing us with rain. As we wandered along Wembley Way, our numbers were once more legion. Meanwhile, sky blue shirts were few and far between.

When it came to the squad, Jürgen Klopp had decided some minor tinkering around the edges would do. So transfer window activity at Anfield provided nothing capable of elevating the pulse rate of a Sky Sports anchor, and to be honest most of us were perfectly happy with that.

Liverpool did add a young Dutch defender called Sepp van den Berg for £4.4m, a kid with a man-bun called Harvey Elliot on a free from Fulham and a couple of goalkeeping reinforcements in Adrián San Miguel and Andy Lonergan.

The boss had declared that the 2018/19 vintage 'deserved to stay together', but only after he had dispensed with a whole raft of fringe players. Daniel Sturridge, Danny Ings, Rafa Camacho, Alberto Moreno, Ryan Kent, Simon Mignolet, and a few others left for combined fees of almost £48m. It meant the Reds were once more showing a profit in the transfer market and some supporters were calling for a statue to be built in honour of sporting director Michael Edwards.

Meanwhile, back at Wembley, we had eventually grown tired of the overcrowded bars and expensive beer and decided to head into the stadium, where we could stand on an overcrowded concourse and drink even more expensive beer. I was in the mood for this game. It might be a 'friendly' but it's a trip to Wembley and I've always felt that once you're there, you want to win it, and you're gutted when you don't; no matter what you might say to the contrary.

In any case, I felt this was a chance to stick it to the nouveaux riche. For all City's protestations and delusions of grandeur, they're not our rivals. At least not in the same sense as their neighbours United are, or our neighbours Everton. Those are truly historic and meaningful rivalries. The one we currently endure with Guardiola's men is more reminiscent of the days when we did battle with Brian Clough's Nottingham Forest or, more recently, Jose Mourinho's Chelsea. They withered and so too would City, I hoped.

Manchester City have essentially won the lottery and have been busy filling their previously humble abode with alabaster bathroom furniture and gold taps. They are the Trump Tower of the sporting world and as far as I was concerned, they needed knocking off their gilt-edged thrones pronto. It was just a matter of who got there first, Liverpool or UEFA.

Inside the stadium, there was the usual pointless pomp and ceremony. Choirs on the pitch and an irritating match announcer doing his impersonation of a circus announcer trying to rev up a crowd who should be able to rev up themselves. This was football after all, not the NFL.

'Please be upstanding for the national anthem,' he boomed. My son and I immediately sat down. It's what we have always done. We have no time for a song that calls upon an imaginary deity to save a woman who frankly does not need saving. It speaks to neither of us, nor does it address any of our concerns. Even if I believed that you need a song for a nation, this isn't it. It is a song for the monarchy.

Therefore, I fully expected to hear an attempt to drown it out with an especially loud rendition of 'You'll Never Walk Alone'. That's what's happened at every cup final I've attended since the early 1980s. Older generations will recall singing 'God Save Our Team'.

Instead, what I heard was loud and sustained booing. This felt new and it marked a significant hardening of attitudes among Reds supporters toward the establishment. Of course, the reaction in the national media and non-Liverpool supporters on social media was entirely predictable and spectacularly failed to ask the obvious question.

Why would the citizens of one of Britain's major cities feel such a disconnect with the country it resides in? Instead of deep soul-searching on behalf of the nation, we would be treated to a mixture of ridicule and faux outrage from the patriotic brigade. I'm told some Manchester City fans joined in the booing, but somehow that got lost in the column inches of condemnation that followed.

It shouldn't surprise anyone that Liverpool has a less than affectionate relationship with the British establishment. Nor should anyone expect anyone else to stand and sing a song if they don't want to. Jürgen Klopp would later agree, saying, 'If Liverpool fans don't want to sing the Queen's song, I respect them for that.'

As is often the case, not all Scousers felt the same way and Liverpool supporters in general had differing opinions on the matter. Those from outside the city and those overseas felt it was a bit disrespectful, like John Whitehead and Ricky Olivares, for example. John, a Red from the Midlands, who was at the game, told me, 'It's our national anthem, whether you like it or not. I wouldn't boo another country's national anthem, and so I didn't boo ours. I joined in with singing it, though I sort of get those from Liverpool booing it though.'

Rick Olivares, a sports journalist and Liverpool supporter from the Philippines, said, 'To be honest, I was surprised by the booing of the national anthem. Having lived in the United States, the Philippines, and Hong Kong, I have not seen anything like it. I cannot claim to understand the dynamic between Liverpool or even England as a whole – politics included. But I still think it is disrespectful. Whatever the grievances, there are proper places to vent one's anger and frustrations.'

Andy 'Toggsy' James, an Australian broadcaster and Liverpool supporter, was similarly surprised, saying, 'In Australia we boo the politicians that hand over trophies or are on stage for presentations. But we don't boo the anthem. We don't sing it as proud as some other countries, but it wouldn't go down well to boo it.'

However, those supporters who grew up in Liverpool throughout the 1980s had much more sympathy for those who decided to boo. Ian Salmon is a Liverpool-born playwright, and although he'd have rather heard supporters drowning out the national anthem with our own song, he found himself in complete sympathy with those who chose to protest. He told me, 'As a city we have been mistreated by the Tory party and the establishment for decades. They have been happy to operate a policy of "managed decline" over Liverpool. We know that our hometown exists in the manner that it does today due solely to the investment of European funding.

'We also know that the abuse we've taken as citizens of the city has increased exponentially in the last couple of years. The "bin dippers" nonsense, the "thieving Scouse bastards" rubbish. The rise of our club has seen this become more and more prevalent.

'The idea that so much of England wants to criticise us as people, as fans, as a football team but then want us in some way to show approval of the country. Ridiculous.'

To many, the royal family and that anthem has come to symbolise the establishment and everything that they perceive is wrong with the country. John Thompson, a Liverpool-born author and Reds supporter, told me, 'It's not just about booing the Queen or the royal family. It's about booing the establishment, the aristocracy and the landed gentry as a whole. My daughter attends Liverpool College, at every formal gathering or prize giving, usually in the big cathedral, they blast out the national anthem. I make a point of remaining seated throughout, a silent booing, if you like.

'The list of reasons why our city should treat them with nothing but disdain, is endless. And, when it feels that Liverpool is being dragged into being just another part of England, the booing of the national anthem fills me with a sense of pride. Wouldn't it be great if we lived in a country where we could be proud of our ruling classes instead of viewing them as the mortal enemies they are?'

So the game hadn't even started and already in the stands the battles lines were being drawn for a season which would see Liverpool and its army of supporters prepare to do battle with the existing order. The pain of another domestic near miss still felt raw, and it was time to lay down a marker. The booing of what is essentially an ode to the establishment felt entirely appropriate in this context.

However, it seemed that the previous season's rulers had one last fight in them. The Reds were sluggish out of the blocks and City seemed well up for the game. They took the lead after just 12 minutes thanks to a Raheem Sterling strike. But in truth they could have been ahead earlier, had Leroy Sané been more clinical instead of hitting his shot into the side-netting. The

Reds had been huffing and puffing their way through each of their pre-season friendlies, and it was starting to look like they were yet to shake off the cobwebs of the summer. As half-time approached with Liverpool a goal down, there was little to offer hope of the perfect season Klopp had called for at the end of the last.

Ninety-seven points hadn't been enough last time. If the Reds were to finally wrest the title from the clutches of City they would have to produce an epoch-defining campaign and reach levels no team had ever managed before. And they would need to do it without having splashed the cash like a drunken sailor on leave, while being chased all the way by a much richer and better-equipped opponent, or so we thought.

None of that looked likely on the evidence of that first half though. Fortunately, there are two halves to every game and the Reds emerged from the break a very different animal. They immediately took the game to City and had already hit the woodwork twice before eventually hitting the equaliser in the 77th minute. Joël Matip pounced on an assist from defensive partner Virgil van Dijk and it was all square, at last.

City seemed to panic, and from my vantage point in the stands, I could see Pep remonstrating and gesticulating to his players and barking instructions they couldn't possibly hear. At least that's what he did when he thought the cameras were on him. As soon as they moved away, he would retake his seat and sit, silently pondering and looking all genius-like.

I would later describe Guardiola as a fraud and a phoney during a conversation in the pub before a home game. Admittedly my assertion was fuelled by beer and it probably wasn't my most insightful piece of analysis. Pep is undoubtedly a great manager, possibly the best. Maybe. But my comments were more to do with his antics on the touchline, that day in August, during the Community Shield.

I get the sense that there's something of the showman in Guardiola, and that he cultivates his image as the tortured genius. What other manager can be described as losing a game because he 'over-thought it'? It's nonsense. I was aware that my analysis of Guardiola was tantamount to heresy, but it would turn into that sort of season.

Meanwhile, those studying Klopp's pitchside behaviour may well accuse me of double standards. After all, there are few managers more animated than Jürgen. However, whereas Pep's demeanour seems contrived to me, there's a natural almost involuntary nature to Klopp's antics. He's more like a supporter in the dugout than a manager, albeit a tactically astute one. The Liverpool boss's genius is organic, not concocted.

For all Pep's protestations and gyrations, his City side were struggling to contain Liverpool in the dying moments of the game. They had the air of a side desperate for time to run out, just like their ideas. Liverpool pressed forward in search of a winner and in the stands there was a growing sense that it would come. In the final moments of normal time, it almost did.

Right at the death, Kyle Walker headed a Mo Salah header off the line to prevent a certain goal. We groaned in disbelief. City had got away with one and they would soon be leaving with the shield.

That glorious missed opportunity was to be the last act of the 90 minutes and Liverpool had done more than enough to suggest that they would once again push City all the way. Whatever happened now, I thought, there is at least pride in matching the champions.

Extra time couldn't separate the sides and penalties beckoned, bringing back bitter memories of that League Cup Final defeat to City back in 2016. The Reds would prove far more efficient and clinical from the spot this time, but the result would be the same.

Sadly, Gini Wijnaldum missed his penalty in the shoot-out, and it would be left for Gabriel Jesus to deliver the winning blow for City. As we filed out of Wembley and contemplated the journey home, we felt we'd seen enough to give us optimism for the season ahead.

Paul Doyle, writing in *The Guardian*, also felt the game was somewhat portentous: 'Call it a phoney war, if you like, but the Community Shield suggested Manchester City and Liverpool are set for another epic battle. One point separated them last season and there was nothing between them on Sunday until City prevailed in the penalty shoot-out. So, Pep Guardiola's side won by the narrowest margin. Again. But there was enough to indicate things could go the other way over the next nine months.'

Neither him, nor us, had any idea what we were in for. And neither did Pep.

Liverpool Football Club were about to mount their most relentless assault on the established order in their entire history. And, in doing so, it would ensure that the record books were rewritten, and both manager and players would achieve immortality.

End of An Era as Reds Announce Sale of Historic Melwood Training Base

In the run up to the Community Shield, Liverpool announced their decision to sell off the land which had served as the club's training base for decades. Melwood, the scene of so much history was to be bought by Torus, a charity based in nearby St Helens which specialises in affordable homes.

The decision represented a significant step in the club's move to a £50m training facility in Kirkby. It also marked a new twist in the campaign by residents to ensure the club did right by them and the history of the site.

In a statement from the club, Andy Hughes, executive vice-president of finance, explained that the club had made the decision to move away from Melwood with a 'heavy heart', but went on to argue that Liverpool had effectively outgrown the historic site. This was compounded by their desire to combine the first team and academy under one roof.

He also went on to reassure supporters that all funds from the sale of the land – believed to be in the region of £10m, – would be reinvested into the first-team squad. These words have proven to be cold comfort to locals in West Derby, who live and work near to the training base.

Ever since the plans for Liverpool to leave the area were announced in 2017, tenants began to voice several concerns. These related to fears that the site could be sold to a high-end private housing developer and the subsequent impact on the local area in terms of increased traffic, schools, and health services.

However, they were also worried about the departure of a piece of the area's heritage. There was a deep sense of loss at the potential bulldozing of what is an iconic and significant piece of football history. These, after all, are people who have grown up within touching distance of one of the greatest sporting locations on the planet. Melwood is the Cavern, the Graceland, or the Abbey Road Studios of the football world.

Many will have lived so close that they could have watched training from their windows, or perhaps stood on rubbish bins next to the giant, grey stone walls in order to catch a glimpse of Bill Shankly, Bob Paisley, Joe Fagan and Kenny Dalglish and their men in training. The likes of Roger Hunt, Kevin Keegan, Ian Rush and Luis Suarez would have been regular visitors to their neighbourhood.

Some will have seen Shankly around the area – his home was in nearby Sandforth Road. They will have chatted to him and many have fond memories of that. There is real history soaked into the ground and countless stories tied up in the walls of the place.

While it's difficult to argue against progress, all Reds want to see the club prosper, heritage and history are important to this club and its people and perhaps more so than at other clubs. Writing in the *Liverpool Echo* in 2017, after the club's plans to leave Melwood were first announced, David Prentice remarked that the place was never just an ordinary training ground: 'It was the birthplace of an entire football philosophy, a place where Bill Shankly hatched and honed his pass-and-move credo – and where world-class players were educated in the Liverpool way.'

The Reds moved into the facility in the 1950s, after previously training on the Anfield grass. However, this was beginning to have a detrimental effect on the pitch and a decision was eventually made to take over a few football pitches in the West Derby area of the city.

The site had originally belonged to St Francis Xavier School and was named after two priests who organised football matches there, Father Melling and Father Woodlock. The first syllables of each of their names had given the site its name: Melwood.

When Liverpool moved in, their would-be training base was in a terrible state. Shankly arrived in 1959 and immediately saw that the three playing fields and adjoining pavilion had not been maintained and the pitches had become overgrown.

In his autobiography, he described it as a 'sorry wilderness'. On spotting what looked like two huge bomb craters in one of the playing surfaces, he asked, 'Have the Germans been here?'

Shankly set about transforming the place into a facility befitting the sporting empire Liverpool would eventually become. Despite the club being in the second tier of English football, his vision convinced the board to rebuild the pavilion and flatten the pitches.

Soon, the players would be boarding the bus from Anfield to Melwood and working on their five-a-side routines and taking target practice against the shooting boards he erected. Then, once training had finished, it was back on the bus to Anfield.

This would ensure the players were properly cooled down after practice. But, more than that, it promoted camaraderie and bonded the players together, as they shared the ride to and from training.

In 2001, Melwood faced another revolution with the appointment of Gérard Houllier as sole manager of the club. Gérard oversaw the further modernisation of the facility which added the Millennium Pavilion we see today.

Melwood has been Liverpool Football Club's official training base for 50 years. But, more than that, it is an important cultural and historical location for West Derby and the city of Liverpool. That's why local campaigners held such strong views about its future.

I spoke to city councillor Harry Doyle about the concerns of the local community and the campaign that has grown up in the area. He told me that he was disappointed with the club's decision to sell the site for housing and felt the club hadn't listened sufficiently to residents' concerns.

'Over the years, West Derby has seen a massive influx of new-build homes which has added pressure to our roads,' he told me.

'These are now gridlocked, particularly at peak times. It can take 20 minutes just to get out of West Derby.

'On top of this, all the local schools and doctors' surgeries are oversubscribed. The medical centre just over the road from Melwood has 12,000 people on their books with only six car parking spaces.

'The final issue, and probably the most important to the campaign group, is the strong connection the local community and fans have with Melwood. Melwood has been a part of our community and many residents have shared memories of Shankly in the area and what a great man he was.

'Local people will be devastated to lose the facility and really wanted Liverpool FC to have a legacy here. The campaign group believed Melwood could have been profitable for the club as a museum or fitness centre.

'I think the sale of Melwood to Torus is no different from a sale to a private housing company. We'll still have all the above problems in the area.'

The issues around the move, particularly the views and concerns of the local community in West Derby, were not entirely understood by the wider community, and indeed the club's global fan base. An opinion poll published in the *Liverpool Echo* found most readers sided with the club. Some felt that 'Liverpool FC isn't a charity'. While that is true, the club has always been a part of a wider community and its activities have an impact on that community for good or bad. When our neighbours feel aggrieved, its important that we all listen. After all, we are frequently told that Liverpool Football Club is the 'greatest football family of all'.

The club maintained that it had engaged with residents over its plans. And, unscientific polls aside, most decent people did have sympathy for the concerns of people living near to Melwood.

That said, this represented another example of the club falling out with sections of the local community. Its plans to host concerts and events in the closed season caused huge local controversy, as did more recent plans to trademark the word Liverpool.

All these controversies had come shortly after Chairman Tom Werner had spoken of FSG's desire to do more in the community, claiming that they understood what Liverpool FC means to the people of the city. Fine words, but this was a community that had grown used to judging people by their actions, not their words.

Future historians will no doubt observe Liverpool FC's necessary and perhaps inevitable move from Melwood with interest. They may reflect on the fact that given Shankly's vision for the club, back in 1959, the old training facility was always going to have a limited shelf life.

The continued growth of Liverpool FC is a testament to its achievements, the genius of the men who built this sporting dynasty and to the players who have and continue to bring us such joy. Let us not forget, though, that this success has also been created thanks to the magnificent community of neighbours that has supported the club throughout its meteoric rise.

We can only hope that those future historians are also able to reflect on how the club left behind a positive legacy of its time in West Derby. And, that it is remembered fondly by those who continue to live there.

ONCE MORE UNTO THE BREACH

Liverpool FC: August–November 2019

Friday Night Lights: Reds Hammer Norwich City and it is Adrián to the Rescue

The European champions got the 2019/20 season off to a flying start with a Friday night game at home to Norwich City. There would be much to celebrate at full time but an injury to a vital cog in the machine that raced to 97 points in the previous season and some familiar carping in the stands cast a shadow over the victory.

In my mind's eye, the first game of the season at Anfield conjures images of sun-baked streets, the Sandon car park packed to overflowing and chippy queues spilling out on to pavements. Not this season though. Instead, on Friday, 9 August, L4 was warm, wet, and muggy as it greeted Liverpool and their adoring followers. In so many ways this was an unfamiliar start to a campaign.

There was even a new object of pilgrimage too. Added to the old haunts – the Shankly statue – the food bank collections, the myriad of pubs, fan zones and the fanzine sellers dotted around the stadium was a giant mural of Trent Alexander-Arnold accompanied by the words 'An ordinary kid from Liverpool, whose dream came true', as the player had described himself. Now those words were permanently etched into the bricks and mortar around Anfield.

Scores of people made their way along Anfield Road to Sybil Road, where they would find a row of terraced houses basking in their new-found fame. To their right, on the opposite side of the road, the great Georgian town houses, a symbol of the area's affluent past stared on in green-eyed envy.

For all the wealth and power of those ghosts of Liverpool's past, they would never have felt the passion and adulation experienced by this working-class lad from West Derby and his team-mates. One by one they queued to have their picture taken in front of his image. In the rain, kids younger than Trent and perhaps dreaming that they one day will adorn a wall, or be idolised by generations, posed in front of the painting. Maybe they fantasised about scoring in front of the Kop and feeling its power rattle their bones.

As I stood in its shadow, I guessed that this was the point of the mural. To inspire, to reach out and say, 'There's a chance for you too. If you work hard and sacrifice like me.' Maybe. But there's no harm in dreams anyway. We know that. At Liverpool, perhaps more than anywhere else, we know that.

The rich merchants of Anfield Road have long gone. It's our place now. That's because each one of us has dreamed of glory, wanted it for ourselves and for each other, and then we've gone out and fought to make those dreams a reality. Just like Trent, Jamie and Stevie and all the others who have graced our history, have dreamed.

So all around me were the old familiar places juxtaposed with the new and the unusual, and the game itself turned out to be a mirror of all of that.

There was the old swagger we had enjoyed in the previous season. That swashbuckling verve was evident in the first half against Norwich, accompanied by the never-satisfied few who bemoan every misstep and proceed to hound their favourite whipping boys throughout the game, irrespective of the quality of the performance.

For example, the sight of Divock Origi being dispossessed, shortly after Norwich had scored their meaningless consolation goal in the 64th minute, was greeted by one inexplicable shout from a fella near me, 'Get him off, he's shite!'

That outburst was greeted with tuts and expressions of disbelief, but it still jarred with me. Another guy had shouted to Jordan Henderson to 'get off and stay off' at half-time. This is a phenomenon almost as old as Anfield itself. For all our famed support and never give up mentality, we have always been 'blessed' with people who will never be satisfied and who revel in their misery.

Jack Balmer, Liverpool's bald-headed striker of the 1930s and '40s, who hailed from the same district of West Derby that gave rise to young Trent, was often on the receiving end of abuse from supporters. Bob Paisley once wrote about how his treatment at the hands of some fans had hurt the player, who had scored 98 goals in 289 appearances for the club.

In the pub, before the game, we had been talking about how Ronnie Whelan had often been a player who could do no right, in the same way that Henderson, the current captain, can never satisfy some people today. You'd be hard pressed to find anyone who watched the game in the 1980s who will admit they did it, but the Irishman would frequently hear their shouts on the pitch.

Just like Henderson though, Whelan would answer his critics by winning the biggest prizes in football. He could do no more. Neither can Jordan and by the end of the season he would have conquered the bloody world.

But, for all the familiar bitter barbs from the minority, the atmosphere during the game was a throwback to the fan-parks of Madrid and the glory of our run to the final. The mosaic displayed at kick-off told the world, as if they didn't already know, that the Reds were back on their European perch. That represented something new in the recent context, a trophy win to gloat about. The monkey is off this Liverpool team's back at long last.

The Kop bellowed, at every opportunity, 'We are the champions, champions of Europe.' If it wasn't yet driving our rivals insane – it wouldn't be long before they were tearing their hair out and declaring that the Reds were 'unbearable'. That's exactly as it should be. We had all decided that we would keep it up for as long as they would if we had lost the final – multiplied by six.

As I joined in with the song, I imagined singing it for 20 minutes solid at Old Trafford or Goodison. I could just envisage the fume and it was an incredible feeling.

Roared on by a jubilant and at times carnival-like Anfield, the players switched through the gears in the first half. That's not to say Norwich were out of it though. They threatened a few times, and Alisson was called upon to twice prevent what looked like a certain goal. One save in particular produced a crescendo of applause from the Kop and repeated chants of the Brazilian's name.

Not since the days of Ray Clemence and Bruce Grobbelaar had Liverpool had a keeper of this quality. In fact, in one of those moments in the game, where your mind drifts, I began to muse on whether Alisson may well be one of the best since the days of Elisha Scott, such is his command of his area and ability to calm his defence.

So the sight of him clutching his calf and falling to the turf deep in the first half was like an arrow through the heart. The sight of him walking off, rather than being stretchered, was the smallest crumb of comfort. We would later learn that we would have to manage without him for an extended period.

What was heartening, though, was the roar of approval for Adrián, the former West Ham goalkeeper brought in for free, and practically under the radar only a matter of days earlier, as he ran on to the pitch. This was the Kop as it should be. Getting behind the man with the Liver Bird on his chest, regardless of any misgivings. I have always held that no matter what my feelings are about the quality of a player, once he crosses the white line, he's one of us and part of the fight.

Back in June, Adrián could scarcely have dreamed that he would be running out in front of a huge crowd at Anfield – for the European champions, and with the team already 3-0 up. The reserve keeper showed no signs of nerves. He could have been forgiven if he had.

Liverpool had gone ahead inside seven minutes thanks to an own goal by Grant Hanley, who had turned in Origi's cross from the left. From my vantage point, it had seemed like the hero of Madrid himself had scored. Others must have felt the same because the Kop began to chant his name. It didn't matter though; he could rightly claim the assist.

Just 12 minutes later, Mohamed Salah got in on the act with the Reds' second. This time it was Bobby Firmino providing the assist, and the Kop didn't seem to know who to serenade most. First, they rolled out chants of 'Egyptian King', following that up with the mesmeric ode to his Brazilian strike partner. These were all welcome signs of the old and familiar Liverpool. The Liverpool of last season, at one with its people and relentless on the field of play.

With barely half an hour on the clock the Reds were three up. This time we were watching Virgil van Dijk score, and Salah was providing the ammunition. His delightful cross from the left was headed home with aplomb and we were all ecstatic. None of us quite knew what to expect before the game. It had potential banana skin written all over it.

However, the Reds had simply picked up where they had left off the season before. Memories of a forgettable pre-season had evaporated, and the explosion of euphoria was reminiscent of much bigger games. Klopp's men were back in town.

The potentially disastrous loss of Alisson was brushed aside when on 42 minutes Origi found the net with a brilliant header, following a superb cross from Trent Alexander-Arnold. The young Scouser was also picking up where he left off last time out and it seemed he wasn't the only player to have found his groove. The Kop, meanwhile, had also raised its level.

Amidst the noise and jubilation, half-time felt like a kick in the teeth. An unwelcome interruption. And so it proved to be.

As I bounced down to the concourse underneath the famous old terrace, I entertained thoughts of a complete rout. Of six, seven, maybe even eight goals. Well, a Kopite can dream. But, while the second half was hardly a nightmare, it was a shadow of the first.

In truth, Norwich deserved their one goal. They had given it a go and some the of the football in the final third was impressive. Their ability to impress and play attractive football, while still losing games, would prove to be a curse for them throughout the season.

For Liverpool, the one bright spot in the second half was Sadio Mané. The last to return to pre-season, he showed no signs of rustiness and was a thorn in Norwich's side from the moment he entered the fray, replacing Origi. Both players received rapturous applause as one departed and the other ran on to the pitch.

The visiting supporters sang 'one-nil in the second half'. You'd imagine that's exactly what their manager will have told his players in the dressing room. Restricting the European champions to just four goals and grabbing a consolation at Anfield had become the benchmark for a team like Norwich. It was also a sign of the progress made by Klopp and his players.

So too are the mutterings and grumbles of some Liverpool supporters, as they left the ground, seemingly unhappy that we had 'settled' for four goals and 'let Norwich back into the game'. Some people are never happy, or maybe expectations have finally reached the stratosphere, after being in the dirt when Klopp arrived. Whatever it was, it felt strange to hear people seemingly deflated after a 4-1 win.

This was the first game of the season. The Reds would surely improve and grow into the campaign, even without their £65m goalkeeper. Adrián, as it happened would prove to be a more than competent deputy during Alisson's spell on the sidelines. There was little to be down about, I thought.

Several messages greeted me as I arrived home. One of them, on social media, was from an Everton fan. It said we had looked like Brazil in the 1970s, during the first half. But it warned of burn-out and suggested better teams would have turned us over in the second half.

Neither assessment was fair in my view. Liverpool did what they needed to do against a plucky Norwich team geed up by the optimism of a new season in the top flight. It was a free hit for them and expectations among their fans were low. That wasn't the case for the six-times European champions (have I mentioned that we won the European Cup?).

For our rivals, those comments would prove to be wishful thinking. For us, it would be fun living inside their heads for the whole season, especially as the rent was so low. It would almost feel like we were squatting at times.

The bar had been set for the Reds now. They ruled over an entire continent after all. Ambitions and expectations were soaring. The fact that some were bemoaning a 4-1 home victory on the opening day of a new season, is perhaps another symbol of the team's rebirth.

Paul Gorst, writing in the *Liverpool Echo*, captured the mood around Anfield after the game: 'Straight to the top of the charts the Reds go, and they will take some shifting, already. Strap yourselves in, Liverpool have gone again.'

Prophetic words indeed, but on that muggy August evening, I'm not sure that even he knew what we were all in for.

Back to the Bosphorus as Reds Lift Their Fourth Super Cup

Liverpool in Istanbul, the game finishing in the early hours of the morning, a victory on penalties and the captain lifting a European trophy – sound familiar? No, I'm not talking about Istanbul in 2005. This was of course another case of history repeating itself, and the story of the Reds' fourth UEFA Super Cup victory.

The venue this time was the uninspiringly named Vodafone Park, the home of Turkish outfit Besiktas. The ground capacity of just over 38,000 made it an insane choice for a showpiece game between two of English football's top sides – Liverpool's opponents, Chelsea, had won the Europa League just days before that night in Madrid. The Reds could have sold out their measly allocation three times over, with many in the region just to be part of the action, even if they couldn't get into the game.

Liverpool's post-2005 Ataturk legacy meant that many locals had fond memories of the club and its supporters, ensuring a warm welcome in the bars and restaurants of Istanbul this time round. All of this would mean that Reds outnumbered the Blues massively in the run-up to the game.

As Liverpool supporters turned Taksim Square red as only they can, I was 5,500 miles away, on holiday in Tenerife. Being away from the action and feeling cut off from the match build-up is agony for me. As utterly illogical as I know this is, I feel in control if I'm able to go through my usual matchday routine, surrounded by familiar places and faces. Take me away from that, place me in isolation – albeit in the glorious Canary Island sunshine – and the nerves increase tenfold.

An all-English final in a European competition has always felt jarring to me. The joy of playing in Continental competition is facing far-flung teams, old European masters and seeing Liverpool test themselves against unfamiliar foe. I won't bore you with how many times the Reds have faced Chelsea in recent years, but we are far from strangers.

As a result, games against the Londoners are usually tight, with both teams cancelling each other out. This one would be no exception.

The mood around the club couldn't have been better going into the tie though. With Liverpool the reigning European champions, Jürgen Klopp had ejected a significant monkey from his back. He hadn't just won a trophy; he had won arguably the biggest of them all.

As I sat by the pool, covered in factor 50 sunscreen and desperately trying to stop my northern European complexion from sizzling, and quenching my thirst with the local brew, I recalled how a friend had once asked me – not all that long ago – whether I thought Klopp was little more than a 'cheerleader'. I laughed at the time, but I could only point to progress and development, and his record in Germany. As I spoke, I knew that until he managed to win something at Anfield, people would always ask those questions.

The same people who may be inclined to downplay, even undermine his achievement in Madrid, were Liverpool to slip up in the Super Cup against Chelsea. Maybe number six was a fluke, they'd probably say. I could almost hear the words, 'He was lucky the opponents were Spurs, a better team would have beat Liverpool.' Of course, such arguments ignore the titanic comeback against Barcelona and the imperious manner with which the Reds had conducted themselves in the last 12 months, but since when has logic had anything to do with it.

Ever since the day Bill Shankly restored Liverpool to the First Division in 1962, won it in 1963 and then secured the club's first FA Cup in 1965, any man brave enough to take the Anfield hot seat has been judged by almost impossible standards. Only two men since those heady days have failed to add to the Reds' trophy cabinet – Roy Hodgson and Brendan Rodgers.

Now that Klopp had joined the pantheon of winners, he would be forever celebrated. But to achieve legendary status, he would need to keep winning. That's football in the 21st century. No manager will get to dine out on past glories for very long. The time afforded to Shankly to build his second great team, and to Ferguson to overhaul Liverpool's achievements, belonged to a different era. Those days were gone.

Suddenly, maybe it was the beer, maybe heatstroke, but I became aware that last season had gone, and our ability to laud our champions of Europe status over our rivals may be tarnished, if we lost the game in Turkey that night. Fellow Reds, gathered around the poolside bar, were far more confident.

One told me, 'They've [Liverpool's players] got the bug now. Once they've tasted that glory, they want it more and more. They'll have too much for Lampard's Chelsea. Most of them are kids, and they're just getting started.'

I could see what he meant. Liverpool's victory in Madrid was the culmination of four years of development under Klopp. In that time, Liverpool had tasted defeat in three cup finals, and had learned from each of them. In Madrid it felt like the squad and the club came of age. It was no fluke.

After what seemed like the longest day, I wandered down the street to a nearby bar and positioned myself on a stool in front of a giant screen. The place was packed and there was a mixture of Liverpool and Chelsea fans in there, as well as supporters of a few other clubs. The atmosphere was friendly, and the usual banter and barbs were in evidence, but nothing untoward.

The Reds were once again facing a game without their £65m goalkeeper, Alisson, who was still out injured. Adrián would make his first full debut in the match, after coming on as a substitute during the season opener against Norwich. Prior to that, he hadn't played a competitive game since January. If there was to be a weak link in the Reds' line-up, logic dictated it would be him. However, as is so often the case when it comes to football, logic doesn't enter into it. Adrián was about to become Liverpool's saviour and hero.

As early as the first half, he was sharp, leaping off his line to prevent Kovacic from scoring. At the other end, Mané had attempted a spectacular bicycle kick after getting on the end of a delightful Henderson cross. The ball appeared to hit Andreas Christensen on the arm but appeals for a penalty were waved away.

For the Reds in the bar, there was consternation, while there were awkward smiles from the rest. Then Salah broke forward and forced a decent save from Kepa Arrizabalaga. However, with N'Golo Kanté starting to exert his influence in the middle, Chelsea began to fashion a few chances of their own.

Pedro hit the woodwork, after Giroud had glided through the Reds' defensive line in what amounted to an early warning of what was to come. The Frenchman latched on to a slide-rule pass from Pulisic in the 36th minute and Adrián stood no chance. The Blues were a goal up.

It felt like a gut punch, and the cheers and high-fives around the bar made it even harder to stomach. This was a Chelsea side who had been beaten 4-0 by Manchester United the previous weekend. Frank Lampard, having taken over as manager with the club unable to reinforce due to a transfer ban, was facing a huge test. I was confident the Reds could get back into the game and was in no mood to surrender to panic. The player causing Liverpool problems was Kante, who looked imperious. Pulisic was also enjoying a decent debut for Chelsea. The American even had the ball in the net only for it to be ruled out by VAR. Despite all that, I felt that if the Reds could reassert their authority in the middle, then we would be okay. Despite a scare when Pulisic netted, seemingly putting Chelsea 2-0 up – his goal being correctly ruled out for offside in the build-up – I was still reasonably confident at half-time. Liverpool made a change at the start of the second half, with Roberto Firmino replacing Alex Oxlade-Chamberlain. His impact was almost immediate.

When Henderson, once again magnificent, lobbed the ball over the Chelsea back line in the 48th minute, the Brazilian was in on goal, Kepa managed to get in his way, but the ball fell to Sadio Mané, who gleefully equalised for the Reds. Chelsea frantically appealed for offside but to no avail.

Liverpool were now in the ascendency, and with the Blues' keeper on his knees, the Reds' captain sent in a fierce shot, but

Kepa somehow managed to parry it away. Minutes later he pulled off a miraculous double stop, beating away efforts from Salah and VAn Dijk, palming the latter shot on to the crossbar and away to safety.

Chelsea tried to hit back by exploiting Liverpool's high defensive line, and Jorginho beat Adrián with a stunning angled shot from 20 yards out, only for his effort to be chalked off for offside. Replays showed that he was. The game was turning into a classic, with both teams going for the win. In truth, neither side would have wanted extra time and penalties, given their commitments in the Premier League at the weekend.

However, that's exactly what they got. Lampard and Klopp would roll their eyes at the prospect of another late night and the disruption to their league preparations, even joking together about it on the touchline.

The tension in the bar was palpable as the referee signalled the end of 90 minutes. There was no animosity on show, but with rival fans in such close proximity, the thought of defeat was perhaps even more unpalatable.

The Reds dominated the first period of extra time and were justifiably in front in the 95th minute, thanks once again to Mané, who hammered home a delightful pass from Firmino. It was a stunning finish and thoroughly deserved on the balance of play. The clock had hit midnight in Istanbul and the Reds looked to be heading into a new dawn with another trophy under their belts. Then disaster struck.

Tammy Abraham, on as substitute for Giroud, found himself in the Liverpool penalty area and going nowhere. As he drifted towards the dead ball line, Adrián rushed from his line and made a lunge at the player, who immediately went down. The referee pointed straight to the spot.

Adrián protested his innocence and I have to say, after watching the replays, I have some sympathy with him. But if you dive in like that you give the referee a decision to make, so he has to accept the blame.

You couldn't hope to find a more contrasting set of emotions than those on display inside the bar in Tenerife, where dozens of us were watching the drama unfold. Within six minutes of Liverpool taking the lead, a self-inflicted wound had cost them dearly. Among the Reds in the bar, there was frustration and disbelief. The Chelsea supporters, who had gone from despair to elation now fancied their team could go on and win it.

Jorginho stepped up and smashed his penalty to Adrián's left. It was a perfect spot-kick and the keeper had no chance. But he should never have put himself or his team-mates in that position. However, such are the margins in football, that a player can be a zero one minute and a hero the next. The Brazilian would prove the point later as the game drifted towards penalties.

Abraham missed another chance to win the tie for Chelsea when the ball fizzed across the Reds' box. Adrián missed it completely and fortunately for him so did the youngster. Then Adrián pulled off a stunning one-handed save from Abraham, who was by now giving Liverpool's defence a torrid time.

Somehow, though, Liverpool saw out the extra 30 minutes and yet another European contest would be decided by the lottery of penalties. The stage was then set for the Reds' deputy keeper to become an unlikely legend.

Penalties are a horrendous way to settle any game of football. However, Liverpool's records in these contests is comparable with the very best. I just always feel supremely confident that we will come out on top, and this was no exception.

Judging by the expressions on the faces of the people around the bar, I wasn't the only one who fancied Liverpool to triumph. The Chelsea fans looked despondent and riven with anxiety, while the Reds were smiling and shouting 'COME ON' at the screen.

Our confidence would be once again justified as Liverpool hit home all five of their penalties. Chelsea had scored four when up stepped Abraham. The youngster looked terrified to me; it was a huge moment in a huge game. Maybe it was my imagination, but as he walked forward to take the spot-kick, I thought he wanted to be anywhere else in the world than there at that moment.

Of course, the keeper can't lose in these duels. Nobody expects them to win. For Abraham though, if he slipped, the trophy was going to Anfield. It was all or nothing, no second chance and no reprieve. Adrián saved.

As he raced out of his goal in celebration, the bar erupted. I didn't see him being mobbed by his team-mates, I was too busy throwing ale in the air and screaming at the top of my lungs. By the time the commotion subsided most of our rivals had left for pastures new, and there were half-consumed beers on the tables and bar.

I frantically reached for my phone. In my semi-drunken state, I had realised that Liverpool had now moved back in front of Manchester United. They were once more the most decorated team in English football history. With blurry eyes, I tapped away at the screen. The result was a tweet that read, 'Liverpool 43 Major honours. Most successful team in English football history. Didn't take long to get back on our perch did it [sic]'

It was posted at 10.55pm local time, and within minutes my phone was going crazy. The tweet received over 12,000 likes and was retweeted over 4,000 times (a personal record). Unfortunately, this wasn't evidence of some new-found celebrity on my part, but the fact that Jamie Carragher had seen the tweet and shared it with his followers and included Gary Neville in the fun.

What followed was a deluge of replies from angry United supporters, claiming that the UEFA Super Cup didn't count, and Liverpool were desperate for even including it in their list of major honours. That was until a few Reds pointed out that Manchester

United did include the trophy on their list of honours, on their official website.

It was all good fun of course, but the irony was that in my half-drunken state, I had got my figures wrong. The Reds had actually won 46 major honours. Jürgen Klopp had delivered once again. However, the boss bemoaned the need for extra time, telling BT Sport:

'It was a very difficult game for both teams. It was all about winning it and we did that in the end. Nobody in the stadium wanted extra time, it was a killer. I'm not sure about the penalty but who cares now.

'We started well then dropped off … we could talk about football but it's too late now. We had to fight, and the boys did tonight.'

In another interview, Klopp would mimic Sylvester Stallone's Rocky, shouting 'Adrián!' into the camera just as the boxer in the eponymous movie had done after an epic victory, as he searched for his wife. The goalkeeper's arrival at Anfield was already something of a fairytale, but after his heroics on this night, his journey had entered the realms of fantasy.

Lampard talked of his pride in his players. There was nothing else he could do of course. But, to be fair, Chelsea had given the Reds a run for their money. Liverpool just had that little bit of extra luck, and perhaps desire too. A commodity they would use to full effect for the remainder of the season.

As the players revelled in yet another trophy lift, Daniel Taylor, writing for *The Guardian*, captured the moments of celebration at the end of the game: 'It was 12.43am local time when the teams were finally prised apart. The players in red had set off on their victory run, all heading to the newest member of their group. Jürgen Klopp was trying to keep up and Liverpool's only problem now is where to accommodate the Super Cup in their already congested trophy room. This was the fourth time they have won this competition, putting them level with Real Madrid and one behind Barcelona and Milan. "European football royalty" to use the words of the public announcer.'

European royalty indeed. But there was more to come. Much more.

Super Sadio Crushes the Saints but Danny Ings Rues Missed Chances

While I continued to sunbathe in Tenerife, the Reds faced a gruelling few days of travel. Their exertions in Turkey behind them, they flew back to England and geared up for a tough test against Ralph Hasenhüttl's Southampton at St Mary's on the south coast. This of course wasn't ideal as far as Jürgen Klopp was concerned, but it is the price of success.

In days gone by, Liverpool would have been almost certain to turn in a lacklustre display in a game like this, probably lose and maybe consider a point a great result. There would have been a ready-made excuse. The players were tired, travelling didn't help, it's still early days would have been stock responses, rehearsed in advance.

Rarely, though, in the last 30 years have the Reds possessed a team as relentless and determined as this one. Long before Mohamed Salah strode on to the Anfield turf, after his team-mates had just overturned a 3-0 deficit against Barcelona without him, wearing a T-shirt with the words 'NEVER GIVE UP' emblazoned on it, that attitude had once more been carved into the ethos of Klopp's Anfield.

It was one the old stadium and its inhabitants had once taken for granted. Ever since Bill Shankly walked through the doors in 1959, surrendering to adversity was simply not an option. It's just that for a while we seemed to have lost sight of it. Now it was back with a vengeance.

We all knew, after a bagging a record 97 points last season and still missing out on the title, that Liverpool simply couldn't afford to drop points against teams like Southampton. In fact, as far as Klopp was concerned, his players weren't allowed to drop points, period. More importantly, his players had completely bought into it too, a victory at St Mary's was not only demanded, it was expected too.

As I sipped my beer and struggled with the heat, my main concern was not player fatigue or a loss of focus, but the fear that Danny Ings, who had struggled with injury at Anfield but who had never lacked for effort and who knew where the goal was, might come back to haunt us. The move to Southampton for £19m was a great one for all concerned; I just hoped I still felt that way at full time.

I would, of course, but Ings would be ruing a missed opportunity to earn his side a great point and inflict a terrible psychological blow on Liverpool. Happily, thanks to a masterclass from Sadio Mané, who scored one and made one, the Reds ground out their second win of the season. As it would turn out, 'winning ugly' had become yet another string added to this team's bow.

The Reds started the game like a team that had travelled thousands of miles and who had played out 120 minutes of gruelling football halfway round the world just three days earlier. Klopp had done his best to provide his men with no excuses, but to be fair they could be forgiven for their heavy legs and weary minds.

However, Liverpool fielded their first-choice front three of Salah, Mané and Firmino for the first time since they had helped lift the European Cup in Madrid. And whereas Southampton would squander the many chances they created, with those three in our team, we always knew we wouldn't need many invitations to score.

And so it proved to be with virtually the last kick of the first half. Mané received a pass from James Milner and curled the ball into the far corner, past the sprawling arms of Angus Dunn in the Saints' goal. It was a stunner, deserving much more than the smattering of cheers in the bar, situated down by the beach and where I had opted to watch the game. I was only one of a handful of Reds in there, with plenty of Arsenal and Chelsea kits on display.

We were a goal up, but things had been far from easy. Still, I had faith, ordered a refill, and stared out to sea while contemplating the walk back to the apartment later. It's a tough life.

The bar had been reasonably quiet in the first half, with those in rival colours paying the game only a passing interest. A few left when Bobby Firmino put Liverpool two goals up in the 71st minute. It was a relief, yet I still couldn't relax. Especially because just seven minutes before the Reds scored, Ings had arrived as a 64th-minute substitute.

Firmino's goal arrived as a result of a Mané assist. The Senegalese striker was in inspirational form, giving Jan Bednarek in the Saints' defence a torrid time and forcing him into a mistake that opened the door for Bobby to score. The Brazilian took the ball past two defenders and unleashed a low drive into the bottom corner.

The Reds looked to be coasting until the 83rd minute, when they – or, more accurately Adrián – pressed the self-destruct button. With the ball at his feet, after a straightforward back-pass from Virgil van Dijk, Adrián had way more time than his behaviour suggested. Instead of spraying the ball out wide, he inexplicably punted it forward and was immediately charged down by none other than Ings.

The ball went straight into the net off the shin of Ings. It was a comedy of errors, again, and cheers once more rang around the bar – not just from the one or two Southampton fans who had so far been inconspicuous, but from the remaining Chelsea and Arsenal supporters who had also been joined by a couple of Manchester City shirts. It seemed like an unholy alliance was conspiring against us, but I had probably just had too much beer in the afternoon sun.

My nerves were now shredded. After enduring extra time and penalties earlier in the week, the thought of the Reds carrying out a desperate rearguard action for the next seven minutes threatened to blow away my earlier confidence. To lose a two-goal lead would have been a terrible blow. Believe, I told myself, and then I ordered another beer.

It was at this point that Liverpool looked to be out on their feet. They hadn't returned home from Istanbul until 4.30am on the Thursday, and here they were just two days later facing the fight of their lives to hold on to a now slender lead. They of course did, but not before they almost gave me a heart attack in the dying seconds of the game.

Ings, who was now giving his former team-mates a hellish time, should have levelled from a centre from Yan Valery. However, he seemed to get his legs in a tangle and failed to make contact with the ball. It sailed mercifully wide, and my heart sighed with relief. Had he got the merest of touches, with Adrián stranded, it would have been a certain goal.

The expressions of disappointment on the faces around the bar brought a warm and fuzzy feeling to my belly, and I looked forward to the walk back and enjoying my evening at the hotel bar with the family, feeling all smug. It was back home to Liverpool the following day, and the journey would be more tolerable knowing the Reds had won.

However, it needn't have been so nervy, and I was frustrated that we had almost surrendered a commanding position. Better teams would have capitalised on our sloppiness, I thought.

To be fair to Adrián, though, he had suffered an ankle injury in Istanbul and had only been passed fit as late as 10am on the day of the game. He had pulled off a couple of decent saves, and I knew the return of Alisson would restore confidence to the back line. It was just a case of getting behind the lad, until Jürgen's first choice was back.

Klopp was equally understanding in his post-match analysis. In the mixed zone after the game, he would be generous in his assessment of his goalkeeping deputy's performance, pointing to his ankle injury as a defence of his error and mentioning that Alisson had made similar mistakes.

He said, 'It's a goalie thing to do at Liverpool. But no problem if we win the games. We played too many balls back to him in this period. I was happy with all of the stuff he did, all of the saves. The other players needed to feel more the responsibility in the build-up. You cannot give all of the balls back to him and hope the painkillers still help.'

Southampton's manager Ralph Hasenhüttl was naturally less content. In truth, he could have no complaints about the result. However, having come so close to snatching a draw from the jaws of defeat, it was undoubtedly hard for him to remain philosophical.

'Ingsy scored once but I think he could have been the big hero for us,' he told the waiting reporters. 'The second chance to miss was unbelievable. We had three men in the box there at that moment but didn't bring the ball over the line. That was really a pity, I must say. I think the guys, for what they invested today, they deserved to take one point and we didn't. That's tough to take, but finally we have to.' For Liverpool, a disastrous result had been avoided, albeit with a huge slice of luck. But, haven't we always been told, luck is a big part of any championship winning season. Didn't we tell everyone that, back in the 1980s? Ian Doyle, writing in the *Liverpool Echo*, summed the matter up perfectly: 'The quality may not always be there at present. But when it comes to digging deep, Liverpool clearly have character in spades. A potential banana skin was sidestepped in what is becoming trademark fashion for a Reds side that, while not fully functioning, are leaning heavily on the growing self-belief that no matter what the situation, no matter how testing the predicament, they know how to get the job done.'

As we would learn as the season wore on, this facet would prove to be the most significant evolution of Klopp's Liverpool. It would delight Reds everywhere and infuriate the rest in equal measure.

Chelsea 1 Liverpool 2: Klopp's Mentality Monsters Make it Six out of Six

By September 2019 chaos ruled in the UK. The government lost its majority in Parliament, which voted that it wouldn't exit the European Union without a deal, while most of its MPs were arguing that leave means leave, and Boris Johnson told so many fibs that even Facebook banned an advert by the Conservative Party. Meanwhile, the highest court in the land said the Conservative government had broken the law. Fortunately, there was one model of consistency and reliability in the land, and that was Jürgen Klopp's Liverpool team.

So, on 22 September, as the Reds made the trip to Stamford Bridge they did so as favourites. They had won their previous five games, following up the victories over Norwich, Southampton and Arsenal with comfortable successes against Burnley and Newcastle. They had also developed a habit of doing just what was necessary to get the job done. Gone was the 'heavy metal' and sometimes chaotic football of the early Klopp era, which was always entertaining if sometimes highly risky.

A 2-0 midweek defeat to Napoli in the Champions League aside, Liverpool supporters had now cast away their nervousness and scepticism about the team. They were at least confident that they would no longer see their side race into a 3-1 lead away from home, only for them to capitulate and lose 4-3, as they had done at Bournemouth in 2016, for example. This was a more reliable version of Klopp's Liverpool.

Their pragmatism would eventually see them soar to a record-breaking lead at the top of the table, but it was in sharp contrast to Pep Guardiola's City side who had battered Watford 8-0 a day earlier. The difference of course was that we knew the Reds' combined strikeforce could always grab an extra goal if needed, with the kind of defensive solidity we hadn't seen for years. City on the other hand had failed to replace Vincent Kompany, a decision that would leave them constantly vulnerable at the back.

It was therefore no surprise when Jürgen appeared unruffled by Pep's rout of Watford. His plan for the season involved winning ugly when necessary, and that would be just fine with all of us. After gaining 97 points the season before, and missing out on the title, we appreciated that there was absolutely no room for error this time out. All that mattered was winning by any means necessary.

However, there was one problem that this Red incarnation was yet to solve, and that was their record against the 'top teams'. Klopp didn't think it was an 'obvious' issue, but results told a mixed story.

As the game got under way, the Chelsea supporters occupying the Matthew Harding Stand unfurled a huge banner of Eden Hazard, the man who had left the Londoners for Real Madrid in the summer, much to Liverpool's relief. Without him, a trip to Stamford Bridge was far less intimidating. The banner did little to worry the travelling Kop, but at least it wasn't made of plastic.

Chelsea looked weak in the middle of the park and Liverpool were dangerous centrally with Fabinho controlling things, and out wide with Andy Robertson and Trent Alexander-Arnold rampaging down the wings. And it was the latter of Liverpool's two full-backs who opened the scoring for the Reds in the 14th minute.

The goal came about after Fabinho had set Sadio Mané off on a run with a brilliant pass; Chelsea seemed to panic, and Andreas Christensen brought him down with a desperate foul.

The resultant free kick was just a couple of yards outside the box, and it seemed like Henderson, standing tall, arms by his sides and chest out was gearing up to thump a shot at goal. Salah to his right, meanwhile, looked only mildly interested. It was a clever decoy because the Egyptian stepped forward and back-heeled the ball to the waiting Alexander-Arnold, who smashed his shot high into the net. It was 1-0 and the game was barely 15 minutes old.

The Reds' clinical ruthlessness was a contrast with Chelsea, who struggled and wasted what opportunities came their way. Their one breakthrough in the first half was ruled out for offside and Liverpool continued to probe. Then Lampard lost his left-back, Emerson Palmieri, to an ankle injury, leaving them vulnerable to raids from out wide.

Klopp's men soon won another set-piece close to goal. This time both full-backs were in on the act. Trent tapped the ball to Robertson who delivered a perfect cross on to the head of Firmino, who managed to out-jump Marcus Alonso and send the away end into raptures.

We were at the half-hour mark and the Reds were 2-0 up. Given the home side's frailties, Liverpool could and should have pressed home their advantage. However, Chelsea made it to half-time with just the two-goal deficit. To Lampard's credit, he somehow rallied his troops and the Londoners came out fighting in the second half.

Liverpool struggled and Kanté slowly started to control the midfield. It seemed a matter of time before Chelsea were back in the game and, to be fair, the goal that cut the Reds' lead in half was a cracker. Kanté was fully 20 yards out when he unleashed a shot that Adrián could get nowhere near.

In previous seasons, Liverpool would have crumbled, and the equaliser would have followed in no time at all. They maybe would have even conceded a later sucker punch and returned home empty-handed. Not this Liverpool team though. Not the mentality monsters, who would hold out for the win.

Paul Gorst, writing for the *Liverpool Echo,* agreed that the Reds had discovered a new-found resilience, saying, 'In seasons previous, the goal for the Blues would have signaled [sic] a Liverpool crumble, but this side is made of sterner stuff. They simply refused to wilt with Joël Matip and Virgil van Dijk in particular thriving.'

The victory, though a little uncomfortable in the end, allowed us all to take to social media and declare in annoying cliché that 'winning when you're not playing well is the mark of champions'. Our rivals would tell us that our luck would run out and that we'd been saved by VAR and all the usual stuff, which of course made the victory all the sweeter. When will they learn?

For *The Guardian,* Jacob Steinberg also commented on Liverpool's 'mental fortitude'. He continued, 'While it was strange to see Liverpool scrambling for control towards the end of this pulsating game the reality was they still possessed the mental fortitude to protect their pristine record at the top of the Premier League. Jürgen Klopp's side simply refused to buckle when Chelsea turned up the heat and, although the European champions were clinging on at times, in the end they were able to celebrate a rare and precious win at the home of one of their big-six rivals.'

The win meant that Liverpool had a perfect start to the season and were now on a run of 15 consecutive victories stretching back to the previous campaign. They had opened a five-point gap at the top and were already looking like champions in waiting. Britain on the other hand, continued to fall apart.

Last-Gasp Milner Breaks Foxes' Hearts as Liverpool Triumph Against Leicester

At the end of September, with the Reds already marching relentlessly towards their first title in 30 years, the world's kids took to the streets demanding action on climate change, forcing the UK Parliament into declaring a climate emergency, before the cabinet succeeded in kicking the matter clear into the long grass. British holidaymakers were being repatriated on a scale not seen in peacetime following the collapse of Thomas Cook, hundreds of homeless people were dying on the country's streets, and MPs decided they'd work weekends – not to deal with the ever-expanding list of crises but to get Brexit done.

None of us would have believed it at the time, but 2019 was but a cakewalk compared to the horror show that would unfold in 2020. Nevertheless, as October got going there was a growing sense that all the grown-ups had packed up and left for the coast, leaving the toddlers behind to run the planet.

At Anfield, of course, Liverpool were in expert hands and no matter what obstacles were thrown in their way, the coaching staff and the players had developed an uncanny knack of overcoming them. That meant a growing sense of confidence, and conversations in the bar before the game, in which we entertained thoughts of going all the way and winning the league.

The Reds were five points clear at the top of the table, they weren't just unbeaten, they had won every game. Sure, they weren't exactly convincing in each of those games, but they had found a way to get the job done. City were playing the following day, against Wolves, so this was a chance for the Reds to stretch the lead and put Guardiola and his players under a bit of pressure. It was a great time to be a Liverpool supporter.

However, after 30 years without a title, after numerous setbacks and near misses, we could never feel completely confident. There was always that nagging sense that something will go wrong. There will be a slip up. That's just who we are, isn't it?

Our opponents on 5 October were Leicester City, their manager was Brendan Rodgers. The man who had given us hope, and who had used that to kill us. Well, not exactly. But the last time I felt this confident, this assured that finally the title was coming home, was after that victory over Manchester City on 13 April 2014.

The Reds had beaten Manuel Pellegrini's side 3-2 and Philippe Coutinho's 78th-minute strike had moved them seven points clear at the top. Sure, City had two games in hand on us, but as I walked from the ground at full time, my eyes welled with tears. This is it, I thought. Finally, the wait is coming to an end. The sense of history in the making was all around me. There were just four games to go, we just had to keep it going, and not let it slip.

Of course, we did just that.

That was then, this was now. It wasn't April, it was October, and we had a long way to go. But that sense of something special brewing was growing and increasingly hard to ignore. Still, on this day we would come face to face with the man who had overseen that terrible fade away, the most painful of endings and the death of a dream. He was a potent reminder that the whole season, all the optimism and hope, could come crashing down around our ears in an instant.

For all the baggage of the Rodgers era, that horrible fly-on-the-wall *Being: Liverpool* debacle, the 'do it for Lucas' and the 'I have an envelope here' nonsense, I confess that I feel a degree of sympathy for him. However, his decision to dump Celtic, who were on the verge of something truly historic, for another tilt at the Premier League top four, didn't help his cause.

The company that makes the spread that resembles tar and tastes like the devil's armpit sweat, Marmite, came up with an interesting and ultimately honest slogan: 'You either love it or hate it'. While it's a strange advertising strategy, it worked. The product has entered the lexicon and is used to describe people who divide opinion. People will say that someone is 'a bit Marmite'.

Judging by the debates I often find myself in about Brendan Rodgers, we'd have to modify the slogan slightly. You either feel sorry for him or you hate him. No, that doesn't have quite the same ring to it does it?

Anyway, for Jürgen Klopp, who was still paying rent to Brendan for the house on Merseyside that he now calls home, all of this was immaterial. All that mattered was the three points. As far as Klopp and his players were concerned, there was simply no margin for error this season. As discussed elsewhere, that meant Liverpool supporters would be watching or suffering through the most incredible and memorable finales to games.

No matter what was thrown at them, this team refused to lie down and accept their fates until the last whistle sounded. And this game would be no different.

Going to Anfield in the 2019/20 season, as it had been the year before, was a joy. For me, it brought back memories of my youth, in the 1980s. Back then, at least according to my rose-tinted spectacles, I would walk to Anfield completely assured of victory. A defeat back then was viewed more with an expression of 'what the fuck happened there' than with anger or rage. That can't be entirely true, memory is a weird thing. But a pilgrimage to Walton Breck Road was always a joyous one back then, and so it is today.

It's worth pausing for a minute and reflecting on just how far we had come under Klopp. Remembering the dark days and the final embers of the Rodgers era, how far we had slipped. And yet here we were, once again crowned champions of Europe and with our sights set on the world title. As I took my seat on the Kop and gazed out over that lush green grass, cast half in the shadow of the Main Stand with the side nearest me bathed in glorious sunshine, at the Leicester fans tucked away in their corner of the Anfield Road, I thought, 'It's good to be a Red.'

Our opponents had been Premier League champions just a few years ago, in what I still regard as a glorious anomaly. I doubted they could repeat the feat but I felt certain that if we could win it this season, and keep hold of Klopp, then we would be no one-hit wonder.

The game seemed to take a while to get going, and it soon became clear that we were going to have to be patient. It seemed most in the Kop felt sympathy for the man in the opposition dugout because Brendan was given a decent reception as he strode out into the technical area. So he should be too; he's no Roy Hodgson after all.

Liverpool's opening goal would prove the perfect antidote to the opening 40 minutes. James Milner, who had toiled relentlessly through a half that offered little to get us off our seats, turned in a sublime left-footed cross that seemed to arc around the Leicester defence before falling deliciously into the path of Sadio Mané.

Suddenly, the grass opened up in front of him and the Senegal hitman raced into the open space. As one, the crowd rose from their seats. Kasper Schmeichel tried to make himself look as big as possible, but Sadio could see the postage stamp-sized spot at the back of the net, where that ball belonged, and he placed it right there.

The cheers left our lungs in an evaporation of relief as much as joy. In days gone by, we had always feared sides who came to Anfield for a point. They would dig in and make it difficult for us, encouraging us to become ever more desperate in our search for a goal, then, late on, they'd try to hit us with a sucker punch.

Leicester, particularly under Rodgers, were no smash and grab artists, but I felt the longer the game went without us getting a goal, the more uncomfortable it was going to get. Now we had that first one, just before half-time, they would have to have a go at us, and with our front three, they would be vulnerable to our pressing and counter-attacks.

The second half was better, with the Reds fashioning a few chances, but after Bobby Firmino had fired wide and Andy Robertson had a shot saved, a little nervousness returned. A 1-0 lead was a dangerous score heading into the final stages of the game. And so it proved to be.

There were a couple of warning signs before the Foxes achieved parity. Jamie Vardy found himself in a glorious position but seemed to take an age before pulling the trigger and the chance was squandered. The Reds' defence, which had been steadfast up to this point – even Dejan Lovren who hadn't started a league game since May was doing well – suddenly looked a little vulnerable.

It would be breached with just ten minutes remaining on the clock, and it felt like a kick in the teeth. In truth a draw at this stage of the season, even one at home, shouldn't set alarm bells ringing. But we all knew how tight things had been the season before and were desperate for the Reds to put clear blue water between themselves and the chasing pack. We would have no doubt viewed a draw as something akin to a defeat. Especially after being a goal up at home.

When James Maddison blasted a first-time shot under the body of Adrián in the Liverpool goal, I was cursing. The people all around me were doing the same. 'Where was Fabinho there?' 'The keeper should have done better.' 'Bloody typical.' Our frustration was writ large in our expressions and screamed into the air, but we knew better than to throw in the towel, not with a full 600 seconds left on the clock.

As it turned out, thanks to the referee playing five minutes of added-on time instead of the four that flashed on the board held up by the fourth official, we would wait a full 900 seconds for our moment of sheer exhilaration.

With time virtually up, and the proverbial fat lady going through her vocal ranges, Mané was once again causing mischief in the Foxes' penalty area. He was out wide on the left-hand side of the box, as we were looking at him from the Kop, and seemingly going nowhere when his legs became entangled with

Marc Albrighton's. Down he went and the referee pointed immediately to the spot.

The ensuing roar was so loud that anyone wandering along Anfield Road or Walton Breck Road at that moment would have been forgiven for thinking the Reds had scored. I would later watch that moment back and think to myself that Mané may have bought that penalty. He got lucky, we got lucky. But he was in the box during the dregs of the game, looking for something for his team, and he found it. If you don't buy the ticket, you don't win the raffle.

However, gone are the days when a referee's word is final, and the inevitable and agonising wait for the obligatory VAR check felt almost unbearable. Had we been denied that spot-kick, it would have felt like the cruellest of blows and the inevitable celebrations in the Leicester section would have been like a kick in the gut.

When, after what seemed like an age, the penalty was confirmed, another thunderous cheer rang around the ground. Now all we had to do was score the damn thing. VAR has introduced many challenges into the game, for supporters who go through the full spectrum of emotions before knowing for sure they can celebrate a goal, and for the players, like James Milner, whose mental preparation time before taking the penalty was stretched almost beyond reason.

This was a pressure-cooker moment for the number seven. With the score tied at 1-1, and this certain to be the last kick of the game, failure from the spot was simply not an option. As I chewed my nails, and prayed to a God I didn't believe in, my stomach did cartwheels.

Inside the ground the noise of the crowd was like the hum of a machine, as voices muttered 'come on, James' or whispered appeals to their own deities. Then, the referee's whistle sounded, Anfield fell silent for an instant, then the thud as the boot hit the ball, the intake of 54,000 breaths and the crack as it hit the net.

Roar! Anfield, like a volcano, rained down joy and sheer relief on the players.

We had done it again. When the game seemed up, when the odds seemed impossible and when nerves and sinews of steel were required, James Milner, the rest of the team and the mighty Anfield had delivered yet again.

If ever anyone asks you why you care so much about football; why you shell out so much of your hard-earned and much-needed pennies to follow the fortunes of these men? show them a moment like that. Tell them, if you can find the words, what it feels like in that instant. There is no better way to win a game than in the dying embers of the fire, when all hope seems lost and the last flame looks to have flickered out.

The sense that this could have been a pivotal moment in the race for the title was overwhelming. That was 17 straight Premier League wins for Liverpool, and they were now eight points clear. There was now clear blue water between us and the rest, and the Reds were ready to set sail for the horizon.

Manchester United 1 Liverpool 1: Solidarity, Food Banks and Another Late, Late Show

Liverpool versus Manchester United is one of the fiercest and most hotly contested matches in the football calendar. The simmering rivalry between the two cities and the supporters frequently boils over, and the desire to win is always huge on both sides of the M62. However, as the Reds travelled to Old Trafford on 20 October 2019, one group of Liverpool fans was carrying parcels of food instead of hate.

Fans Supporting Foodbanks, an initiative set up by a group of fans who follow both Liverpool and Everton, regularly travels around the country supporting similar initiatives in towns and cities across the land. Ian Byrne, Dave Kelly, Robert Daniels and a host of others established the campaign in response to a genuine crisis on the city's streets and in its homes because of the UK government's controversial austerity programme.

The UK, at the end of the second decade of the 21st century, was the sixth-richest nation on Earth. However, there remain people – many of them in work – who don't have enough money to feed their families. Estimates suggest that as many as 14.3 million people were living in poverty, including 3.9 million children.

Robbie Daniels, an Everton supporter and co-founder of Fans Supporting Foodbanks, summed-up those behind the organisation's work and explained why football rivalry should be secondary when it comes to supporting those in need: 'There is a need for communities to come together in common cause. Austerity, Universal Credit the Bedroom Tax and the massive underfunding of city councils is hurting the people we care about.

'The power of football supporters through fan activism should never be overlooked, and I'm proud that in times of trouble the fans of this great city come together as one to support the most vulnerable in society. It's the right thing to do, the moral thing to do and it's the Scouse thing to do.'

Fans Supporting Foodbanks took its inspiration from the Celtic fan group, The Green Brigade, which regularly holds collections in its own communities. The spirit of solidarity in Glasgow and the belief in communities coming together to support each other was something that resonated strongly with the lads.

Ian and Robbie were adamant that rivalry should exist for 90 minutes only, saying, 'For 90 minutes, on the pitch and in the stands, we celebrate our rivalries and support our teams. But, after that, we would urge working-class supporters across the country to understand who our real enemies are.

'The people who propagate austerity and policies like zero-hours contracts that drive working families into poverty and food banks, they are the people we should turn our anger on. Not each other.

'Race, religion and football allegiances, these are all just ways in which we can be set against each other. When we fall for it, it makes implementing austerity easier. Our message is to challenge this false narrative and to always remember that unity is strength.'

As he boarded the coach, travelling to Old Trafford, Ian Byrne told TV crews covering the campaign, 'My enemy is not someone who speaks with a Salford accent or a Geordie accent. I don't care if you're a Cockney either. My enemies are the people who make me do this, who drive my community to food banks. They are also enemies of the people of Manchester too.'

Such community spirit is commendable and the idea of football supporters setting aside their differences in the interest of a wider issue helps restore faith in humanity. It does not mean we can't be rivals for 90 minutes though, and that was exactly the case as the two sides faced off in Manchester.

Liverpool had won their opening eight games. They hadn't lost a league football match since January and sat at the top of the table. Confidence was high, even though their recent record at Old Trafford was less than impressive. This Liverpool team was vastly superior in every way to Manchester United, and *this* United team were in 14th place, just one point above relegation.

Facing Jürgen Klopp in the home dugout was Ole Gunnar Solskjær, a man whose previous assignments included managing the United reserve team, Norwegian side Molde, and Cardiff City. He had been appointed caretaker manager at Old Trafford after Jose Mourinho was sacked following a particularly chastening defeat to Liverpool at Anfield. Eventually, United awarded him a permanent contract, much to the delight of Reds supporters everywhere.

This was a managerial mismatch of epic proportions. Logic dictated a Liverpool win. However, football has an annoying habit of serving up illogical outcomes. And, so it was to be at Old Trafford. David Hytner, writing for *The Guardian* after the game, agreed: 'By any objective measure, this had seemed like an away banker during a fevered build-up. Manchester United, mired in their worst start to a season since 1989/90, were goal-shy, their confidence seemingly in pieces. Liverpool were supposed to roll up to Old Trafford and extend their run of consecutive wins in the Premier League to a record-equalling 18th game. Solskjær, the eternal optimist, had claimed that "this is the perfect game for us" but, to put it bluntly, nobody believed him. Perhaps they should have done.'

That may have been over-stating things a little. This was far from a 'perfect game' for United, but neither was it for Liverpool. The Reds started sluggishly and laboured through the first 30 minutes of the game. Then disaster struck, as it so often does for Liverpool on this pitch.

All the Reds had to show for the opening half-hour was a tame Roberto Firmino shot at David de Gea that did little justice to a flowing move and cross from Sadio Mané. With the game struggling for a defining moment, one was provided in controversial circumstances in the 38th minute.

Another Liverpool move broke down when Victor Lindelöf clumsily tackled Divock Origi from behind. With the striker lying crumpled on the turf, clutching his ankle, the referee simply waved play on. Suddenly, Daniel James swept out to Liverpool's left, with defenders racing to get back into position, and sent a delightful pass that eluded everyone. Racing into the box was Marcus Rashford, who dispatched his effort past a helpless Alisson, who was playing his first game after being injured in the season opener against Norwich City.

It was 1-0 to United and their supporters could scarcely believe their luck. There won't have been many occasions in the last 30 years when they would have trudged their way to Old Trafford fearing the worst. But this would surely have been one.

Liverpool under Jürgen Klopp, though, had developed an incredible knack of finding their way out of tricky situations. No team playing against the Reds was able to relax until the final whistle sounded, even if they were ahead. It would lead to the development of an all-consuming fear factor in their opponents, and an unassailable never-say-die spirit that coursed through the veins of each and every member of Klopp's squad.

To put it simply, if even a 3-0 advantage for Barcelona was not enough to vanquish this Liverpool side, then a lesser team like United could ill afford to rest easy with a simple 1-0 lead. With time running out though, and the clock ticking towards the 85th minute, those in the Stretford End must have started entertaining thoughts of a famous victory, and months of bragging rights. Not to mention another opportunity to say they had dented yet another title bid.

Their hopes would have hit the stratosphere when Mané had a goal ruled out by VAR for handball. On the bench, Solskjær began to dream. Fortunately for those in the away end, Andy Robertson and Adam Lallana had other ideas.

Mané found himself with the ball at his feet 25 yards out and opted to slide it out wide to the advancing Robertson. The Scotsman took it on a few feet and whipped in a delightful cross, which left the United defence looking like statues. Ghosting in at the far post was Lallana for the simplest of tap-ins.

The travelling Kop went ballistic and in the commentary box, Gary Neville punched his desk, while Jamie Carragher silently revelled in the moment. Liverpool had been having a very rare off-day yet United had squandered their opportunity.

The Reds had come bearing gifts off the field, but on it they were proving as stingy as ever. That's exactly as it should be of course.

In the closing moments, Klopp's side could have won the game and many people, back on Merseyside and beyond, would bemoan the two dropped points. However, the fact that a draw at Old Trafford was now seen as a source of disappointment for Reds fans and celebration for United supporters was perhaps a marker of Liverpool's continued rise.

However, the progress made in the months ahead would show everyone that we hadn't seen anything yet. Klopp's juggernaut was only just getting started.

Liverpool 5 Arsenal 5: Liverpool Kids Emerge Victorious as Anfield Basks in Ten-Goal Thriller

On 30 October, Parliament had held its last Prime Minister's Questions before the country went to the polls on 12 December, football clubs were handing out food parcels to hungry families, and we were about to witness a campaign for the soul of the nation which would eventually, it seems, be claimed by the bony hand of the devil. Meanwhile, the Reds got ready for one of the most remarkable nights in the history of the League Cup and Anfield.

With victories over Genk in the Champions League and Tottenham in the Premier League under their belts, Liverpool turned their attention to the Carabao Cup. It was of course a competition that Klopp suggested the Reds may not participate in, before settling on a very youthful line-up to take on Arsenal.

The Reds handed a debut to 17-year-old Neco Williams, and gave starts to Caoimhin Kelleher, Sepp van den Berg, Harvey Elliott and Rhian Brewster. There was also an explosive substitute appearance by young Scouser Curtis Jones.

They would all play key roles in what would become the highest-scoring fixture in the history of the League Cup, and as such have written their names into the history of football and the legend of Anfield.

The game ended 5-5 in normal time, and it had everything, including a last-minute leveller, following an assist from a debutant. The Reds then edged a dramatic penalty shoot-out thanks to the heroics of a local lad, in front of his beloved Kop.

Liverpool reached the quarter-finals of the competition, sparking scenes of wild celebration on the pitch and in the stands.

Writing in *The Guardian*, Andy Hunter captured the magic of the evening: 'Unai Emery [Arsenal manager] could point to Caoimhin Kelleher's penalty save from Dani Ceballos in an otherwise flawless shoot-out as the fine margin that often separates teams at this level. It would not be entirely true.

'His team traded ten goals with Liverpool, ranging from ugly to stunning and including everything in between. They traded dreadful mistakes and blows from beginning to end of an enthralling cup tie too. But only one side possessed the belief that the game is never over, and it was not the team that led from the 26th minute until the 94th, that led 3-1, 4-2 and 5-4 in stoppage time.'

The Reds were already developing a winning mentality and penchant for going to the very end in games. The win over Spurs three days earlier had shown how they could come from behind and the victory over Leicester had illustrated their never-say-die attitude, as would many more games to come. What this night showed though, was that these qualities were not limited to the first team. Liverpool's refusal to accept defeat and fighting spirit ran right through the entire club and was evident at all levels.

This was a cup tie that swung back and forth and put supporters through every emotion possible. For those on the Kop it ended in ecstasy, for the travelling Arsenal fans, it brought agony. But it was always enthralling.

Even those on the defeated side would acknowledge what a thrilling experience it had been. Héctor Bellerin, who had captained the Gunners, said, 'I have to say it was great to play this kind of game. The tempo of the play, the goals – this is football. This is what you play football for, for nights like this. Whatever the score, today we're gutted, but I'm sure there's going to be nights that go in our favour.'

The average age of Liverpool's starting line up was 23, compared to Arsenal's which was almost 25. And another hero on the night would be Kelleher, their 20-year-old third-choice goalkeeper, whose penalty save in the shoot-out set up the opportunity for Curtis Jones to fulfil a lifelong dream.

However, Liverpool had only been granted the opportunity to contest penalties thanks to the brilliance of young debutant Williams and a stunning volley from Divock Origi. It was the perfect ending to regulation time, and had it been presented as a script idea to a Hollywood producer, it would have been flatly rejected as too far-fetched. Not that anyone on the Kop would have been surprised though, these sorts of dramatic climaxes are now our stock in trade.

Time was almost up. Arsenal had led 5-4 from the 70th minute and the game headed into the 90th. A night that had been a free hit had become a must win, and as Liverpool's second and third strings combined to create the equaliser that would take the game to penalties, the supporters in all four corners of the ground lapped it up.

On the touchline, Klopp grinned. He was revelling in the spectacle and willing his charges on. As far as he was concerned, they had already done themselves proud, and delivered more than he could ever have expected. He would tell journalists after the game, 'I don't know when I had so much fun at a football game.'

Who could blame him? Liverpool had gone ahead in the sixth minute thanks to a Shkodran Mustafi own goal, before going 3-1 down. Suddenly, Klopp's decision to make so many changes looked to have backfired, but this game had more than a few twists and turns left in it.

The Reds seemed to temporarily fall apart and their touch and passing seemed to have deserted them. However, a run by Harvey Elliott into the Arsenal box in the closing stages of the first half resulted in a foul by Gabriel Martinelli. Andre Marriner immediately signalled a penalty, which James Milner put away with ease. The first half had been pulsating and thrilling, and with the score at 3-2, no one could wait for the second period to start. However, Liverpool were presented with another mountain to climb just nine minutes after the restart when a mistake by Milner gifted Ainsley Maitland-Niles a goal and Arsenal had four.

Liverpool, determined that their opponents would not have the last word, picked themselves up and fought back. Just four minutes later Oxlade-Chamberlain unleashed a thunderous 25-yard shot that rifled into the top corner of the net.

Curtis Jones, a young Scouser who had once supported the Reds from the Kop, had already joined the action from the bench after an injury to Naby Keïta in the 55th minute. He soon had a hand in Liverpool's fourth and equalising goal. The youngster's pass found Origi on the edge of the Arsenal box, and the Belgian escaped his marker and smashed a shot past Martinez.

It was 4-4 and if the referee had blown the whistle then and there, we would have all felt we had received full value from the game. But there was even more drama to follow.

Arsenal's fifth goal even drew appreciative applause from some on the Kop, having been scored by Joe Willock, who had ridden a coach and horses through the Reds' midfield before unleashing a fantastic shot from 30 yards into the Liverpool goal. It was an absolute stunner and good enough to win any ordinary game, but this match was far from a normal one. And this was Anfield.

With seconds remaining on the clock, Williams found himself out on the right, deep in the Arsenal half. Looking up, with all the presence of thought of a seasoned pro, he spotted Origi lurking in the penalty area, and sent in a stunning cross. The Belgian did the rest, volleying the ball into the back of the net to an explosion of joy behind the goal.

The celebrations on the pitch were equally joyous, but nothing compared to those at the conclusion of the resultant shoot-out. A miss by Dani Ceballos saw the scores tied at 4-4 as Jones stepped up to take his spot-kick in front of the Kop.

Supporters held their breath as the youngster stood hands on hips and waited for the referee's whistle. If he was churning with emotion inside, there was no outward evidence of that. With a puff of his cheeks, he raced forward and smashed his penalty into the net and immediately reeled away in celebration with the cheers of thousands in his ears. It must surely have been a dream of his, and it had now been fulfilled.

He told reporters, 'Being a local lad, it's always been my dream to get an appearance at Anfield. To get an assist to give us a chance and then to score a penalty is just a dream come true. I was calm, I picked my spot and I was fortunate enough that the winning penalty went in. This is just the beginning. I'm just a young lad and I've still got a long way to go. Any opportunities I'll take with both hands. This is what you play football for.'

Moments like that are why people like me watch football too. Klopp was in fine form as he greeted journalists in the post-match press conference. Grinning ear-to-ear, he told them, 'I enjoyed pretty much each second of the game. I was so happy for the kids that they will remember their first night at Anfield for the rest of their life. In the end they made it a proper special football night. Everybody who came tonight saw 19 goals, including the shoot-out, that's pretty special. Really perfect, absolutely perfect. Maybe as a manager I should think more about or worry about the goals that we conceded but I couldn't care less to be honest. I couldn't care less tonight.' Nobody was worried about defence or goals conceded. They had paid to see a cup tie, to be entertained and to see a glimpse of Liverpool's future. They had been amply rewarded, and on the evidence of this game, the future was a bright one.

THE WORLD IS NOT ENOUGH

Liverpool FC: November 2019–January 2020

The Lost Shankly Boy, Robbo and Mané: Liverpool Vanquish Villa with Late Salvo

On 2 November 2019, Britain was still enthralled with Brexit controversies and gearing up for a General Election. October rain had battered the country, causing floods, and prompting a series of bizarre publicity stunts featuring the country's oafish prime minister, Boris Johnson, a mop and bucket and an incredulous camera crew. Little did any of us know but to our eventual horror he would get the job on a permanent basis just in time for Christmas.

Liverpool had gone 27 games without defeat and were now immovable at the top of the table. It seemed nothing could stop them, and 200 miles to the south, Arsenal fans were haunted by nightmares which involved their 'Invincibles' being usurped by the 'Inevitables', led by a grinning Klopp.

Meanwhile the Reds had travelled to Birmingham to take on Aston Villa, and I was on a train to Liverpool city centre to meet a forgotten player from the Shankly era. I would leave that meeting having agreed to collaborate on his autobiography, but events in the Midlands provided even more excitement on my journey home. We'll get to that in due course.

As I sat in the Merseyrail carriage on my way into town and staring blankly out the window watching raindrops tracing their way down the glass, I began musing on whether all those years ago, in the 1960s, some sort of deal had been struck with the Devil. Perhaps Liverpool are only allowed to be successful when the country is ruled by an evil Tory government, I wondered. Nah, we did all right under Harold Wilson and Jim Callaghan, I told myself.

I got off the train at Moorfields and began walking in the winter drizzle towards the Shankly Hotel on Victoria Street. It was nearing kick-off time and tourists raced past me, their suitcases bobbing behind them on wheels, as they sought out bars and hotels where they could watch the game. I walked on towards my meeting with George Scott.

George was one of Bill Shankly's first signings. After a few exchanges on social media and a couple of phone calls, I had become convinced he had a fascinating story to tell. I was keen to get his views on the current season and explore how he felt Klopp compared to the great Scot who laid the foundations all those years ago. In my mind, I thought it would make an interesting article. It would end up being much more than that, of course.

By the time we sat down to talk, the game was already under way. It wasn't being broadcast live, and instead the TV screens dotted around the bar area featured *Gillette Soccer Saturday,* and between the constant temptation to check on the score and frequent interruptions from supporters who had recognised George, I realised this meeting would run much longer than I thought. What could I do but sit there and drink beer and chat about the glory days of the 1960s. It's a tough life, but I'm dedicated to my craft.

Klopp had gone for a strong line-up. The inclusion of Dejan Lovren in defence, in place of Joél Matip, had led to the usual despair on social media. But this was a strong Liverpool side that would surely strike terror into the hearts of Villa's players and fans, or so I thought. I decided to relax and allowed myself only a momentary glance at the TV screen nearest to our table.

George and I began by reminiscing about an incredible night at Anfield just a few days earlier, when a group of Liverpool youngsters had triumphed at the end of a ten-goal thriller against Arsenal. George had been a promising youngster, full of hopes and dreams and he knew only too well the dangers of getting too carried away. Nevertheless, even he was excited by the development of players like Neco Williams and Curtis Jones.

As we chatted away, we were completely oblivious to the fact that the Reds' senior team were also putting our travelling support through a rollercoaster ride of their own in the Midlands. In addition, we had no idea of the huge VAR-inspired controversy that could so easily have robbed Liverpool of another three points.

I watched the game later, on TV, and was incredulous at how the experts at Stockley Park could have disallowed a perfectly good first-half goal, scored apparently as a result of Bobby Firmino's offside armpit. The decision to rule out his strike would force the Premier League into all manner of contortions as it attempted in vain to justify the obvious injustice.

'The red line signifies Firmino and was aligned to his armpit, which was marginally ahead of the last Villa defender,' read the statement. So that's where we were, in 2020, armpits could be offside. Perhaps our enemies were right after all, maybe we would struggle once VAR came into effect. The trouble for them of course was that they had now changed their tune and were arguing that VAR was part of an elaborate plot to guarantee Liverpool a 'tainted title'.

The Reds had struggled to settle initially but had still managed to test the Villa rearguard a couple of times, with Mané and Salah going close. I was of course oblivious to this and when I looked up at the TV, 20 minutes into the game, I was horrified to see that the home side had taken the lead through Trézéguet. Liverpool had conceded from a set-piece and Jeff Stelling, underlined by the Sky Sports scores ticker tape, was in animated mode.

Above the clatter of glasses, I informed George that we had gone behind. We both rolled our eyes and got back to the beer and conversation. I guess we just weren't that worried.

'The thing about Klopp that really reminds me of Shankly,' said George, 'is that he won't tolerate the players giving in or their heads going down. He always believes that you keep going until the final whistle.

'He demands that of the supporters too, but I'm sure he trains the lads with that in mind. They are so fit, and that allows them to keep scoring late goals. The opposition are just worn down.

'It was like that under Shanks. He ran us into the ground in training, but we knew that would make us stronger and give us more endurance than our opponents. It worked and that was the real start of the "never give up" mentality of the club.'

Apparently Villa's goal had also been subjected to a lengthy VAR check but eventually the genius that is Martin Atkinson, this time armed with a video camera and not a whistle, the man who had been the villain of the piece at Old Trafford, the scene of Liverpool's only dropped points to date, felt it should stand. He was of course far less generous when Firmino converted a Sadio Mané assist, and to all sane people equalised for Liverpool. So Klopp's team would have to dig deep once more, draw on their reserves of belief and fight to the death if they were to get anything from this game. Wijnaldum, Mané and Salah all wasted glorious opportunities to level and Villa's goalkeeper Tom Heaton proved impregnable for much of the second half.

The introduction of Alex Oxlade-Chamberlain and Divock Origi almost bore fruit, and I later watched as the former blasted two shots at a Villa defence that was, by that stage, 11 strong and permanently camped in its own 18-yard area. Then Lallana missed from close range after a good work by Bobby Firmino.

As the travelling Kop doubtlessly began chewing through their nails, George and I continued our chat. Although the glances at the television became more frequent and angsty. The game was heading to a conclusion and the Reds were still behind.

Eventually it was time to leave, and with a gentleman's agreement for us both to work on George's autobiography sealed with a handshake, I made my way forlornly back to Moorfields station.

I was excited at the prospect of another project and was eager to get in touch with my publisher, but I always get this churning in my stomach when Liverpool are losing. It's like hunger pains that gnaw at you until the next opportunity to put things right. With our next game being against Manchester City, the thought of going into that on the back of a miserable defeat to Aston Villa just deepened the pain and intensified the gnawing. I couldn't think about anything else as I boarded the train home.

I took my seat and didn't bother looking at my phone. I was deep beneath the city's streets and knew I'd get no signal until the train emerged into the watery sunlight and approached Sandhills station. So, I sat there staring at the window again and praying for a miracle. My watch told me that if one were to arrive, it would need to get a move on. There were just minutes of normal time left.

Then the carriage filled with light and I looked at my phone, waiting impatiently for the 4G indicator to appear, announcing that I had signal and could check what I felt must be the final score. It eventually did and I opened the Twitter app immediately and began furiously refreshing my timeline.

A single tweet, I think it was from James Pearce of The Athletic, caused my heart to soar. It simply said 1-1. I punched the air and shouted 'Yes!' Fortunately, there was no one else in the carriage. Scrolling through numerous tweets I could see that Andy Robertson had scored an 87th-minute leveller.

I'm not a religious man. I have been an atheist for most of my life and I reject all forms of mysticism. However, when it comes to football, I'm not confident enough in my convictions to take chances. Some things are just too important, and cockiness often comes before a fall.

I could probably write a book on the bizarre football-related rituals I have allowed to consume me over the years. I once even decided that it was the rituals themselves that were bringing Liverpool bad luck, and that if I could force myself to stop, we'd start winning trophies.

That was at the start of the 2000/01 season. I managed to keep it up for a while, until my friends convinced me that my television was lucky and I had to leave it on, set to the channel that was broadcasting our games, even if I was out at work or at the game.

Anyway, this tendency to become consumed with superstition and the irrational belief that my actions somehow influence the outcome of sporting events taking place hundreds of miles away caused me to turned off my phone and put it in my pocket. The equaliser had been scored while I wasn't looking at it, I reasoned, therefore if I didn't look at it during injury time, well who knew what might happen.

The remainder of the journey was spent telling myself that a draw away from home wasn't all that bad. And, the psychological lift of snatching a point from the jaws of defeat would give the lads a lift going into the all-important game against City the following weekend.

I got off the train at Fazakerley and debated whether it would be good karma to wait until I was back inside the house before checking the phone, or if I could safely do it now. I couldn't wait and pulled it out of my pocket, hastily switching it back on.

I couldn't believe my eyes. It was 2-1. Liverpool had won a corner, after Trent Alexander-Arnold, making his 100th appearance for the club, saw his free kick deflected wide. As the ball sailed into the box, Mané ducked his head and flicked the ball over his shoulder, past the helpless Heaton and into the net. The away end at Villa Park filled with red smoke as supporters celebrated deliriously. Liverpool had snatched all three points and in the most dramatic way possible. More importantly, they had maintained a six-point lead over their nearest challengers, Manchester City.

Pep Guardiola's men had won narrowly against Southampton, and Mané's late winner would have hurt them as much as it delighted us. That presented Jürgen and his boys with an opportunity to go nine points clear. Surely that was too much to ask. Wasn't it? As I put the key in the door, my phone pinged. It was a message from George Scott, a lost Shankly Boy: 'What a team we support Jeff. Just like the one I joined in 1960.'

There could be no better endorsement of Klopp's Liverpool than that.

Liverpool 3-1 Manchester City: Pep Fumes as Reds Set the Benchmark

The Reds went into their clash with Manchester City on 10 November on the back of two narrow wins. It was still early days in terms of the destination of the Premier League championship, but the media were already billing this as a title decider. Images depicting the fine margins by which Liverpool lost to Pep Guardiola's team at the Etihad a season earlier were replayed endlessly in the pre-match build-up.

Discussions about what might have been dominated the chatter in the pub. Liverpool, it's true, had been just millimetres from earning a valuable point that day back in January 2019. It had been their last defeat. Had they managed a draw, the league title would have arrived at Anfield a year earlier.

For all the hollow bragging of United and Everton supporters, who managed draws against Liverpool and proceeded to claim they had cost us the championship, the simple truth is we lost it at the Etihad on that wintery evening in Manchester.

There was also the question of the Community Shield defeat in August. We all pretend not to care about that, but if you make the trip to Wembley you want to win the thing. Losing it is a bitter disappointment, especially on penalties. The journey back had been a miserable one and the hangover the following day ferocious, so I yearned for vengeance for all of that.

Liverpool led City, who were in second place before the game, by six points. They now had the chance to go nine clear of Guardiola's expensively assembled team. All the ingredients necessary to ensure a combustible encounter were present, and all that was needed was the referee to blow his whistle and light the blue touchpaper.

City fancy themselves as rivals of Liverpool. In truth, that's something they are never likely to be. Just like Chelsea before them and Nottingham Forest in another era, they have proved to be nothing more than a transient irritant. The nouveaux-riche outfit, funded by the wealth of a sovereign state, will have to splash the cash for a generation before they will ever be considered a real rival.

For most Reds, our club only has two genuine historical rivalries, Everton and Manchester United. I cannot see that changing any time soon. These things can't be invented, they must emerge organically. Nevertheless, they had proven themselves to be a worthy adversary and one we would have to beat if we wanted to claim the ultimate prize in May.

To that end, the atmosphere inside the stadium at kick-off was so thick it felt heavy. Watching the game, courtesy of Liverpool FC, was Sean Cox and his family. The Irishman had suffered a traumatic brain injury after being attacked by a group of AS Roma fans outside the Kop before the 2018 Champions League semi-final at Anfield.

The roar as the game got under way was so loud that it left my ears ringing and everyone around me seemed to be wearing a grimace on their faces. The Kop was like a huge army on a hillside, ready to charge, and Liverpool flew at City.

City looked decent, and they had their moments in the opening exchanges. But it took the Reds just six minutes to breach their defences. We'd barely drawn breath when the ball fell to the feet of Fabinho. He looked to be 30 yards out from my perspective, but his shot was like a laser and it flew past the outstretched arm of Claudio Bravo, deputising for the injured Ederson,

We celebrated in a tumult of hugs and fist punching as some climbed on their seats to wave their scarves, which had been tied to wrists like some homage to the 1970s, jubilantly in the air. Few of us noticed there had been a VAR check and none of us in Block 109 had realised that Trent Alexander-Arnold may have handled the ball in the build-up.

The goal was eventually given and we got to cheer once more. On the touchline, Guardiola once more went through his repertoire of theatrical histrionics and his players shook their heads as the game got back under way. We didn't care. Nor did we have any idea that there was a chance the goal could be ruled out and the ball taken back to our penalty area for a City spot-kick.

Again, City went on the front foot in search of a quick equaliser, but this is a Liverpool team that thrives on playing against open, attacking opponents. Just seven minutes later they plundered another goal when a superb ball by Andy Robertson was headed home by Mohamed Salah.

In the past, I think we'd have been nervous. Despite the two-goal lead, we'd have feared a City fightback. But this season all that had gone. There was something different about this Liverpool team, something relentless, ruthless, and ready for anything that came their way.

City huffed and puffed, and Guardiola fumed, but there was a growing sense they had nothing we couldn't handle. Even when Sterling went close and Agüero's shot was deflected on to the upright, nobody worried because we knew that the Reds always had another goal in them.

A two-goal lead at half-time can be a dangerous one. The first ten minutes after the break is often crucial. Had Liverpool conceded early in the second half, who knew what could happen. Had they scored a third, we would all have been in dreamland. It came as no surprise that it was the latter.

In the 51st minute Henderson sent the ball into the City box. Bravo hesitated and Sadio Mané headed into the net, right in front of a jubilant Kop. It was 3-0 now and Liverpool were cruising. City did manage a reply with 12 minutes left on the clock, through Bernardo. Liverpool had probably been guilty of easing off after their third and had allowed City too much possession. Still, the goal came too late to threaten to spoil the party.

There was still time for another controversial moment when Alexander-Arnold appeared to have handled in the box. The City players appealed furiously for a penalty, but referee Michael Oliver waved them away. It was a moment that almost caused Guardiola's head to explode and he would become an instant meme as he thrust two fingers in the air and stared skyward, screaming 'twice, twice' into the abyss.

Behind him, Main Stand residents chuckled and on the pitch the Reds just got on with winning the game. Andy Hunter, writing in *The Guardian,* described Pep's furious outburst: 'Guardiola lost himself in fury on the touchline because the Liverpool full-back had got away with something similar at the start of the game. Nobody knows how fine the margins might have been if City had been granted the late penalty or, indeed, the early one and the visitors did have a couple of flickers in the closing stages, when Liverpool looked heavy-legged. Yet Klopp's team were able to close out the result and he was entitled to say that, until Silva's goal, it had been Liverpool who were in control.'

Guardiola couldn't let go of his anger and it would continue to bubble and boil after the final whistle. The BBC's Phil McNulty captured the manager's rage in his post-match report. He wrote: 'Guardiola was fuming at the final whistle, appearing to thank referee Michael Oliver sarcastically before leaving the pitch, shortly after being enraged when another penalty claim against Alexander-Arnold was waved away.'

As we filed out of the ground and headed for our after-match celebrations, all of us sensed something had finally shifted in the title race. More than that though, it felt significant in so many ways. Too often in the past, when faced with an opportunity to take advantage of an opponent's stumbles, or stamp their authority, Liverpool have faltered.

However, when presented with the chance to hammer another nail in the coffin of City's title defence, this time the Reds had grasped it with both hands. They looked at long last like the real deal. McNulty agreed: 'The manner in which Klopp and Anfield celebrated this victory said everything about its magnitude – if self-belief was not surging through them before, then it surely is now after last season's champions were overcome.

'A huge roar went up from the Kop as Liverpool's players gathered in front of it after the final whistle. Such is their form this season, with 11 wins from 12 league games, that it is surely their title to lose now. This is a team who have lost one of their past 51 league games – where will the numerous slips needed for them to lose this lead come from?'

Jürgen Klopp, speaking on BBC Radio 5 Live, was in triumphant mood and lauded his players: 'What a game. If you want to win against City you have to do something special and we had to be intense. When City started to control it more in the last 15 minutes, it was tense, but then you saw the quality and what the boys can do it. The boys did 75 minutes of unbelievable stuff.'

The defeat had put clear daylight between the Reds and the chasing pack. They were now eight points ahead of second-placed Leicester. City had lost significant ground, however, and had now slumped to fourth place behind Chelsea. As I made my way home later, it was hard to escape the significance of this moment. It really did feel like we had taken one giant stride towards number 19.

Liverpool 'Reserves' Tarnish Marco's Silva Lining

On 5 December, the *Liverpool Echo* carried a back page that would have cut like a knife through the hopes and aspirations of Everton supporters. Above the words 'In the ZONE' was a picture of a jubilant Xherdan Shaqiri leaping into the arms of Sadio Mané. Underneath that, a disconsolate and despairing Marco Silva, arms outstretched at his side, screamed from the touchline at Anfield. Accompanying this tableau were the words 'In the DROP zone'.

Liverpool, fielding what was to all intents and purposes a second-string XI, had destroyed Everton 5-2. The defeat had plunged the Blues into the bottom three. The Reds, meanwhile, were sitting pretty, eight points clear at the top of the table. Yet, the pre-match omens had been so good for Everton.

Blues had been dining out on their 'epoch-defining' draw at Goodison Park in the previous season, a result they claimed had robbed Liverpool of the league title. With Liverpool seemingly invincible, they will have been desperate to throw another spanner into the gears of this red machine. When they saw the team sheet, hopes of a first win at Anfield since 1999 and first anywhere over the Reds since 2010 were sky high.

Klopp's men were not exactly in scintillating form. They had managed to grind out wins over Crystal Palace and Brighton and Hove Albion in the Premier League. Meanwhile, a disappointing draw against Napoli at Anfield had left them with much to do in the Champions League.

The Blues were struggling for points at the bottom end of the Premier League table. A victory, even a draw against a Liverpool side playing within itself and fielding a weakened team, would have been a huge shot in the arm to a club that looked further away from achieving their much vaunted 'power shift' than ever before. Liverpool's 'reserves', however, had other ideas.

In truth, the backdrop to this fixture was a sombre one. For all the point-scoring and stick dished out around the derby, Everton fans have always shown huge solidarity with Liverpool on the issue of the Hillsborough stadium disaster.

In the lead-up to this encounter, the former match commander at Hillsborough, David Duckenfield, who was on duty on the day of the tragedy, was found not guilty of gross negligence manslaughter at a retrial at Preston Crown Court. It was a decision that caused anger across the city. Both sets of supporters planned to hold a banner across the Anfield Road end and the matchday programme carried a tribute to the 96 on the front cover.

On the pitch, Everton's miserable run at Anfield would enter its third decade. Liverpool would also score five goals against them for the first time since 1982. For all the claims that Liverpool's side was a team of expensive superstars and narratives about a 'people's club' going up against the super-rich, the team fielded by Marco Silva was no bargain basement outfit.

The likes of Jordan Pickford, Gylfi Sigurdsson and Richarlison had all cost in the region of £30m to £40m. Liverpool's starting line-up that night featured only one player whose fee exceeded that amount. Virgil van Dijk had cost them £75m, but the Reds had largely financed that deal with the sale of Philippe Coutinho. There could be no excuses this time.

For Blues supporters, Silva's decision to go with an ultra-defensive line-up was heavily criticised. Andy Hunter, writing in *The Guardian*, had pointed out that Klopp had selected a first XI that didn't include six of the men who had won the Champions League in June and containing five changes from the side that beat Brighton the week before.

One seemingly myopic Everton fan told me, 'We were virtually playing your reserve team. He should have gone out all guns blazing.' I could only smile and imagine what we could have done to an Everton side set up to attack us. How Liverpool runners would have exploited the gaps left behind, had they not started with five in defence and four in midfield.

The fact they came for a point and still got hammered said more about the relative state of the two clubs than perhaps anything else has in the last ten years. However, for all of that, both sides would serve up perhaps the craziest first half in a Merseyside derby in living memory. It was a six-goal thriller that effectively ended the game early for those who had travelled across the park.

The Reds dominated from the start of hostilities. They took the lead in the sixth minute of the game and following Everton's first raid on their goal. As their move ran out of steam, Adam Lallana took over and immediately fed Sadio Mané, whose curling pass to Divock Origi was stunning.

Jordan Pickford, miles off his line, tried desperately and in vain to deny the Belgian, but Divock simply sidestepped his advances and slid the ball into the unguarded goal. With the away end reprising their roles as zombies in the TV show *The Walking Dead*, the rest of Anfield didn't know whether to laugh or cheer. It had all been too easy.

Mané was in incredible form and Everton had no answer to him. They could at least be forgiven for that, because frankly no other team had been able to deal with him all season. He also created Liverpool's second, latching on to a brilliant cross-field ball from Trent Alexander-Arnold, sidestepping the advances of Everton's midfield and feeding a slide-rule pass to Shaqiri. The Swiss international ran on to the ball and deftly slipped it into the far corner. The Reds were 2-0 up inside 17 minutes, and we were all starting to fantasise about a cricket score.

This was still a Merseyside derby though, and no matter how bad Everton get, you always expect some kind of response from them. Four minutes later one arrived. It was more frustrating than anything else, a fly in the ointment, an irritant; yet it briefly threatened to spoil the party.

Everton swept forward, perhaps provoked into action by the sneers and angry appeals from their own supporters. Alex Iwobi sent a low cross into the Liverpool penalty area and the defence went AWOL, allowing Michael Keane to smash a decent shot into the roof of the net. After being utterly dominant, Liverpool's lead had now been halved and, for a brief instant, the Everton faithful had hope.

But, as David Moyes had once quipped, 'It's the hope that kills you.' I doubt whether six words could ever sum up life as an Everton supporter as much as those did. Those hopes will have risen and crashed when Dominic Calvert-Lewin blazed through on goal before misfiring under pressure from Van Dijk.

The Kop began idling through its derby day hit list. 'You haven't won a trophy, you haven't won a trophy, you haven't won a trophy since 1995' was given a good airing. As was 'Snow is falling, all around us, Kopites singing, having fun, 'tis the season of love and understanding, merry Christmas, Everton.' The Blues in the Anfield Road end just glowered and swore, flipping the occasional bird our way.

Liverpool's third was a thing of beauty. This time none other than Dejan Lovren was in on the act, sending a delightful long ball down the centre of the field to the waiting Origi. He escaped the attentions of Keane and controlled the ball sublimely with his left foot before lobbing the onrushing Pickford.

As the ball nestled in the back of the net, there was a huge roar around the ground, and chants of 'going down!' rang out as Reds looked to rub salt in gaping wounds. For Blues in the away end, this was torture, but it was about to get much worse.

Mané, who had given Everton a torrid time, bagged the Reds' fourth after being teed up by Alexander-Arnold. His fierce low shot into the bottom-left corner from 18 yards drove an arrow through the hearts of the visitors, that hurt so much they would be unable to celebrate Richarlison's consolation effort on the stroke of half-time.

I still recall, with utter amazement, looking over to the Anfield Road end from my seat in the Kop, as the Brazilian got Everton's second and made the score 4-2, and witnessing not a flicker from the Goodison faithless.

The goal had gone in on the stroke of half-time, it had the potential to lift spirits and the Everton dressing room could maybe have been rallied ahead of the second period. A two-goal deficit is not so big that it can't be overcome. Yet so despondent were the Blues, so utterly unconvinced were they that they could get back into the game, that the goal barely registered with them.

Little wonder then that Everton's approach to the second half was damage limitation rather than bloodcurdling attempt at a fight back. They had gone to a 4-4-2 formation towards the end of the first half, but they continued to look disjointed and lacking in purpose throughout.

The game had become so easy for the Reds that Klopp decided to risk Roberto Firmino, who had been warming the bench most of the night, and was doubtless itching to get at this inept Everton line-up. It was a little disappointing, however, that he chose to hook off Origi who was now on a hat-trick.

Firmino, though, would help confirm Liverpool's rout by setting up the fifth goal right at the death. The Brazilian utterly humiliated Mason Holgate right in front of the Kop, before steering the ball to Wijnaldum who fired a low drive into the far corner. The expression on Gini's face told of how much he understood a goal in a derby meant for any player.

Five goals against Everton is a hugely significant figure. Psychologically it is the most damaging and conjures memories in the minds of a certain generation of a disastrous day at Goodison when Ian Rush scored four. For Liverpool fans, it is a dream come true and it would make my week.

If I could have found a Blue on social media in the days that followed, I would have given them a dog's life. Sadly, there must have been significant Wi-Fi outages in Evertonia because I couldn't find a single one. Never mind.

Marco Silva must have sensed the writing was on the wall, and his termination notice had already been signed. The Everton boss left the field without the customary applause for the travelling support. He would indeed be sacked in the morning.

The contrast for Klopp could not have been starker. The German had bought and sold well. So many of his signings had turned to gold and he was now firmly a darling of the Kop. This had been his 100th victory as Liverpool manager, achieved in 159 games. No one else in Reds history had done that. He was untouchable.

Andy Hunter, writing in *The Guardian*, summed up both the significance of the victory for both halves of the city, as well as lauding Klopp's achievements: 'Bragging rights barely covers the latest rewards for Liverpool from a Merseyside derby. Emphatic victory in the 234th episode protected their eight-point lead at the Premier League summit, extended their unbeaten league run to a club-record 32 games and brought Jürgen Klopp his 100th league win as Liverpool manager. It is also likely to herald another period of expensive upheaval for their distressed neighbours.'

Liverpool followed up their derby victory with wins over Bournemouth, Red Bull Salzburg and Watford as they marched towards the Club World Cup in Qatar. While Everton continued their perpetual rebuilding under the surprising leadership of Carlo Ancelotti, the Reds were about to conquer the bloody world.

Injury Time Madness in Qatar as Monterrey Fold and Reds Book Date with Destiny

As December began, Britain was cloaked in a veil of sadness. After a horrific terrorist attack at London Bridge left two people dead, the nation's terror alert status was at its highest. The country was also heading towards a General Election, with opinion polls – inexplicably to people like me and many others – seemingly indicating that Boris Johnson's Conservative Party was headed for victory.

With so many people struggling, some dying on freezing cold streets, and the NHS in perpetual crisis mode, it seemed unfathomable that the government responsible for all these things could stand a chance of being re-elected. However, that's exactly what happened.

In the Premier League, Liverpool had marched on through November. The crazy victory over Everton at Anfield was followed by routine triumphs over Bournemouth and Watford, and qualification for the knockout phase of the Champions League courtesy of a 2-0 win over Salzburg. Now the Reds had a date with the Club World Cup in Qatar, with the first game taking place against Club de Fütbol Monterrey at the Khalifa International Stadium in Qatar on 18 December.

There was just one problem; they had also reached the quarter-final of the League Cup and were scheduled to play Aston Villa at Villa Park on 17 December. Two games, almost 3,500 miles apart and within 24 hours of each other meant that Jürgen Klopp had a huge decision to make.

With pundits, some in the press and many rival supporters suggesting that the trip to Qatar was nothing more than a money-spinning exercise, a 'meaningless friendly', there was a certain amount of pressure on the boss to field a strong side in the League Cup.

When he inevitably refused to do so, those same voices accused him of disrespecting the competition. I witnessed many social media posts and received more than a few texts from people who had – after the Reds lifted the League Cup under Kenny Dalglish in 2012 – told me that it didn't matter, because it was a third-rate trophy, and who were now its greatest defenders.

For Liverpool fans, like me, who have memories of the Reds' encounters with the various incarnations of the Club World

Cup down the years, thoughts of the competition are always accompanied with pangs of regret. Defeats to Independiente and Flamengo in the 1980s hurt me as a kid. I was also gutted when São Paulo beat Rafa's Reds in 2005. So I was desperate for us to win it, and be able to proudly declare that Liverpool were world champions.

By qualifying for the competition, Liverpool would now have the opportunity to avenge their defeat to Flamengo in 1981. It had been the Brazilian outfit's greatest achievement, at least in the eyes of their supporters, and they had dined out on their 3-0 victory for way too long. They needed putting in their place.

The trophy represented a gaping hole in our collection of silverware, and the chance to sing that we were champions of the world at every game was just too big an opportunity to pass up. It seemed that Jürgen agreed. He took his entire first team to Qatar and left a youth team, marshalled by under-23 coach Neil Critchley, to defend the club's honour against Aston Villa.

The kids crashed to a 5-0 defeat, but they earned huge praise for their efforts and many felt the scoreline flattered the Midlands club. What many people, throwing around the 'disrespect' arguments, ignore is the question of how academy coaches and young players are supposed to get their breaks unless they are given the opportunity to test themselves at a higher level. Is it not disrespectful to them, to moan when they are selected?

Before Liverpool could contest the Club World Cup Final, they would have to negotiate a semi-final against Mexican side Monterrey. With a chance to face compatriots Flamengo in the final, Alisson, Fabinho and Firmino would have been eager to make a statement, and they did.

However, as they so often did, they would leave it late before putting Reds supporters and Monterrey out of their misery and booking their date with destiny. There was no contemplating defeat in this game. Having abandoned a domestic trophy to play in the competition, going out of the competition in their first outing would have invited a great deal of criticism, and potentially could have robbed the team of their momentum.

The Reds were facing something of an injury crisis, particularly in defence, with Matip and Lovren out with knocks and VAn Dijk missing through illness, and Trent Alexander-Arnold starting on the bench. That meant Jordan Henderson would have to put in another huge performance, this time at centre-back. It is typical of the man – so often unfairly maligned in the past – that he delivered in spades.

If the reshuffle in defence was understandable, the changes up front were not. The decision not to start Firmino and Mané was confusing and a little worrying.

The game was far trickier than any of us had anticipated, and when Rogelio Funes cancelled out Naby Keïta's opener within the space of two first-half minutes, my heart sank. Liverpool stumbled their way through this one, with Alisson pulling off a string of saves to keep his team-mates within sight of the final.

Eventually, in what seemed like one of the longest 90 minutes in football history, extra time seemed inevitable. Would they have the energy to see it through? They wouldn't need to, thanks to Roberto Firmino.

The Brazilian had only just been introduced from the bench when he poked home a Trent Alexander-Arnold cross seconds into added time. He was immediately mobbed by his team-mates, who were no doubt grateful they wouldn't have to play another 30 minutes.

Writing in the *Liverpool Echo*, Ian Doyle summed up what this victory meant: 'Klopp said before the game Liverpool hadn't flown thousands of miles just to put on a show – they are here in Qatar to win. Flamengo await on Saturday, 1981 and all that. Destiny is calling.'

Just three days later, Jürgen Klopp and Liverpool would become the best team on the planet.

Reds Conquer the Bloody World and Settle an Old Score

Liverpool lined up to face Flamengo in the final of the FIFA Club World Cup at the Khalifa International Stadium on 21 December. It was a game that will be remembered for some atrocious refereeing, a titanic performance from captain Jordan Henderson, and another match-winning strike from Roberto Firmino. It was also an incredible experience for those lucky enough to see it first-hand.

With the game taking place thousands of miles away, and on top of Christmas, the number of supporters travelling from Liverpool would have been far fewer than the average cup final jaunt. That would mean it was over to our supporters in Africa, UAE and the Middle East to take up the baton, and they did in huge numbers. However, one group of Scousers who did make their way out there were the crew from Redmen TV.

Ross Chandley, a writer for the site and the team's social media and marketing manager, found the whole experience captivating and one he would never forget. However, one aspect of the trip that completely took him aback was how united the local population and supporters of all teams were in their adulation and respect for Mohamed Salah.

'Something which really struck my colleagues and me was the support for Mo Salah,' Ross told me. 'Being a short tournament, all fixtures obviously relied on the outcome of the earlier games. There were no guarantees as to which teams would be at the latter stages. This meant that there were a large number of neutral supporters at the majority of games.

'Yet, every time Mo Salah's name was announced the noise would be deafening. It really hit home how big Salah is and the influence he has on the world. Every time he touched the ball the crowd roared, and the response was the same when he received an individual award at the end of the tournament. It was spine-tingling.'

I asked Ross how the atmosphere compared to other trips following the Reds, like the ones across Europe for example. Presumably, there wouldn't have been as many of the usual crowd out there. Did that feel strange?

He said, 'I'm not sure if it was a little strange or just different. Maybe both. For the games leading up to the final there were pockets of fans dotted around which made it difficult to generate any sort of atmosphere. And again, those fans in the stadium were often fans of teams which were not participating.

'The atmosphere was undoubtedly different and much better in the final and not just because of Liverpool fans. The Flamengo fans were there in their tens of thousands. We spent around a week in Qatar and the standout feature was the Flamengo fans, they were everywhere. Flags, shirts, songs, you name it, they were there. Given it would have taken them 15-plus hours to get to Qatar, it was incredible, and that made the trip special.'

Clearly the competition was a big deal in Brazil. The team and their supporters took it seriously, and they desperately wanted to win it, in much the same way Reds fans view the European Cup, the status of being crowned world champions is much coveted in South America.

We are now used to fan parks in Europe generating atmosphere and stories that will travel through generations of families; I wondered if supporters in Qatar were provided with the same opportunities. What was the fan park culture like out there, and how did the way the South Americans followed the club differ to ours? Again, Ross was completely taken with the support shown by the Brazilian supporters, which drew admiration from many Reds.

'The atmosphere they created in the fan parks was sensational,' said Ross. 'At one point there was a crowd of Liverpool fans, including myself, filming them as they took over a bar and spent over an hour singing. They were genuine football fans who loved their club and it showed. And despite them singing a song about them beating Liverpool many moons ago they were friendly, welcoming and gracious in defeat.'

The trip was not without its funny moments though. Ross recalls with amusement the stadium announcer's attempts to stoke up the atmosphere: 'Undoubtedly the funniest feature of every match was the stadium announcer during the build-up to the games, half-time and then again at full time. They'd obviously gone for an American slant on marketing, atmosphere and culture generation. And that was something we weren't used to at all. But his over-exuberance and energy did get people going; even if we ended up laughing it was very much a talking point.

'He would pop up at different spots in front of the crowd, and despite being on a big screen we spent a great deal of time trying to spot him. It's 100 per cent not something that would go down well at Anfield and in England, probably, but it added to the experience.'

For Reds fans there were the usual fan parks and pre-match entertainment on offer. In that sense, the experience was very familiar. However, there were logistical issues in terms of getting around. Travel from the hotel to the park would take 45 minutes, then another hour to the stadium. That meant potentially big nights, featuring Reds-supporting artists like the Lightning Seeds and Jamie Webster, saw the fan zones only filled to half their capacity.

This game mattered to so many though. Liverpool's decision to prioritise this competition is vindicated by the joy it brought so many, and it would have been hugely disrespectful to the supporters who spent small fortunes to get out there, and to the

Flamengo fans who made it such a tremendous occasion, had they not done so. However, for all of that, the event was almost ruined entirely by the standard of refereeing.

The *Liverpool Echo*'s Paul Gorst captured the feelings of every Red when he penned these words about what was a refereeing disaster-class: 'It was a big game that needed a big official. Abdulrahman Al Jassim – the man in possession of the whistle – was not that man. Tasked with taking charge of this Club World Cup Final, it was surely a career highlight for the Qatar-based referee. A feather in the cap of the 32-year-old, no doubt.

'It was not, however, a vintage performance, to say the very least. The referee spent the game leaving Liverpool's players, supporters and management team perplexed with a string of odd calls.'

A series of bizarre decisions, eerily reminiscent of the incompetence on display when Rafa Benitez's side contested the 2005 final in Japan, only worse, were capped by one of the most baffling calls I have ever seen in the final moments of the game.

Sadio Mané had burst through on goal and looked certain to score. However, he seemed to skew his shot wide. The referee immediately pointed to the spot amid protests and incredulity from the Flamengo players.

Replays showed that Mané had clearly been fouled. The only question to be resolved was whether the infraction was inside or outside the penalty area. With the referee spending some time staring at multiple slow-motion replays of the incident, it seemed that the very worst that could happen would be Liverpool being awarded a free kick on the edge of the area.

Yet, bizarrely, inexplicably and infuriatingly, he waved away his original penalty award, handed the ball back to Flamengo and simply resumed play. No penalty, no free kick, not even a goal kick to the Brazilians. All Klopp could do was smile ruefully, the Liverpool players were incredulous, and they were right to be.

If Laurel and Hardy had been given the job of officiating the game, they'd have surely made a better fist of it than this buffoon. Fortunately, his display couldn't prevent Liverpool lifting the trophy, but that decision meant they would have to contest an additional 30 minutes of extra time.

Liverpool had almost gone ahead in the first minute of the game when Firmino blasted a shot over the bar. Alexander-Arnold and Naby Keïta also wasted opportunities to put the Reds in front. But Flamengo gave as good as they got in the early exchanges.

In the second half, Bobby struck the woodwork and Mo Salah planted a shot wide of the target, before the Brazilians came back again. This had the potential to be a great game of football. But for the increasingly bizarre intervention of the man in the middle's whistle, it would have been.

With 15 minutes remaining, Alex Oxlade-Chamberlain crumpled to the ground clutching his ankle. It was another blow for him and for Reds, and it proved to be his last involvement in the game. Lallana replaced the former Arsenal man.

Liverpool went close again as the imperious Henderson, who had been everywhere, mopping up at the back and starting attacks all over the place, unleashed a powerful curling thunderbolt which the Brazilian's keeper did well to tip over the bar.

As the final whistle sounded, and the teams got ready for another 30 minutes of action, the stage seemed set for someone to make themselves a hero, or perhaps a villain. This was now high stakes for Jürgen Klopp and Liverpool. After placing all his eggs in FIFA's basket and sacrificing the League Cup, defeat at this stage would have been excruciating.

Harry Poole, reporting for the BBC on the night, wrote, 'Manager Klopp said he wanted to change perceptions of the Club World Cup in Europe as his Liverpool side prepared to face a Flamengo squad who had been given "a clear order to win it and come back home as heroes".'

Clearly feeling the weight of an entire continent on his shoulders, not to mention the expectations of millions of Liverpool supporters, the boss rallied his troops for extra time. Each of them seemed to sense the hand of destiny though, and two men who had more than any others driven the Reds to new heights combined to win the game.

In the 99th minute, herculean skipper Henderson sent a delightful ball to Mané, who slid it inside to Firmino who took huge pleasure in smashing his shot into the net. The Brazilian had beaten the Brazilians. There was a beautiful symmetry to that, and the ghosts of 1981 had finally been exorcised.

The Reds had become the reigning European and world champions, and after winning the Super Cup earlier in the season against Chelsea, they had completed a continental treble. Henderson's trophy lift shuffle was fast becoming a delicious habit, but there was just one more piece of silverware to go. It was one we all craved more than any other – the Premier League. If our captain could lift that one before the season was over, he would become immortal. The whole team would.

For all of us and for this Liverpool team, the world was not enough.

Jet-Lagged Reds Blow Away Leicester City

As they flew home from Qatar to a heroes welcome, Liverpool players may have had a ready-made excuse for succumbing to a festive hangover on Boxing Day. Next up was a trip to Leicester City, their nearest challengers, just five days after an energy-sapping 120 minutes out in the Middle East.

The Reds' challengers had failed to narrow the gap significantly and Klopp's men had a chance to go 13 points clear at the top of the table. In doing so, they would make this one of the greatest Decembers in the club's history. However, most of us were convinced this would be no walkover.

The cost of defeat of course would see our lead cut to a mere six points. Even though we would still hold a game in hand on the Foxes who sat in second place, going into the second half of the season that might have been damaging to both morale and momentum. We needn't have feared though, as Liverpool blew away their jet lag to produce a masterclass at the King Power Stadium.

According to the BBC's Phil McNulty, the Reds 'produced a performance of such stature and dominance it is almost impossible to see how they will not claim their first title in 30 years'.

The idea that Liverpool would finally end 30 years of pain was becoming increasingly hard to ignore. Not that we didn't do everything in our power to tell anyone who would listen that it was too early to talk about titles, of course. The truth was, however, that this Reds side were starting to look invincible. Their consistency was staggering.

Consequently, most of us were already quietly starting to dream that our wait would soon be over. In fact, so impressive was Liverpool's march, many had moved beyond what felt like an inevitable title, and on to dreams of surpassing Arsenal's 'invincibles' tag. What we saw at Leicester did nothing to dent our silent confidence. The Reds, who would have to wait until the game against Wolves on 29 December to display their world champions emblem on their shirts, went into half-time leading by a single Bobby Firmino goal. That barely came close to reflecting their dominance though. They were moving through the gears, delighting the travelling Kop and making light of any suggestions that they would pay the price for their Qatar jaunt.

Several Evertonian friends of mine had tried in vain to undermine Liverpool's participation in the competition, claiming it was a 'glorified friendly'. Others laughed at the idea that winning it meant we were the best team on the planet, and perhaps more tellingly, all of them forecast it would derail Liverpool's title charge.

'The players will be knackered after that,' read one text message. 'You've been lucky with injuries,' came another bizarre claim, ignoring a catalogue of injuries to first-choice stars, including our £65m goalkeeper. 'This will mess up the season now. Should have stayed home and respected the League Cup,' was another one, and who could forget, 'Watch your lot bottle it now.'

They were of course living in the past. Such 'rules' only applied to Liverpool teams of the past. This vintage had matured beyond all expectations, into a machine that seemingly could not and would not be stopped. In fact, so relentless was this side that a new conspiracy theory – or as I prefer to call it, delusion – was born. Liverpool were too good; they must be doping.

To be fair, given the fact that the media, referees, Stockley Park, UEFA, FIFA and the Premier League were all moving heaven and earth to ensure Liverpool would win the league, at least according to these tinfoil-helmeted numbskulls, it hardly seemed worth the team resorting to performance-enhancing drugs. I mean, talk about overkill.

In the second half, Liverpool toyed with the home side some more, before winning a penalty in the 71st minute after Çaglar Söyüncü handled in the area. Maybe the conspiracy ran so deep that even some of our opponents were in on the act.

James Milner, who had only just come on as a substitute, stepped up to take the resultant spot-kick. He did not disappoint and the Reds were now in cruise control. Three minutes later, Trent Alexander-Arnold, who had provided Firmino with the assist for his first, duly delivered another for his second.

Leading 3-0 and absolutely bossing the game, Liverpool looked imperious. Firmino immediately ran to the touchline and hugged Jürgen Klopp. It was a touching moment, but none of us understood the significance of it. Klopp later revealed that Bobby had been concerned about his lack of goals, but afterwards the boss told him he hadn't even noticed that his striker was having a drought – so good was his all-round game. That seemed to have lifted the weight from the player's shoulders and the resultant four goals in three games told its own story.

It was hard to believe that a side who had travelled 7,000 miles, and played 120 minutes just five days earlier, could perform like this. Yet here they were blowing Leicester apart. Alexander-Arnold was also having an incredible night and he sealed a mesmeric performance with a stunning finish to make it 4-0 in the 78th minute.

Liverpool had destroyed Leicester in a seven-minute spell that left the travelling Reds fans breathless. It would also be a devastating blow to the chasing pack, and all those who had hoped their title march would come to a screeching halt as a result of their dalliance in Qatar. Liverpool had now dropped just two points in 18 games this season. They had only lost one game in the entirety of the previous one. Their lead at the top was 13 points, and soon supporters would no longer be able to hold their tongues. Klopp was delighted with his team's efforts and obvious resilience, he told the waiting media: 'I am happy about that. I appreciate it because I do not take it for granted and the boys have to do it every three days. We had big chances at the start of the game, did not score with them but stayed in the game and controlled it.'

All Leicester's Brendan Rodgers could do was recognise Liverpool's brilliance, saying, 'We played our last two games against two of arguably the best teams in the history of the Premier League.'

Leicester had also been beaten by Manchester City on the night Liverpool were being crowned champions of the world. They had managed to lay a glove on Guardiola's men that night, losing 3-1. They got nowhere near Liverpool though. Rodgers knew this only too well, telling *Match of the Day*, 'People were trying to put us in a race with Liverpool, but we know where we are.'

The Reds were out on their own, and this was shaping to be one of the greatest seasons in their history. Hard as it was to believe at this point in the campaign, there was even more to come.

Everton Humiliated at Anfield as Klopp's Kids Trump Carlo's Blues

There are many peculiar dynamics to the recent rivalry between Liverpool and Everton. Some of them are unpleasant, some fascinating but most are just plain hilarious. The game on 5 January 2020 epitomised one of the funniest facets of the 21st-century encounters with the Blues.

I am of course talking about the FA Cup fifth-round tie, when Jürgen Klopp fielded a team barely out of sixth form. Well, that's possibly a slight exaggeration, but not by much.

As has become their way, Evertonians drifted into the fixture like unsuspecting dupes convinced that this one would finally be *the* one to end their drought. The Blues had not won at Anfield since 1999, something we frequently pointed out, and as they stared in disbelief at our grinning coach's team selection, they must have been dancing inside.

In truth, they were in ebullient mood before they arrived at the stadium. With Carlo Ancelotti the closest thing to a nemesis Klopp had encountered now inexplicably in the Goodison hot seat, their optimism engulfed social media and they would christen their new boss 'Carlo Fantastico', much to our amusement. To be fair to them, convincing Carlo to join Everton is an achievement that belongs in the realms of the fantastical, and it is a huge coup on the part of the Goodison hierarchy.

And, I must confess that as I looked at the team Klopp had selected, my heart sank. Not out of any disrespect for the youngsters, who have been fantastic and who had earned their places. It was just that being a veteran supporter who has followed Merseyside derbies for over 45 years, I knew that any manager who underestimated the enemy would usually come unstuck.

As bad as the Blues had been, it only made them hungrier for an Anfield scalp. They would have vengeance for decades of hurt on their minds, and Jürgen's team would look like an open invitation to deliver the killer blow. But what the hell did I know?

Instead of motivating the Everton squad, the sight of so much youth in the opposition ranks seemed to increase the pressure on their heads. And, in the face of it, they wilted.

Klopp could justify his team selection on the basis of injuries and with so many of his stars running on empty, and with a league title to clinch there was no point taking risks. There were three teenagers in the starting XI and five of the men who lined up against the Blues had barely featured all season.

Liverpool were further undermined by the loss of the experienced James Milner due to a hamstring injury just eight minutes into the match. Yasser Larouci deputised. However, the star of the evening was Curtis Jones. The 18-year-old was making only his third start and the Blues had no answer for his tale of the unexpected in the 71st minute.

Ancelotti's men did have a number of opportunities in the opening half, but they were wasteful and, as the game wore on, the sense that another memorable victory was on the cards grew. In the second half, they simply failed to turn up, and as the away end grew increasingly impatient and frustrated, the Liverpool second-string took control.

The coup d'état was delivered with 20 minutes left on the clock. David Hytner described the moment for *The Guardian*. He wrote, 'Curtis Jones knew exactly what he wanted to do and so did the whole of Anfield. It is one thing to think it and quite another to execute but that is exactly what the 18-year-old Liverpool midfielder did.

'Accepting the ball from Divock Origi on the edge of the Everton penalty area, to the left of centre, Jones shaped to bend a right-footed shot into the far top corner of the net.

'It arched in exquisitely, kissing the underside of the crossbar on its way down and in past Jordan Pickford for added show-stopping value, and the Liverpudlian had a first senior goal to savour. It deserved to be the winner and it was.'

It was a sumptuous moment, and the youngster celebrated just like you would expect him to after scoring the winning goal – his first senior strike for the club – in a Merseyside derby at Anfield. Not for the first time, our jubilation would be mixed with mirth. There will come a time when Everton finally end their derby misery, the law of averages says it must happen. But until then, there will always be a sense of tragicomedy for them.

Their high hopes and low points are a constant source of amusement for us. Whenever that comes to an end, we will always have a treasure trove of hilarious memories to keep us warm. This was a glorious one though.

Klopp told the BBC that his reserve side had been 'sensational'. Showering them in praise he said:

'I saw a sensationally good performance of a not very experienced team with a lot of players playing for the first time on this kind of stage, in front of this crowd, against the opponent. It was outstanding. I loved it – I loved each second of this game.

'If you want to be a Liverpool player, you have to respect the principles of this club. We cannot always play the best football in the world, but we can fight like nobody else. And as long as we use our principles, we will be a difficult opponent to play against.'

The young Reds had certainly outfought and outplayed their opponents, especially in the second half. Most Blues would acknowledge the ignominy of the defeat, and their rage was a joy to behold at times. Of course, the win would allow Liverpudlians to reprise a famous old Shankly quote: 'In all my time in Liverpool, I always said we had two great teams. Liverpool, and Liverpool reserves.'

Not for the first time, the great man's words would resonate through the ages. Oh, how he still makes Kopites happy.

Under a Blood-Red Sky: United Vanquished and the Kop Senses Holy Grail is Within Reach

It is often said that football is cyclical. I guess by that, people mean that all good things come to an end, and we shouldn't be too upset by that, because our day will surely come again. Of course, there are those who argue that while that may be true of the biggest clubs in the game, it doesn't necessarily apply to the rest. However, when it comes to Liverpool's rivalry with Manchester United, it definitely feels like a case of what goes around comes around.

When I was a kid, I wasn't too bothered by United. The big rivalry for me was always Everton. I was too young to know about their glory years under Matt Busby, and their victory over us in the FA Cup in 1977 was painful, but never terminal. Had that defeat come against our neighbours across Stanley Park, it would have hurt far more.

Of course, I would get my baptism in this inter-city rivalry in the 1980s. Many away trips to Old Trafford taught me that there was certainly no love lost between us. Those experiences heightened the desire to win and increased the joy of any victory over them. That's why the Kop would sing 'are you watching Manchester' as they watched their team dominate English football. It was our way of rubbing their noses in our superiority.

So, when Alex Ferguson managed to lift United from the doldrums and eventually usurp Liverpool at the top of the English game, it hurt deeply. In the last 20 to 30 years it has been very difficult to believe the 'football is cyclical' mantra. Even when Ferguson proclaimed that 'Liverpool will come again' I wished I shared his optimism. Ryan Giggs's declaration that United would never fall apart like Liverpool did in the 1990s now seems incredibly foolhardy, but at the time, while I may have scoffed, I feared he may be right.

United seemed to be getting everything right on and off the pitch, while the Reds struggled to keep pace. But it appears that Giggs was wrong, Ferguson was right, what goes around does indeed come around. Football is cyclical and Liverpool are back. There is no stronger evidence of that than the game against United at Anfield on 19 January.

As the final whistle sounded, and under a blood-red sky, players leapt from the turf and punched the air. Supporters danced and embraced in the stands, and the Kop bellowed with all its might, 'WE'RE GONNA WIN THE LEAGUE, WE'RE GONNA WIN THE LEAGUE,AND NOW YOU'RE GONNA BELIEVE US, WE'RE GONNA WIN THE LEAGUE!' It felt like a bold statement at the time. Too bold for some.

Upon hearing the deafening roar, the lad who sits next to me simply smirked and said, 'I'm not singing that yet.' However, he was swimming against a vast red tide that had been swept up in belief and by the incredible team they support.

For the United supporters, there was only silence as they exited the stadium and, it now seemed, their perch. Their journey home would be a miserable one for them and the Kop's chants would hurt even more, because deep down they could see it was true. After 22 games, Liverpool were an astonishing 16 points clear of Manchester City at the top of the table, and a colossal 30 points ahead of United.

Andy Hunter, writing in *The Guardian* after the game, captured their despondency perfectly: 'For Manchester United fans, it is the hope that kills them. The hope Ole Gunnar Solskjær can find the answers, that the flickers of promise from his tenure can morph into meaningful momentum, that the romance inherent in his appointment can somehow override the problems and the drift at the top of the club.' It was, on the evidence of this match, a forlorn hope.

I had gone with the usual trepidation a fixture against this particular foe engenders. It wasn't so much that I feared them, I didn't anymore. This United team were an average one and on paper I felt the Reds would have too much for them. But these encounters always create a sense of anxiety because the rivalry is so intense. Losing, or even drawing, would have felt like a hammer blow.

My nervousness was heightened by the fact that the chasing pack had already dropped points. Leicester had been beaten; Manchester City had drawn. This was a real chance to solidify our position at the top of the table and send out a real message to the rest of the country. Win today and surely we would have one hand on the trophy.

This was the best Liverpool team my mates and I had seen in many years. We argued over whether they had surpassed the relentlessness of the 1978/79 side or the flamboyance of the 1987/88 group. I argued they were a hybrid of the two. Ah, but they need to win the league came the reply. They will, I thought, but I didn't dare say anything out loud.

It felt like nothing could stop us. At least nothing football-related anyway. The world was a volatile place, and some had feared that US president Donald Trump's apparent desire to start a war with Iran may escalate and force an end to football. 'Just our luck,' someone in the Cabbage Hall pub said, 'we're on the brink of winning our first league in years, and World War Three breaks out.'

We laughed. None of us believed it would come to that. We were a little more concerned about news of a deadly virus that had emerged in Wuhan in China and talk of it becoming a global pandemic. When someone mentioned that this was more likely to disrupt our ambitions there was still amusement, but the laughter was a little more nervous.

The Reds were enjoying the best start of any team in all five of the top European leagues, having won 20 out of 21 games, amassing 61 points in the process. That record eclipsed the 59 points achieved by Manchester City during their 2017/18 title run. Liverpool were now unbeaten in 38 matches; they hadn't lost a game in over a year and had won 12 games in a row. They had become invincible and the title seemed inevitable.

Their last outing, a 1-0 victory over Spurs at the Tottenham Hotspur Stadium, filled us with belief and we were quickly able to shake off any sense of foreboding. There was a game against one of our biggest rivals to think about after all. And, despite our confidence going into the match, we had to accept that the only points dropped up to this point had come against Manchester United back in October.

That 1-1 draw had been celebrated by United fans like a victory but it felt horribly frustrating for their Liverpool counterparts. So, as we walked towards the ground, there was a feeling that we had a score to settle.

Though the statistics suggest that the Reds struggled for shots on goal in the first half, the experience inside the stadium tells a different story. The opening exchanges were a breathless affair and Liverpool's players hunted in packs as United failed to gain even the most meagre foothold in the game. Liverpool's passing and overall play was far superior, and although United fans may have comforted themselves with the idea that they were the only side to take points off the Reds to that point, their players were looking like they had no chance of repeating the feat.

It took just 15 minutes for the hosts to break United's resistance. When the Reds won a corner, down at the left-hand side of the Anfield Road end, the crowd rose in anticipation. Trent Alexander-Arnold jogged over to it and gleefully accepted the applause and adulation from those sat in the Anfield Road end and Lower Sir Kenny Dalglish Stand, before sending in the perfect centre. Virgil van Dijk rose above the United defence and powered the ball home. It was his fourth of the season and as he raced along the touchline, baiting the Old Trafford faithful, the ground was a picture of red celebration. Liverpool now had the bit between their teeth and the crowd began to sense a mauling could be on the cards. When Bobby Firmino curled an absolute beauty past David de Gea just on the half-hour, it seemed we might be right. However, Stockley Park once again made a mockery of claims that Liverpool were somehow benefiting from VAR. In the build-up to Firmino's finish, a perfectly legitimate challenge by VAn Dijk on United's keeper was adjudged to have been a foul. The goal was ruled out. It robbed Liverpool of the comfort their performance merited and gave hope to the visitors that they scarcely deserved.

The *Liverpool Echo*'s Paul Gorst felt the decision would do little to persuade conspiracy theorists among the Reds' rivals, however, writing, 'The facts, however, are only likely to get in the way of the half-baked conspiracies, so dense "LiVARpool" wisecracks will continue to be made between now and May, whatever happens.' Then Liverpool had the ball in the net again, after Gini Wijnaldum beat De Gea once more. This time the linesman ruled him offside, even though the gentlemen at Stockley Park's evidence appeared marginal at best. Liverpool were now everywhere and United could get nowhere near them. It was all enjoyable stuff, but the longer we went without adding to our tally, the more the chance of an undeserved equaliser grew.

Half-time would have come as a blessed relief to Solskjær and his players. However, the opening exchanges of the second would have filled him with dread as within ten minutes Liverpool had seven shots on goal.

First Salah seemed to get his feet all tangled up and scuffed his shot, when a goal seemed certain. Then, moments later, captain Jordan Henderson crashed a fierce effort from distance against the upright. The Kop collectively held their heads in their hands. Wave after wave of attack reigned down on the United defence, but somehow Liverpool couldn't find the breakthrough. It was now perfectly clear that there was only one side who wanted to win the game. Perhaps the United manager could be forgiven for his tactics. Staying in the game as long as possible and hoping for a smash and grab at the death was possibly his best hope. However, it was all a far cry from the all-conquering United teams of the Ferguson era. How the mighty had fallen.

Klopp ran through the substitutions as he went in search of a crucial second that would render Solskjær's strategy null and void. He sent on Adam Lallana for Alex Oxlade-Chamberlain, and later removed Origi and Fabinho, replacing them with Mané and Firmino.

Nervousness began gnawing at the stomachs of Liverpool supporters as the game wore on. As if sensing this, United began to mount a few meaningful attacks but Alisson and Mohamed Salah had things covered.

With the game edging towards its close, United wasted another foray into the Reds' box. Alisson held on to a weak shot and immediately launched it to the waiting Egyptian, who was deep in the United half and facing the Kop end.

As the ball landed at his feet and he raced forward, it seemed like the whole stadium rose to its feet at the same time. The sound of the plastic seats clicking back into their upright positions almost drowned out by the sharp intake of breath of 53,000 supporters. With United's midfield and defenders trailing in his wake, Salah rounded De Gea and slotted the ball into the empty net.

It must have felt like the resultant noise was going to blow him over, as he raced towards the Kop, heart pounding, chest out and chin up. He ripped off his shirt, tossed it to the ground and accepted the waves of applause and cheers that rained down on him. His goalkeeper, who had of course provided the assist, raced from his line, and led the charge of Liverpool players who would mob their striker.

The game was now up and United were down and out on Merseyside, again. Liverpool were on top of the world, and as the players walked back to the centre circle for the pointless restart, the Kop roared, 'AND NOW YOU'RE GONNA BELIEVE US, WE'RE GONNA WIN THE LEAGUE.'

Solskjær's bizarre claims that Liverpool had shown his side respect aside, the Kop now clearly believed that a first league title in 30 years was written in the stars. Given the flame-red sky over Anfield at the final whistle, it seemed the heavens also agreed.

A TEAM FOR THE AGES BUT A STORM IS COMING

Liverpool FC February–March 2020

Records Tumble as Second-Half Blitz Stuns Saints, and a Statue of Two Anfield Greats is Unveiled

As the sun set on another Anfield victory, on 1 February, the Kop, the nation's press and everybody else had declared that Liverpool were champions-elect. After the Reds had dispatched Southampton 4-0, with 13 games to go, and with Jürgen Klopp's side needing to win just over half of them to guarantee a first league title in 30 years, who could blame them.

Liverpool had gone in on the back of victories over Wolves and West Ham. They had gone 41 matches undefeated in the league, including 36 victories. That represented a win ratio of almost 88 per cent, with 113 from a possible 123 points on offer.

However, it was a run of games that had begun at the start of December 2019 and stretched to 16 in all competitions that had caught the eye of journalists and supporters. Despite playing on average twice per week, travelling all over the world and managing injuries and fatigue, they had won all but one of them. Their only defeat had been to Aston Villa in the League Cup when they fielded a virtual youth team.

At the start of that run, which also included the FIFA Club World Cup in Qatar, games against Everton (twice), Leicester, Manchester United and Tottenham Hotspur meant most of us would have been grateful if Klopp's men had simply remained in title contention by spring. Instead, they would emerge 22 points clear at the top of the table.

While the result against Southampton may have somewhat flattered the Reds, their record over a long period did not. Klopp was now on a run only bettered by Bill Shankly in 1972, and he was all set for immortality.

It seemed that nothing could stop the Reds. With City's task of hauling in Liverpool's 22-point lead now declared impossible on a *Liverpool Echo* back page, under the headline 'Catch 22', talk had now switched to whether the leaders could go the rest of the season unbeaten or whether they could eclipse Manchester City's record of 100 points in a single season. They had after all now taken 100 from a possible 102 in a run that stretched back to the season before.

Emma Sanders, writing for the BBC, pointed out that Liverpool had now opened up the biggest lead at the top of the league in British top-flight history. Young supporters, born after 1990 and having been bored to tears by listening to tales of the glory years from their parents, now had a team of their own that could stand up to the best of the past.

All Klopp's charges needed to do was go out and win the silverware to prove it. If they could add the English championship to their world and European crowns, then those millennials would be boring their own kids and grandkids for years to come.

I had already called it, telling my son that he was watching something truly special. Not that he needed much convincing. 'Treasure them,' I told him. 'Teams like this don't come along often. This is as good as anything I have ever seen.' I meant it too. I have been privileged to have watched first-hand the great Paisley team of the 1970s and early '80s. I revelled in the flamboyance and majesty of Dalglish's 1987/88 side, but this team could go toe-to-toe with all of them.

I didn't think anything could stop them. Nothing in the world of football could. However, there was something else brewing that would threaten the whole season and could, if some had got their way, have declared Liverpool's most remarkable season null and void.

We had all become increasingly aware of the growing coronavirus threat. Britain had confirmed its first two cases at the end of January and within days of this game, more people would test positive. I admit that, at the time, we tried to play it down, at least in our pre-match conversations.

We were still naïve as to just how bad this could get, and the newspapers and politicians were still consumed with domestic matters. On 31 January, the country had begun an 11-month process that would see it leave the European Union. It would be weeks before the true horror became clear to us all.

Our main priority, as we supped beers in the Cabbage Hall pub prior to the game, rested on Liverpool getting a win ahead of the mid-season break. The Premier League had finally introduced the rest period, insisting that clubs refrain from even playing in friendly matches. The move had been welcomed by Klopp, who had long been critical of English football's seemingly crazy schedule.

In fact, he was so determined to adhere to the break that he would incur the wrath of football purists by promising to field a youth team, managed by their coach, in the forthcoming FA Cup tie against Shrewsbury Town. Amid claims that Jürgen was 'disrespecting the FA Cup', the manager was unrepentant. Liverpool went on to win it anyway.

Opinion was split among supporters, with some arguing that with the 'title sewn up already' he should play the first team. Winning the FA Cup, some said, would be great for the club. I had visited the ground hours before the game, to take in a new statue that had been erected outside the club store. It was a fitting tribute to Liverpool's most successful manager, Bob Paisley, and featured the former boss carrying an injured Emlyn Hughes from the pitch on his shoulders.

It's a truly iconic image and encapsulates not just the selflessness of Paisley, but the spirit of Liverpool Football Club too. I reflected on the fact that Bob had never won the FA Cup, as a player or a manger, and wondered what he would have made of Jürgen's decision. However, I couldn't help feeling that right then, at that point in our history, the league was a far greater priority.

With Manchester City not playing until the following day, this game against Southampton represented an opportunity to put pressure on Pep Guardiola's players. Win this, and we would also have an eye-watering 22-point lead at the top. It barely seemed believable, and yet here we were.

The first half was a dull affair, with Southampton creating the best chance through Danny Ings, but they were regularly held back by the interventions of Virgil van Dijk and Alisson, who came to the hosts' aid again after another Saints raid.

Liverpool thought they'd won a penalty after Firmino appeared to be fouled, and Van Dijk attempted an impudent back-heel that was saved by Alex McCarthy, but this was sub-par stuff. Anfield, though, is a different stadium than it was even a year ago. Gone are the days when impatience reigned, and frustration usually won out on the terraces and began to interfere with play on the field.

It is now a place where, for the most part, supporters understand that there are 90 minutes in a game. So what if Liverpool are not 3-0 up by half-time, there's another 45 minutes plus stoppage time to go, after all. These are thoughts most were incapable of in days gone by.

Klopp and the players had earned such patience. Even their sternest critics in Block 109 had seen the light. And so, as the half finished, most of us felt intensely relaxed. In truth, even if Liverpool had been a goal down going into half-time, few of us would have been panicking. And, as ever, the players would emerge in the second half and totally justify our confidence.

In fact, it took them just two minutes. The ball fell to Oxlade-Chamberlain at the edge of the 18-yard box and facing the Kop. We could see he was shaping to shoot so got to our feet. He then unleashed a fierce low drive that left the keeper rooted to his spot. Liverpool had started the game without the inspirational Sadio Mané, who hadn't even made the bench. Any team would miss a player of that stature, but former Arsenal man Oxlade-Chamberlain had filled the hole left by the Senegalese striker, proving that though the faces may change, the same old Liverpool just carries on.

The Reds were then robbed of arguably the goal of the season. Alisson had turned defence into attack, distributing the ball with ease to Salah who put it into the net, before being adjudged to be offside after a VAR check. However, they would not be denied a second, and a great combination between Oxlade-Chamberlain and Firmino ended with Henderson smashing the ball home.

The captain was imperious in this game, and even his greatest critic (who happens to sit next to me on matchdays) turned to me and said, 'What a player!' You could have knocked me down with a feather, but there was no arguing with the assessment.

In his post-match report for the *Liverpool Echo*, Paul Gorst said the skipper's performance 'typified everything good and great about the Reds skipper this campaign. The England midfielder is in the form of his career and those calls to make him Player of the Year are only continuing to grow.' Jordan was everywhere and he gave Southampton no time on the ball, while conducting the game from the middle of the park. This is a player who had converted his doubters and cemented himself in the affections of his long-time admirers. When he was substituted for Lallana with two minutes left the applause was thunderous, with every Red in the ground standing to show their approval.

It was a thoroughly deserved ovation, and by this time Liverpool were 4-0 up thanks to a brace by Salah. They were his 17th and 18th goals of another incredible campaign. Liverpool had won by a comfortable margin but in truth they had played within themselves.

Southampton had given a good account of themselves and better teams than them had struggled more at Anfield. Their manager, Ralph Hasenhüttl, was rightly pleased with his team's performance, if not the result: 'Maybe the result is a little high, but I would like to watch this game if we had gone a goal up. The best team in the world for 50 minutes had no real chances and we had a massive one.

'But in the end, it was a deserved win for Liverpool. We played the best we can, so I am very proud.'

Jürgen Klopp agreed that Southampton had fought hard, but also had great praise for his own players. When asked what was the key to the victory,? he told the BBC, 'The readiness to improve in the game and learn from the game. The set-up of Southampton I could not give more credit to. What a strange result in the end. It's deserved because we score the goals, but what a team.

'They had too many shots on target and we had to change in the second half. That helped massively and when we are rolling it's difficult to stop. Even when it was 4-0 Southampton did not stop and I have so much respect for that.'

It had taken a second-half blitz to see off the Saints. However, the fact Liverpool had conjured a win with consummate ease was so gratifying. Emlyn and Bob would be so proud.

Liverpool Storm to 'Insane' 25-Point Lead as Mané Becomes a Centurion

By the midway point of February Liverpool were seemingly hurtling towards the finish line. All around them the storms were raging and their quest for glory was becoming one of the most dramatic in the club's history, if not the history of the game.

Just a week earlier, Storm Ciara had blown Manchester City's fixture with West Ham off course, allowing Liverpool to take a commanding 22-point lead at the top of the table. Guardiola's date with the Hammers was rescheduled for Wednesday, 19 February, meaning Liverpool would have to brave Storm Dennis in East Anglia with the chance to go 25 points clear at the summit.

In Europe, UEFA was also blowing ill winds in the direction of the Etihad. On the eve of Liverpool's visit to Norwich the governing body had announced a two-year Champions League ban for City, accusing the Citizens of false accounting and breaches of Financial Fair Play regulations. With talk of Premier League points deductions and demotions to League Two swirling around their heads, the hierarchy at City assembled the squad for a crisis meeting.

CEO Ferran Soriano was reported to have told the assembled players and staff, 'Trust me, as I trust you, this will be dropped.' His assurances would have sounded somewhat hollow when Pep Guardiola stood up to say, 'Whatever league we are in, even if they put us in League Two, I will still be here.'

Liverpool's nearest rivals were being swallowed by the storm, but at Anfield the story was very different. It seemed they could withstand anything the gods threw their way. Klopp had ridden out a mini-tempest over his decision to field a youth team in the FA Cup fourth round replay against Shrewsbury, and much to the ire of the world's punditry he also left the managerial reigns to under-23 coach Neil Critchley. The captaincy was handed to Curtis Jones, making him the youngest skipper in Reds history.

While social media went into meltdown and trolls – of all people – waxed lyrical about 'respect', the kids simply hurried and harried Shrewsbury into submission and took the tie 1-0. Meanwhile, Jürgen and the boys decanted to – in some cases – sunnier climes and prepared themselves for the title run-in.

The contrast between the title rivals could hardly have been greater. After pipping Liverpool to the championship just a matter of months earlier, City's charge had blown itself out, while Liverpool were gaining hurricane-force strength.

The Reds were beginning to see daylight in terms of their injury list, and Klopp had the luxury of choosing from a virtually fully fit squad as he contemplated the challenge ahead at Carrow Road. Only Xherdan Shaqiri remained on the treatment table. With Sadio Mané only just back to his fighting best, the boss opted to keep him in reserve and on the bench for the evening kick-off. It would prove a masterstroke.

The game got under way in the glow of the floodlights in front of a crowd of 27,000. Norwich had given Liverpool a good test at Anfield right at the start of the season. Klopp acknowledged in his pre-match press conference that the 4-1 scoreline back then did the Canaries something of a disservice. They had caused the Reds enough problems to warrant respect on home soil.

However, this was a clash between top and rock bottom. The gap between the two sides – 55 points – was of historic proportions. Surely the Reds would have too much for Norwich and the result would be a formality. As ever, it would prove anything but that. For all the talk of a weakened Premier League, teams in the bottom half of the table had developed a stubborn tendency to refuse to surrender without a fight. And that's exactly what happened here.

Perhaps hampered by the wind or maybe they were looking to catch Norwich off guard, Liverpool opted, maybe on too many occasions in that tempestuous first half, to go long. The Reds were enjoying tremendous success all season by being unpredictable. While the manner of their wins wasn't always spectacular, as in this game, the variety of their tactics and their ability to win in different ways from one week to the next was proving their most powerful weapon.

However, in the first half at Carrow Road at least, it wasn't working. The Reds were dominating but the final pass or the final shot simply wouldn't come off. Norwich dug in and had chances of their own. One move in particular produced a save of supreme quality from Alisson.

Liverpool were on their way to ten clean sheets in 11 games. Much of the talk around their defensive prowess centred on the return to the squad of Joe Gomez and the imperiousness of Virgil van Dijk, but the contribution of the goalkeeper cannot be overstated. With Liverpool's defence so resolute, he isn't called upon often but when he is, his levels of concentration and ability to time his interventions to perfection are second to none.

Such was the case in the first half when Lukas Rupp broke the Reds' high line and was through on goal, so Alisson came flying out to narrow the angles. In all black he is an imposing figure and his actions will have sown the seeds of doubt in Rupp's mind. Instead of shooting, he opted to square it to Teemu Pukki, the Finn who had scored the Canaries' consolation at Anfield, for what seemed like a tap-in. Alisson, looking like a cross between James Bond and Stretch Armstrong, had other ideas.

Somehow, the Brazilian stopper stretched out his right arm, which seemed to grow in length as he dived across his box, and palmed the ball from under the feet of Pukki. It was a breathtaking moment that exemplified his class and ability to do absolutely the right thing at completely the right time. Norwich's chance had gone, and it was to be their best one of the half.

At the other end, former Newcastle goalkeeper Tim Krul was also performing heroics, pulling off an incredible double save. His first denied Salah and the second prevented Keïta from profiting on the rebound.

While some – particularly on social media – may have been growing frustrated with the Reds' inability to blow Norwich away in that opening half, those in the away end were more relaxed. The cry of 'we're going to win the league' whispered quietly by a mere few a matter of weeks ago was now being belted out at full throttle. Gone were the superstitious, afraid to speak too soon or jinx the Reds' run. There was no more talk of 'bottling the title' anymore.

Those hardcore veterans of the Liverpool away-day scene had more than most seen the true glory of this team. They knew that no matter what obstacles were hurled at their feet, this group would always find a way to overcome them. They had seen it at

Aston Villa, and they had seen it elsewhere. Even if Norwich had scored you would have been hard-pressed to find a single travelling Kopite who wouldn't be utterly convinced that their side would score two, even if there were only minutes left.

In the second half, Liverpool upped their game considerably and Norwich began to struggle to break free. That they did on a couple of occasions was testament to their resilience and rendered their league position a perplexing one. The Canaries played good football and but for the often-callous nature of the game at this level, they would be continuing to do so in the Premier League for years to come. However, against teams like Liverpool, who only need one moment of brilliance in a game, attempting to match their attacking style can seem like folly.

They continued to press their case nonetheless, and Todd Cantwell sent a shot against the side-netting after one breakaway and Alexander Tettey crashed another effort off the woodwork. However, while commentators and pundits like Sky Sports's Martin Tyler were seemingly fantasising that the Reds' long unbeaten run was about to end, declaring with relish that 'the longcr this gocs on, thc morc you get the feeling that this could be the day', Klopp was preparing to pull out his trump card.

On the hour mark, the German sent on his Senegalese marksman to wreak havoc. The sight of Sadio Mané emerging from the bench must have been a harrowing one. Tired legs and minds, players who had given everything to earn their parity with the Reds, would now have to contend with arguably Liverpool's most dangerous player of the season. As it so often has against so many teams, Mané's intervention proved too much for the Canaries to handle.

Within 20 minutes he had delivered the killer blow, and not even the faint anxiety of a VAR check could rob Liverpool of all three points. With just 12 minutes remaining, Norwich's resolve was finally broken. Though the goal belonged to Mané, the assist had come from Jordan Henderson.

The number 14 sent a delightful ball down the inside-left channel and into the box. Mané controlled it beautifully, spun on a sixpence and smashed his shot on the half-volley into the net. A despairing Krul could only grasp at thin air as he was beaten at the near post.

Frustration and rancour momentarily erupted among the home supporters, but even some of them could find something to enjoy in the brilliance of this Liverpool team. Post-match television footage captured a rare moment of sportsmanship as Canaries fans pleaded with Klopp to pose for selfies and asked to shake his hand. It seemed they knew they had been privileged to play their part in what was becoming a historic season for the Reds.

In the build-up to his strike, Sadio had appeared to place his hands on the back of Norwich defender Christoph Zimmerman. However, it was the slightest of brushes and it would have been a crime if a goal of such brilliance had been chalked off by the men at Stockley Park. It was his 100th goal in the Premier League. Sadio was now a centurion.

All that remained was for the peerless Bobby Firmino to pass up a glorious chance to place the cherry on top of the icing on the cake, to torture a metaphor. Assist-king Trent Alexander-Arnold whipped a fantastic ball across the six-yard box with just four minutes remaining. With the goal at his mercy, all Firmino had to do it seemed was to make contact and it would have been 2-0. Perhaps there was too much pace on the cross, maybe Bobby lost concentration for a millisecond, whatever it was somehow the striker put his effort wide.

Klopp declared his side's lead at the top of the Premier League to be 'insane'. Maybe, in the eye of this Red hurricane, Liverpool's achievements seem nothing short of madness. To be 43 games unbeaten and counting is beyond the expectations of even the most fervent supporter, but once more, with his half-time reset and decisive substitution, Jürgen proved there is method in that madness.

Liverpool 3 West Ham 2: Strange Days and Scary Nights but Reds are 12 Points from Heaven

As Anfield got set to welcome the visit of David Moyes's West Ham United on 24 February, all the talk in the football world was of course centred around Liverpool's inexorable march to their first league title in 30 years. David Moyes was apparently telling his players and any journalists who would listen that the game was a 'free hit', a warm-up in readiness for the ensuing relegation battle ahead.

Outside of football, Britain was being battered by Storm Dennis, with over 600 flood warnings in place. Austerity was leading to a growing divide in terms of social inequality and for the first time in a century, life expectancy in the UK had stalled. Amidst the chaos, football was fast becoming my last refuge from the storm.

Prior to kick-off, Liverpool sat 19 points clear at the top of the table, had kept ten clean sheets in their previous 11 games, had won 20 home matches in succession and were unbeaten in their previous 43 outings. Meanwhile, the Hammers were third from bottom. Nobody, it seemed, could see anything but a routine home victory. Nobody, but me.

These were strange days to be a Liverpool supporter. Thirty years without a league title does strange things to a fan. Accustomed as I am now to also-ran status in the Premier League interspersed with all too infrequent title challenges and heroic but ultimately crushing near misses, the sight of my team apparently cruising to the Premier League championship is, well, a little unnerving at times.

Surely there's a banana skin around the corner. We had become so accustomed to false dawns over the years that it seemed certain our hubris would be punished at some stage. Sure, the Liverpool I grew up supporting won titles and trophies with a regularity that became, well, almost boring, but the Liverpool of my adulthood did things very differently indeed.

I'd grown to understand that if the Reds were to win silverware, they would do so in the most excruciating way possible. We had to go behind by a seemingly insurmountable margin before returning from the dead in a logic-defying comeback before we could get anywhere near the prize. Games must be won in the final moments, with goals scored by improbable players, or opposition strikes had to denied by our goalkeeper, performing the seemingly impossible. This was the Liverpool I had grown accustomed to over three decades without a league title.

In short, the Liverpool of the late 20th and early 21st centuries did not coast. To paraphrase a banner on the Kop, the Reds have always climbed the hill their own way, which usually meant via the most treacherous and circuitous route. Off the field, the club had an unerring ability to fly by the seat of its pants also.

In the days of David Moores and Rick Parry, they would rest on their laurels and dine out on past glories, squandering opportunities to capitalise on success. Under Tom Hicks and George Gillett, they squandered those reserves, failed to invest and flirted with administration. I had come to believe that this was the new 'Liverpool Way'. The hard way.

The sight of my team marching towards inevitable glory, their rivals trailing in their wake and falling to pieces in the process, just felt too good to be true. The Reds were now the epitome of success both on and off the field, while their closest rivals were a train-wreck in terms of corporate governance and still living off past (albeit recent) glories on it.

In the week after the game against the Hammers, Liverpool posted profits of £42m despite spending £223m in the transfer market. Plans for a new training complex in Kirkby were well advanced and a planning application to expand the Anfield Road stand, bringing the overall capacity to 61,000 had already been submitted. Matters on the field could not have been better either.

Meanwhile, Manchester City announced that they had lodged an appeal at the Court of Arbitration for Sport after UEFA had issued a two-year Champions League ban on them for over-stating sponsorship revenue and breaching Financial Fair Play rules. On the field, they were a shadow of the team that reached 98 points the previous year.

So, what did I have to worry about? I couldn't put my finger on it. I just had a bad feeling about this game. This seemed a little too easy, and perhaps I had been conditioned to believe that they never could be, or even shouldn't be.

Whatever it was, I was not good company in the pub. 'I wasn't nervous until you started going on,' said a mate, as we downed beers in the Cabbage Hall. 'Don't be daft, Moyes hasn't won a game at Anfield in his entire career,' said another.

Still, I couldn't shake it.

As I took my seat on the Kop, I continued to share my maudlin attitude, declaring, 'I'm really nervous about this one,' to the guy who sits next to me. He simply turned to me with a smile and said, 'I'm not mate. We'll blow these away.'

In his pre-match notes, Jürgen had called for the crowd to play their part. 'It's a Monday night under the floodlights,' he declared, 'we need everybody to play their part.' Did Jürgen have the same sense of impending doom that I had? Fortunately for Liverpool, they are blessed with a manager who doesn't believe the hype.

When reminded at the end that Liverpool needed just four more wins to clinch the title, his response was simply, 'Yes, but we still have to win them.' Until they were won, there was no way he was going to relax and that meant his players couldn't relax, and neither, it seemed, could I.

Within nine minutes of the start, it seemed all my fears had been swept away. Three minutes later they came flooding back with a vengeance. By the 54th minute my pre-match tension was beginning to feel prophetic.

The night got under way with the Reds attacking the Anfield Road end. Our traditional anthem had not long died away when Trent Alexander-Arnold was chasing the ball as it seemed to be rolling out for a corner. Most of us expected him to leave it but instead he turned and whipped in a low cross. The ball evaded the Hammers' defence and was met brilliantly by Gini Wijnaldum.

His header was point-blank and the goalkeeper should have palmed it away, but his wrists seemed too weak and all he could do was help it on its way into the net. The whole ground roared with approval, and I cried out in relief. I had been worried for nothing, I thought.

For a team who had seemingly accepted their fate prior to kick-off, West Ham were uncharacteristically adventurous. Michail Antonio was giving Andy Robertson a tough time out on the left. It was on this side of the pitch that the Reds conceded a corner just three minutes after going ahead.

They were no longer the soft touches they once were from opposition set-pieces but they had succumbed to a corner at Atlético Madrid a matter of days earlier in the Champions League. Even I though, despite my nerves, considered that to have been an anomaly. I retained my faith in Alisson, Joe Gomez and Virgil van Dijk regardless.

As the ball floated in, Liverpool looked less than assured and this time it was Alisson who should have done better. Issa Diop rose highest for West Ham and powered in a fierce header. The ball sailed past the outstretched hand of Alisson and the away end could not believe what they were seeing, ironically singing, 'We've scored a goal, we've scored a goal, we've scored a goal.'

These days no goal seems final, and the inevitable VAR check that follows brings hope to one team and fear to another. The goal stood, and as Salah and his team-mates raced back towards the centre circle, those nagging doubts returned to the pit of my stomach.

Later, with the game won, Klopp and his players spoke of the 'incredible atmosphere' that drove them across the finish line. Jürgen said that we set the stadium on fire after the Hammers drew level and did so again after they had pulled ahead. For the sake of clarity, and in case future historians get the wrong idea, the truth was a little more nuanced than this.

It's true that, for a Monday night game against relegation fodder, the atmosphere was lively. The Kop did roar into action, somewhat briefly, after Diop levelled. However, for the remainder of the half the mood was fractious, frustrated and a little grumpy. I think we could all be forgiven. After all, we were not used to having to fight this hard at home. It was a strange feeling.

Still, with the arrival of half-time, I felt reasonably confident that Klopp and his backroom staff would have identified where their charges were going wrong. Liverpool always improved after the break, and their fitness usually ground down the opposition whose legs and minds eventually buckled. Of course, this would again be the outcome, but not before another almighty scare.

The second period continued where the first had left off. The crowd did its best to get behind the lads, but it just wasn't happening. Liverpool, missing Jordan Henderson in midfield after he had sustained a hamstring injury in Madrid, struggled to keep the ball and the Hammers seemed to find it too easy to play through them. In the stands, the mood grew anxious and supporters struggled to contain their nerves.

There would be groans as a move broke down or a pass went astray, followed by chants of 'we love you Liverpool, we do' as fans struggled to make their minds up. In truth, even an improbable defeat wouldn't have proved terminal in the Reds' quest for their first title in 30 years. The men from Anfield would have remained 19 points clear. However, such is the flawless nature of their pursuit, we feared the deflating effect a setback could have. After the carrot of coasting to the title had been dangled, the stick of once more having to deal with uncertainty and nerves, no matter how ridiculous that sounds, seemed too hard to bear.

West Ham may have sensed the uncertainty in the stands and, perhaps buoyed by the Reds' indecisiveness on the pitch they took the game to Liverpool in the early phases of the second half. And, then, after an incisive move in the 54th minute, Pablo Fornals put the visitors in front. We were all in uncharted territory.

The Kop tried once more to rally, but the atmosphere continued to fluctuate between incredulity, anger and irritation. Klopp had seen enough. The midfield just wasn't dealing with the Londoners and they were winning all the second balls and cutting through Liverpool with too much ease.

Keïta had not had a bad game, despite the post-match post-mortem. However, his style of play wasn't what we needed if Liverpool were to pull level and eventually go ahead. The boss turned to Alex Oxlade-Chamberlain. His impact was immediate and, as the Reds began to reassert their game, the crowd did respond.

For the last half-hour, Anfield once more felt like it was home to a team chasing the biggest honours, like it knew it had a job to do and its team needed it. Just ten minutes after the introduction of Oxlade-Chamberlain for Keïta, Liverpool were level.

In one of many forays into the opposition area, which had led to a succession of corners, Andy Robertson found an injection of pace out wide on the left. Leaving his defender for dead he pulled short of the dead-ball line and squared a pass to Mohamed Salah. The Egyptian's shot lacked power and was straight at the keeper, but it completely outwitted him.

Lukas Fabianski has been a great stopper for the Hammers, saving them on many occasions, including at Anfield. However, on this occasion he had a nightmare. As he bent to pick up the shot, he completely misjudged it and the ball rolled between his legs and into the Kop net. All around me we leaped to our feet, fists pumping the air.

The relief, the ecstasy, the emotion of it all is hard to explain to anyone who doesn't follow football. In quiet moments alone, I struggle to explain it to myself. However, the moment the football trickled through Fabianski's legs the euphoria was palpable, and belief returned in spades.

In truth, after the indifferent first-half display and the lacklustre start to the second, I'd have gladly taken a point at that moment, were one offered. A draw would have left Liverpool unbeaten and still 20 points clear at the summit. However, this team never settles for a point while there's still time to claim all three.

The Reds went on the front foot as they searched for the winner, and the Kop rolled out renditions of 'Allez, Allez, Allez', booing the Hammers whenever they were in possession. At last, we could sense another late show would seal an improbable win. And, so it proved to be. It was probably this shift in mood that convinced Klopp the atmosphere had been 'on fire'.

The pressure was beginning to take its toll on West Ham, who in truth would have also gladly walked away with a point if one was on offer. It wasn't.

In the 80th minute, Gomez took a shot at goal from the edge of the penalty area. It took a wicked deflection and rebounded into the path of Trent, who lobbed over Fabianski at his near post, leaving Sadio Mané with the simplest of tasks and the striker tapped the ball over the line.

This time the celebrations were as full-blooded as any we have seen before. Once more, while playing well below the standards they themselves have set, Liverpool had found a way to win. It had been this way all season, and at full time Klopp would hail his side's ability to win every type of game, even the 'grumpy' ones. I knew exactly what he meant.

The game at times had been excruciating and even in that final ten minutes plus an inexplicable five minutes of added time, there was still time for the Reds to have a goal disallowed and for West Ham to be denied by the brilliance of Alisson. None of that mattered, nor did the at times excruciating nature of the win. In the final analysis, all that counts are the numbers. These may be strange days, and this was a scary night, but Liverpool had gone 22 points clear of Manchester City and just 12 points from heaven.

Watford 3 Liverpool 0: Reds Show Human Side as Fans Deal with a Very Rare Defeat

On 29 February 2020, Britain had just recorded its first death from the deadly coronavirus. The victim was a man who had been quarantined on the *Diamond Princess* cruise ship, and the country had been drenched by the wettest month on record. All around us, it seemed as though the world was in chaos.

At 5.30pm on that wet Saturday evening Liverpool travelled to Vicarage Road, Watford, for what should have been a routine victory. Of course, football is famed for failing to follow a script, and on this occasion, it would veer wildly off course. As a result, Liverpool suffered their first league defeat of the current season, and their first in over a year. To say the reaction was over the top was an understatement.

The love all supporters have for their football teams borders on the irrational at the best of times. During the worst of times, some fans race across the border of irrational and headlong into Bizarro Land. When Liverpool left Vicarage Road with their tails planted firmly between their legs and their heads bowed after a 3-0 defeat, the population of Bizarro Land grew massively.

A combination of defensive calamity, midfield anaemia and a bluntness in attack on Liverpool's part, coupled with intense focus, hard graft and ruthlessness in front of goal from Watford led to two goals from Ismaila Sarr and another from Troy Deeney. The Reds had no reply.

It meant Liverpool had just ended a run of 18 straight wins and 44 games unbeaten. They sat at the top of the league, 22 points clear of their nearest rivals, with ten games to go. This had been a remarkable sequence that had seen them not lose a league game since January 2019. Yet the reaction of some Liverpool supporters on social media was eye-wateringly ridiculous. At the Lingmel Inn, in the Norris Green area of the city, the scenes were reminiscent of a Wild-West bar-room brawl.

Maybe this stuff happened in the halcyon days of the 1970s and '80s, I just have no recollection of anything that came close to it. I didn't frequent pubs back then of course, as I was too young. And there were no such things as social media of course. The closest thing to that was the school playground or the works canteen. I definitely don't remember witnessing the sort of meltdowns that have become commonplace on Twitter and Facebook these days, when Joe Fagan's treble-winning heroes lost 4-0 away to Coventry City in 1983, or when Bob Paisley's magnificent 1978/79 team lost four times on the road to the likes of Bristol City, Aston Villa, Nottingham Forest and Sheffield Wednesday. Back then, we simply went to our rooms and sulked. And, in school or at work, we just took our medicine.

The simple reality is that Jürgen Klopp and the boys had created something so ridiculously special that the thought of defeat – never mind the real deal – had become so alien to many, that when the inevitable eventually happens, they lose their collective minds. It was by no means everyone, of course, and there were plenty of Reds offering up some much-needed perspective. It's also easy to understand that the 30-year wait for a league title, coupled with the internet platforms we are all given to vent our frustration can distort attitudes and behaviours.

I wouldn't want any future social historian, who is hopefully still able to get hold of a copy of this book, to think that we had all taken leave of our senses. But, if you're reading this in 2050 for research purposes, suffice it to say that quite a few Reds embarrassed themselves after this result. And understand that even saying that doesn't quite do it justice.

Liverpool were poor in every department at Watford. Klopp had opted to bring in Dejan Lovren to partner Virgil van Dijk, in place of the injured Joe Gomez. The moment the team sheet was announced, there was consternation at the change, especially as Joël Matip was given a place on the bench.

Lovren is nowhere near as bad a defender as some would have us believe. However, he hadn't played for a long time and his inevitable ring-rustiness would prove a huge problem. Still, it was unfair to hang all the responsibility for the defeat solely at his door. Everyone in a red shirt had a bad game at Vicarage Road.

Van Dijk struggled, Trent's passes went astray too often, Alisson wasn't his usual imposing self and Robertson fell short of the gargantuan standards he has set for himself. In the middle, Liverpool seemed to be missing something, I wasn't quite sure what it was, but it was shaped a bit like Jordan Henderson. The captain had now fully completed his transformation into Ronny Whelan, another player some people will never appreciate until he is out of the team, and even then, some of them won't realise it. Up front, Mohamed Salah, Roberto Firmino and Sadio Mané inevitably struggled because of all of the above.

Of course, none of this should take anything away from Watford. They were magnificent and fully deserved their win. There was nothing lucky about it and nothing for any Liverpool player or supporter to complain about. It was a fair result.

The media were unanimous beforehand in declaring that for the Hornets to win, they needed to play the game of their lives and Liverpool to have a rare off-day. That kind of 'perfect storm' hadn't happened for 422 days, of course, but it did on 29 February – Leap Year Day. It was way overdue.

Liverpool had flirted with this sort of result all season if truth be known, winning 14 games already in the campaign by just a single goal. Their penchant for lulling teams into a false sense of security before stinging them at the death was becoming the stuff of legend – the mark of champions, we said. Trouble is, you can only get away with performances like that for so long, and Liverpool had enjoyed more than their fair share of getting away with the odd off-day.

In addition, thoughts of setting a new benchmark as the new 'Invincibles' and eclipsing the great Preston North End and Arsenal teams, who went a whole season without defeat, had become something of a millstone and was adding unnecessary pressure to what was a remarkable season regardless.

John Barnes, a veteran of the majestic 1987/88 team, declared that he was glad it was over as he now felt the Reds could just focus on getting the job done. Stan Collymore, of the 1990s Roy Evans team, tweeted, 'Best thing that could happen to Liverpool. New sensation to deal with ahead of CL [Champions League], no more invincible talk, a reset in every way.

'Incredible to get this far, now they get to react to something that they haven't experienced this season.

'And good sides react well. Win, win.'

Chris Bascombe, Merseyside football reporter for *The Telegraph*, offered some much-needed perspective and pointed out the magnitude of the Reds' achievements to that point, saying, 'And after they've been yelled out for being so abysmal, they should be applauded for what they have achieved in this unbeaten run. Probably never see it in another Liverpool team.

'Shit happens … usually more often. Move on to next game.'

Klopp was typically straight-talking in his assessment, declaring that he 'wasn't bothered' by the loss of the unbeaten record, but was just determined to learn lessons. Congratulating Watford for their win, he claimed the Liverpool display was not good enough and looked forward to playing 'freely' and winning games unencumbered by talk of records and the unbeaten run.

Virgil van Dijk led the response from the Liverpool players, saying, 'It is unacceptable to lose 3-0. We need to strike back, and we will.'

In the coming days, the Reds would fall out of the FA Cup, thanks to a 2-0 defeat at the hands of Chelsea. They got back on track in the Premier League with a victory over Bournemouth. However, there were darker days on the horizon.

In the wake of the results, all of us had to come to terms with the fact that this Liverpool team were indeed human after all, just like their predecessors in the 1970s and '80s were. Most of us could find it within ourselves to do that. The least said about the rest, the better.

Liverpool 2 Atlético Madrid 3: The Game that Turned Anfield into a 'Biological Bomb'

They would call it the match that should never have happened, or that should have at least been played behind closed doors. Despite being in the grip of a global pandemic, which had prompted the Spanish government to ban internal travel and had already seen death counts in Madrid soar, UEFA and the British government saw fit to allow the game between Liverpool and Atlético Madrid to go ahead.

Public health experts called the decision reckless and were incredulous at the apparent laissez-faire attitude to allowing thousands of supporters, who were not even allowed to travel in their own country, to visit Merseyside. Photograph's of Madrid fans crowding bars and marching through the streets of the city centre filled the internet and local press.

We will never know how many staff in Liverpool's hospitality industry were exposed to the virus because of these decisions. However, at the time there were many voices even at this early stage of the UK's COVID-19 outbreak who argued the game would lead to a spike in infections. A month later, with the infection and death rate on Merseyside climbing and even club legend Kenny Dalglish contracting the virus, the government's chief scientific advisor described the possible link as 'an interesting hypothesis'.

The mayor of Madrid went a little further than that, describing the decision to let 3,000 supporters from the Spanish capital to fly in to Liverpool John Lennon Airport as 'a mistake'. That was probably a little too polite, with others preferring to refer to it as an act of criminal negligence. Some estimates would suggest that up to 41 deaths could be attributed the decision to allow the game to proceed.

So it was, amidst an emerging public health crisis, that on Wednesday, 11 March 2020, Anfield got ready to host Atlético Madrid and hordes of their supporters for the Champions League round of 16, second leg. With the Reds trailing from the first leg at the Wanda Metropolitano, the stage was set for another incredible night. However, this time it was Diego Simeone who would be grinning at full time.

Of course, Anfield responded as it always has on nights like these. The pre-match welcome was as passionate and fierce as ever, even if for those responsible for stewarding inside and outside the stadium there was more to consider than usual. Those yellow-jacketed men and women, whose job it is to maintain crowd safety, who often do their jobs so well we hardly notice them, had been placed in harm's way alongside the more than 53,000 who attended.

1995 My son Joe's journey begins. Here he is with me, in his first Liverpool kit.

Me, Joe and my daughter Mollie aged 9 and 7 in 2005 at Homecoming Parade

Mollie Goulding 2005 Champions League Homecoming

My son, Joe, before the Champions League semi-final clash with Chelsea at Anfield in 2007

Joe, Me and Mollie 2009

Joe at Wembley 2012 Carling Cup Final

Me and Joe before 2012 FA Cup Final

My daughter Lucy in 2012 aged eight, in her King Kenny shirt

Joe (centre) with the family Blues, John Colquhoun (left) and Harry Colquhoun (right)

Joe Goulding at Wembley for the League Cup Final 2016

International Champions Cup, 2016. Joe and me taking in Liverpool versus Barcelona at Wembley

Munich 2017 L-R Me, my son Joe and my Dad Billy

On my 50th birthday in 2017, now forever part of the fabric of Anfield

L-R Joe Goulding, Ian Rush and me

My youngest daughter, Sophie, at her first match with big brother Joe on the Kop in 2018

The Klopp mural, near Liverpool's Baltic Triangle

Me (right) with my mate John Stulberg in the Sandon Car Park prior to the live screening at Anfield of the Champions League Final in Kiev 2018

Sending the boys off to Madrid at the final game of the 2018 2019 season

Homecoming 2019

Waiting for the six times European champions on the Strand, Liverpool waterfront

The returning heroes 2019

The captain holds the cup aloft

A new mural is unveiled at Anfield for the first game of the 2019/2020 season against Norwich

My son, Joe, (left) and me at Wembley for the 2019 Community Shield

Finally we did it. The wait is over and the Reds are league champions again

A 5-year-old Ross Chandley of Red Men TV in his Liverpool kit

Ross Chandley from Red Men TV (right) with his dad, Mark, on the Kop for the live screening of the final in Kiev

A young Paul Salt with his brother and the old league title in 1990

BBC Radio Merseyside Sport's Paul Salt and his son Matthew on the Kop at the start of our title-winning season

LFC History's Christopher Wood with the old league trophy in 1990

Christopher Wood in 2019 after Liverpool had won their sixth European Cup

Liverpool FC Historian Kieran Smith in 1990

Kieran Smith, his wife Georgina, and their children, Charlie, George and Emily in 2020

L-R Stu and David Gouding holding their late father Jimmy's shirt, Harry, Alfie, Jake and Louie Goulding

John Whitehead and friends; Morgan; Jaz B; Old Big Ears; Manoj; Andy and Jaz S, deliver a gift to the Bernabeu Stadium following Liverpool's triumph in Madrid 2019

Louise Lacey and her daughter Emily at Anfield

Bundesliga journalist Chris Williams pops the bubbly in his garden as the Reds declared champions for the 19th time

Dhriti Bania on her Red travels

Copa 90's Ben Webb celebrating number six

The family of 1920s Reds title winner, Walter Wadsworth. Centre stage is Walter's son, Bill Wadsworth with his daughters Jacqueline Wadsworth on the left and Susan Wadsworth on the right.

Former Liverpool reserve and one of Shankly's first signings, George Scott, with his grandsons Callum and Charlie on the Kop

Justin Shanahan with his son Euan

Fionn Nolan and his father, Dermot, celebrate number 19

Stephen Lawrence and Tracey Murray receiving their father, Reds legend, Tommy Lawrence's banner from Peter Carney and Spirit of Shankly before Crystal Palace game

Keith Salmon with his son, Charlie, at the Wanda Metropolitano, Madrid in 2019

Linn, Emil, Asa, Alexander and Andreas Beijer celebrate in Sweden

L-R Peter Kenny Jones, Ajay Shah, Tommy Jones Snr, Tom Jones Jnr at Madrid 2019

Peter Carney and his son Tom with their new Champions banner

L-R Tony Zeverona, Michael Grierson, Chris Grierson, Conor Hill, Joe Zeverona, Peter Collis, Dave McLoughlin, Ricky Gambrill

Matthieu Pierre in Augsberg Main Square 2016

The Echo's *Dan Kay, arms aloft, with L-R Dean Harris, Ste Moon, Grant Bryce, Mark Currie, Richard Bryce, Clare Hanson and Andy Dunbar at the Super Cup Final in Istanbul*

This is Anfield's Joanna Durkan and her mum Bev at the match

The Voice of Anfield, George Sephton live on BT Sport celebrating as Liverpool crowned champions for the 19th time

Dublin lad, David King, with his daughter Alice, who has now seen the Reds win the league title for the first time.

Fahd Basheer and his wife, Nahala attending a game against Huddersfield at Anfield, in 2019, which ended 5-0 to the Reds. They also took in the 4-0 against Barcelona

The Anfield Wrap's Aaron Cutler with a banner that sums up how we all feel

Joe Goulding and Sean MacGregor in Madrid for the Champions League Final 2019

Celebrating on the streets of Woolton, Liverpool

Australian Reds, like Amanda Ellem (L) and Belinda Kimber, celebrated number 19 in fine style

Lee Tracy, grandson of 1920s Liverpool FC captain, Tom Bromilow, celebrates number 19 surrounded by his grandfather's memorabilia

For Gary Stanford, a crowd safety steward in the Anfield Road end, and his colleagues, it was a night like no other. Concerns had already been raised a week earlier, prior to the Bournemouth game, and the presence of COVID-19 meant his job took on a whole new dimension. Gary explained, 'The week before was a strange one. During the Bournemouth game, searching became an issue. I work on the response team. There's about 40 of us, and we search all away fans, as well as managing the concourse and the stairways in the away end. We did raise issues about search practices but were told government advice was business as usual, apart from hand sanitiser.

'When their main group of Atlético supporters got to the search lines, they stormed it, and we spent five minutes fighting them back. The same thing had happened against Everton in the league. We knew we couldn't let them through and get crushed at the turnstiles. In the ground they were decent, until they scored. Then we did the usual pushing them back.

'The difference here was that we knew where they'd come from [Madrid, with its high infection rates and death count]. As supporters, they were sound. There was lots of laughing, taking pictures and so on. Some of the stuff before the game was out of order though.'

Video footage would later emerge on social media, showing the desperate lengths people like Gary went to in order to prevent injuries outside the ground, coupled with the risk posed to their own safety. Many stewards had expressed concerns prior to the game. However, government advice had not been helpful, and those who look after supporter safety love their jobs, and many felt not turning up for duty was simply not an option.

After the game there was heavy praise for their efforts, with club CEO Peter Moore even singling them out for thanks. Many had gone above and beyond to ensure order was maintained in the away end. In doing so, they had placed themselves in harm's way. Gary is grateful that to the best of his knowledge, none of the team became unwell because of their work that night.

I went into this game with the usual sense of destiny and a huge amount of optimism. I've just seen Liverpool pull it out of the bag so often, and from much worse positions than this one. There's always a nagging sense that the laws of probability suggest that this uncanny knack must have a shelf life, sooner or later the streak will come to an end. Still, I was reasonably confident that Liverpool would do it again. And for 94 minutes, they were nothing short of perfect, before disaster struck in extra time.

The Reds took the lead through Gini Wijnaldum, whose header in the 43rd minute drew the tie level. It was on, and Atlético looked like they were rocking. Their fans, though they never fell silent, became edgy. Perhaps they too sensed the hand of destiny was once again on Liverpool's shoulder.

They needn't have worried as their club had previous for breaking Kopite hearts late in the game. None of us will ever forget Diego Forlan's 103rd-minute equaliser in 2010, that sent Rafa Benitez's Reds out of the Europa League at the semi-final stage, on the away goals rule. Surely, this Liverpool team couldn't fall for another sucker punch. They could of course, and the pain would be even greater.

That Liverpool side of 2010 was in decline. A Europa League final would have papered over the cracks of a club and a team that was a shadow of the one that hit the heights in Istanbul in 2005. Though the devastation was palpable, the feeling was more one of resignation. Under Klopp, expectations have soared, victories are expected, and our emotions lay forever on the edge of joy and despair.

As the game wore on, it was all about Liverpool. We were immaculate and our passage to the next round of the competition felt assured. The 90 minutes ended with parity achieved, now extra time and the possibility of penalties beckoned. Still, we weren't worried. We'd been here before, so many times.

Just four minutes into the first period of extra time, Bobby Firmino sent the crowd into ecstasy as he put the Reds 2-1 ahead on aggregate. With Liverpool marching towards an inevitable domestic title, the realisation that they were on the brink of progressing to the quarter-finals of the Champions League caused hearts to soar. This could be one of the greatest seasons in the history of the club, on a par with 1977 and 1984. This team could match and even eclipse the likes of Paisley and Fagan and we celebrated like we believed it.

Wijnaldum had been the provider. The hero of the previous season's epic tussle with Barcelona had powered down the right flank, hurtling towards the touchline at the Anfield Road end. His cross was met by the head of Firmino, but the ball hit the upright. The crowd held its breath as the rebound fell at the feet of the Brazilian. In an instant it was in the net and the place exploded.

It was thoroughly deserved. Liverpool had squandered several gilt-edged chances, and none more so than a 67th-minute header crashed against the crossbar by Andy Robertson. The full-back had been gloriously placed, and when the ball crashed off the woodwork, hands flew to foreheads and a collective gasp rushed around the ground. Now Bobby had made his chance pay, and with the Reds consummate on the ball and the defence barely troubled all night, hopes were high that they would see the game through or even add to their lead.

Job done? No, not at all. We never saw it coming, but when it arrived the Madrid sucker punch floored us all. It was of course entirely self-inflicted. The only way Liverpool could lose this tie was if they pushed the self-destruct button, and that's exactly what Adrián, in for the injured Alisson, did when he accepted a back-pass from Alexander-Arnold. He just had to take his time and then either clear upfield or pick out a Liverpool player. Instead he rushed his clearance low and shanked it straight to João Felix, who moved it to the substitute Marcos Llorente.

It all seemed to unfold in slow motion and my stomach lurched as the midfielder, who joined Atlético last summer from Real Madrid, took one touch to set himself before banging his shot low into the bottom corner. Adrián would compound his error by appearing to dive in stages to reach the ball. He got nowhere near it.

On the pitch players in red stared at the heavens, perhaps asking for just one more miracle, one more heroic finale. In the stands, shoulders slumped and hands covered eyes. Could a goalkeeping calamity really rob us of European glory again? It could.

With the Reds now having to force the issue, they left themselves vulnerable at the back. Atlético plundered another two goals, creating a hugely flattering scoreline and sending their hordes of followers into delirium. Once more they had struck late on to torture Liverpool and end a European campaign.

Writing in *The Guardian*, David Hytner summed up the night with these words: 'Liverpool ought to have won this game several times over. They attacked in waves, battering Atlético, testing their resilience to the limit. The most influential player on the pitch was the visiting goalkeeper, Jan Oblak, who made a string of excellent saves.'

It was all so hard to take. Had Liverpool struggled, been outplayed or outfought, I could have accepted it eventually. But to lose in such circumstances, to have come so close to the prize only to have it snatched from us was a crushing blow. To have been the architects of our own downfall only made matters worse.

Sympathy for Liverpool came from the Devil, as far as Reds were concerned. It was strangely Diego Simeone of all people who offered words of comfort in his post-match press conference.

'What I have to say and will be saying at the next UEFA coaches' meeting, is what I think is unfair,' said the Atlético boss.

'Today was unjust because we had 30 minutes of extra time to score three away goals. Liverpool never had that. We had 30 more minutes to score an away goal and Liverpool didn't. That's not fair.

'The rule favoured us today, but it might go against us in the future. Liverpool had 30 minutes fewer to score an away goal. That's wrong.'

It would do little to salve the wound his men, aided by our goalkeeper, had inflicted. In the aftermath of such a harrowing defeat, all proportion goes out of the window. The emotion magnifies the sense of loss and I remember, as I drifted away from the stadium, feeling as though the season was falling apart. Though we were streets ahead in the league, uncatchable and without equal, we were now fighting on just one front. The dream of a glorious domestic and European double was no more.

I was of course being ridiculous. We would surely be English champions for the first time in 30 years, I would tell myself. We were just two games from heaven and surely nothing could stand in the way of an epic celebration in May. But what about COVID-19? My head was in turmoil.

The days running up the game had been filled with talk of the season being cancelled, postponed, or even declared null and void. Rival fans, who had slowly come to terms with Liverpool ending 30 years of pain, had been openly discussing going into hiding, emigrating, or booking stays on the international space station. Liverpool supporters had been declared 'The Unbearables' but we preferred the honorific 'The Inevitables'.

Now with arguably the greatest team in the club's history in danger of missing out again, some could barely hide their glee. After achieving a club-record points total, Liverpool had been pipped by a Manchester City team that managed just a single point more in 2018/19. They had responded by becoming a relentless juggernaut, hurtling to a 25-point lead at the top, which had seemed impregnable. They had become a team so good that only a global crisis could stop them. The fact that one had come along right on cue seemed delicious to some.

Just two days later, Arsenal manager Mikel Arteta tested positive for coronavirus. Others followed and, perhaps inevitably, football was suspended. Jürgen's quest for the holy grail hung in the balance. Former Manchester United player and Sky Sports pundit Gary Neville posted a photograph of him popping a champagne cork on social media and the sense that our bitterest rivals had been handed a get out of jail free card was palpable.

Could such a momentous season really end like this? Could anyone really begrudge us the title after such an incredible campaign? When weighed against the magnitude of the pandemic, these questions bordered on the irrelevant, of course. However, as Jürgen Klopp himself said, 'Football is the most important of the least important things.' Surely, we would get our chance, wouldn't we?

Amidst the turmoil and horror of the pandemic, Europe was facing an apocalypse with Britain not far behind. Most of us felt torn between the common sense realisation that the safety of the people had to come first, and a desire to see the season played out, even if that meant we would do so behind closed doors. It was a forlorn hope and reality would soon bite.

None of us could imagine that the death toll in Britain would surpass that of every nation, except the United States, and that the north-west and Liverpool would be so badly hit by the disease, and that we would ultimately have to accept that football must go into lockdown, along with the rest of the country.

Dreams can never be locked down though. And, although arguments would rage for months over whether the season should be completed, or if it should be voided, in the eyes of Jürgen's army of believers, the title was already won.

ANFIELD UNDER LOCKDOWN

Liverpool FC: March–June 2020

Delayed Gratification and Lockdown Emptiness

On 13 March 2020, the Premier League announced that it would suspend all games until at least April. Three days later, the UK government announced new restrictions to try to combat the spread of COVID-19. This became a full-scale UK-wide lockdown on 23 March. The impact was huge and wide-ranging.

Suddenly people were panic-buying toilet rolls and hand sanitisers, and supermarket shelves were stripped bare in no time at all. The number of cases of COVID-19 escalated and the death rate climbed as the realisation that our worst fears were coming true sank in.

The prime minister took to the airwaves to calm the nation, only to declare that 'more of your loved ones are going to die before their time'. This was of course borne out by events, but what we didn't realise at the time was that had the government instituted lockdown a week earlier, the eventual death toll could have been halved. Whether this was due to callous indifference, incompetence, or a mixture of both will be debated for years to come.

The public, confined to their homes, took to their doorways weekly to applaud NHS workers. It was both a morale-boosting act of solidarity and a grim reminder that these workers were putting their very lives on the line to protect the nation from this virus. It wouldn't be long before news began to emerge that some of them had paid the ultimate price.

The loss of football matches pales in comparison with loss of life and the impact of all this on the mental health of the population. Social isolation, though necessary, led to anxiety in people young and old. Anywhere from 40,000 to 50,000 people in the UK had lost their lives at the time of writing. Across the globe, the death toll was staggering.

In this context, it seems frivolous, even disrespectful to talk about sport and recreation. However, a life spent in isolation or at least socially distanced is a miserable one. It eats away at your mental wellbeing. The loss of the things that once acted as a distraction or an escape, gave meaning or purpose to life or helps to forge bonds with others, made coping with any crisis much harder to bear.

This is the function that football has served in my life. Going to the match, writing, or talking about the game, meeting friends in the pub before and after it are all aspects of what constitutes normality for me. COVID-19 robbed families of loved ones, but it also stole our normality. Whatever that may be for different people, it took away the things that anchor us and give us meaning.

That was me for much of this period. But if I was struggling, then my children were suffering far more. All of them faced significant challenges, whether that was fears about their own health, or their parents'.

My youngest became increasingly anxious during the lockdown and enforced absence from school – away from her 'normal'. We noticed that the number of times she told us and her sisters and brother that she loved us had increased dramatically. We saw it as something comically endearing at first, until we slowly came to understand what lay behind it.

My wife and I both work in the National Health Service, which puts us in direct contact with the disease – my wife, as a result of working on the frontline, more so than me. However, to my daughter's young mind we were at risk of becoming ill and dying every time we left the house.

When we finally got her to talk through her feelings, she told us that every time she went to sleep or said goodbye to us in the morning, she thought that may be the last time she would ever see us. She wanted us to know how much we meant to her, and for 'I love you' to be the last words we heard from her. She is ten years of age.

In families and homes across the world, conversations like this were happening. Minds filled with secret fears and concerns for friends and loved ones. My father, who is approaching 75, feared living out the remainder of his life in isolation and unable to hold his family, to kiss his grandchildren. All these things render sport and football irrelevant. And yet, they're not.

Football is my escape, but it's also my way of expressing myself. Of course, I'm not defined by it. I am many things besides a Liverpudlian. My profession is nursing, my job is managerial, I am a husband, a father, and a friend. We are, all of us, all these things and more. But if I'm honest, if I am forced to say what truly defines who I am, my values and beliefs, what drives my passions and my desire to write, for example, I would have to say that being from Liverpool and supporting Liverpool Football Club has been the major driving force in my life.

Football is the closest I get to the spiritual. It makes no sense and even as I write this I feel it sounds grandiose, ridiculous even. I cannot deny it though.

That place on Walton Breck Road, named after a hill in South Africa, the scene of so much bloodshed during the Boer War over a century ago, is home. I am so familiar with the place; I feel I know every brick in its walls and have walked over every paving stone on the way to those turnstiles. It is filled with ghosts, of long since departed Reds, some of them friends, some of them family, some of them both.

Then there are the phantoms of games lost and tremendous victories, of songs sung and banners unfurled, and of quips and sayings from a cast of thousands who have stood and sat next to me for decades.

I carry all those ghosts with me every time I go to that magical place. To be locked out of it was painful.

Many supporters have shared with me similar feelings. In *Red Odyssey II*, we met Tony Zeverona on his many European travels. In a conversation conducted online he told me, 'I think lockdown has been difficult for everyone. We miss the social interaction.

The match, the pint before and after the game with the lads and the mickey-taking that we all get every week.

'I have been working from home, so it hasn't changed for me work-wise, but it has been difficult not to have that social interaction. Social media has provided a platform for people to look back on happier times and Reds have been posting pictures from here there and everywhere, looking back and looking forward to these games and trips returning, which they will. It really has underlined how lucky we are to support and follow Liverpool.

'Not being able to be there when we win the league will be the hardest thing to take for me. That feeling you get when they lift that trophy is a feeling that should be shared with your mates. When it happens, I should be having a pint with the people I care about, looking back on the most incredible season and talking about our favourite moments; the ones that will live with us for ever.

'We have waited 30 years for this moment, but if it is not to be, then that's fine. It's not the best scenario, but it's one we will accept.'

This is Anfield's Joanna Durkan told me how she had experienced a whole range of emotions during football's hiatus.

'The simplest way to describe it would be a rollercoaster,' said Joanna. 'Missing football was one thing, but Liverpool being so close to the holy grail and the uncertainty which followed formed the basis of my emotional journey.

'You have to in some way grieve an image in your mind that you had conjured up for years, with mass celebrations and scenes of jubilation no longer possible; which takes you through the webs of anger, frustration and then ultimately must come acceptance.

'I'm lucky that my job centres around football and Liverpool and so I did not feel the full brunt of its absence, but it made me appreciate the little things – the social interactions, the banter, the one-upmanship and the "normality" it brings to everyday life.

'You saw the very best of people and of football fans of whom many in this country still paint in the same light with an old, stale brush – like Klopp says, it's "the most important of the least important things", but it gives so much to so many and that escapism was sorely missed.'

Others, like author Steven Scragg, had experienced personal tragedy during lockdown, and had found that the absence of football had impacted, even compounded the grief and loss.

'Lockdown has been surreal,' he told me. 'We were just two wins away from the title when football ground to a halt. Of course, there are more vital things in life, but you shouldn't undersell how important football is to people.

'It is crucial to my relationship with my father. As a widower, it is his social life and I was delighted that we were going to be able to see the team we love lift a first league title in 30 years. At almost 82, I really didn't think we'd get the chance to share another title together.

'During our enforced time apart, his brother, my uncle Dave, died. It was something my dad had to absorb on his own. As it was me that was receiving updates from my cousin, Neil, I effectively had to give my dad a running commentary on the death of his brother.

'My Uncle Dave loved football, he loved Liverpool FC and he talked about them to his very last lucid day on this earth. He'd want Liverpool to see this title win over the line and it has made the null and void campaigners' desperation to deny Liverpool all the more distasteful. Unique circumstances and a "new normal", have still not been enough to eradicate ingrained hatreds and reactions that speak of a lack of common sense.'

Graeme James Strain, a veteran of that magical night in Madrid, told me about how closely interwoven the fortunes of the club and his life are.

He said, 'Lockdown and the cessation of football has shown to me just how linked my happiness is to the Reds, and how much of an impact they have on my mood. How much I need to go the match with mates and have that whole experience. I have tried to use it all as a positive. I have used the time to watch retro-games, shown my lad some of the classics from when I was his age and younger, I've read more about the Reds and just appreciated how much they have done for me, how many times they have made me cry and how many times they have taken me to places I never thought I would see.

'However, all I want is to see football and Liverpool back and I'm desperate to see us win the title. Frankly, after 30 years, Hendo could do his shuffle on the moon and I wouldn't care. I just want to see that trophy come to us as soon as possible.'

Writer and football historian Peter Kenny Jones had also felt the loss of a loved one during the period of social distancing and had attended a funeral limited to only ten mourners. He told me of a poignant moment, as he and his family said farewell to their loved one, as the song 'You'll Never Walk Alone' played in the background. Football is never far away in Liverpool, from the cradle to the grave. Peter told me, 'Lockdown was obviously a time that was worrying and scary for myself, my family and everyone worldwide. There would be nothing more my Auntie Pat would have loved than to have seen Liverpool win the league again. It's heart-breaking that she will never see that.

'I haven't missed a game at Anfield since 2011, the thought of life without football is just awful. But what I do know is I can live without football for a few weeks as long as it helps bring this pandemic to a halt.

'I can't wait for football to return though. The lockdown has made me realise how much I love Liverpool, how much I hate missing them play and how much joy you get from enjoying the best moments with the most important people.'

I also caught up with George Sephton, often referred to as the voice of Anfield having been Liverpool's stadium announcer since 1971. He told me, 'Being in self-isolation for 12 weeks, my emotions were in a tangle. I was devastated when the Premier League was suspended, so close to the winning line for my Reds. Double-devastated, as my poor grandson Thomas, who is just eight years old, had tickets for the centre of the front row of the Anfield Road stand to watch the title being won at Anfield! He was distraught of course.

'Into lockdown and the first priority was to survive and hopefully be fit and well for the restart whenever it came. My wife and I obeyed the rules and she did a terrific job of looking after me so the first bit was completed successfully, although I had been very worried about the physical contact I'd had with the Atlético Madrid fans on 11 March.'

Like George, all Reds would gladly wait for the holy grail of a first league title in 30 years, so long as it meant gaining control of a deadly virus. However, all of us were given a stark reminder of how important our club is to us, how our lives and our moods are all wrapped up in the fortunes of our team, and how lost we feel when all that is taken from us.

Furlough Fury: The Own Goal that Raised Questions About Football's Ethos

Barely a single facet of our lives went untouched by the coronavirus pandemic. In difficult times major sports like football have been an important form of escapism and release. Yet, even this has been taken away, at least temporarily. Not since the war has a global event interfered on such a fundamental level with our way of life.

Of course, sport pales in comparison with the human cost of the disease. Meanwhile, the economic burden, which threatened to plunge the world economy into recession and even depression, would have a human cost of its own.

In response to this many economies around the world were forced to intervene in ways that would have been unthinkable only months earlier. In the UK, the government announced that it was introducing a job retention scheme, which paid 80 per cent of employee wages up to a maximum of £2,500, and initially for three months. The scheme applied to all companies affected by the crisis and who needed help to pay staff costs.

A number of high-profile companies applied to the scheme, with some coming in for criticism, and others accused of profiting from a crisis. Among these were Tottenham Hotspur's Daniel Levy, and Mike Ashley, owner of Newcastle United. Their decisions meant staff at those clubs would only be paid 80 per cent of their wages.

When, on 4 April, Liverpool Football Club announced that it would furlough staff while topping up their salaries, ensuring they would lose no income, the reaction was ferocious. Many – me included – argued that in choosing to access the public purse to pay their staff, the club has betrayed the values of supporters.

Others pointed to Liverpool's claims of a socialist ethos and its vision statement, 'We Are Liverpool, This Means More', as evidence that the club's acts were hypocritical and lacking in class. The outpouring of anger and condemnation led to a reversal of the decision and an apology to supporters just two days later. A statement on the club's official website read, 'We believe we came to the wrong conclusion last week to announce that we intended to apply to the coronavirus retention scheme and furlough staff due to the suspension of the Premier League football calendar, and are truly sorry for that.'

While many praised the club for listening and acting on concerns, others felt there had been irreparable damage done to its reputation. The whole episode was felt to have made a mockery of CEO Peter Moore's words, uttered as recently as October 2019: 'The success of Liverpool Football Club is based on socialism.

Bill Shankly, a Scottish socialist, built our foundations. Today too, when we speak about business questions, we ask ourselves: what would Shankly have done? What would Bill have said in this situation?'

While this was accepted by many without question, even welcomed with pride by some, it was for me a remarkable and unprecedented statement from a Liverpool CEO. I couldn't in my lifetime recall any board member publicly identifying with socialist ideas or principles. Not in the days of John Smith and Peter Robinson, David Moores and Rick Parry and certainly not under the stewardship of Tom Hicks and George Gillett.

The club may have felt like a family to a generation of supporters like myself, but I would argue that this owed more to the bond between fans, the manager and the team, than it did to any corporate identity. Back in the glory days of the 1970s and '80s, supporters barely paid the owners of the club any attention. So long as they stayed out of the way and ensured there were enough tickets for cup finals, we were content to leave them to it.

Clearly Liverpool have, like every other Premier League club, always been a footballing enterprise run by venture capitalists. Its very birth is owed to a boardroom dispute between rival businessmen and the club's first owner was a Tory mayor, brewer and freemason. He would hardly have found sympathy with Shankly's philosophy.

That Peter Moore should profess that socialism was the guiding principle of the business, while welcome, was also jarring. Particularly when juxtaposed with the club's failed attempts to raise some ticket prices to £77 and to monopolise the name of our city. In a region that features some of the poorest neighbourhoods in the country and a sense of civic pride you'd go a long way to better, this was always going to be met with fury and protest. And it was.

When stacked up alongside the latest debacle, these 'mistakes' start to look like a pattern of evidence that the club lacks class and that the business isn't being run with a conscience. That supporters care about this is both interesting to me and commendable.

Steven Kelly, a columnist with the *Irish Examiner*, agrees that there is a contradiction, and that Liverpool Football Club is primarily a capitalist enterprise, at least as far as its owners are concerned. However, he feels that supporters are entitled to pick and choose their battles, citing the longstanding campaign against the S*n newspaper paper a case in point, and suggests the club is rightly held to a higher standard.

'I think you pick and choose, knowing, as you say, this is a capitalist enterprise. Primarily. Boycotting *The Sun*, even though a lot of newspapers wrote awful things is an example of that,' Steven pointed out. 'We walked out because of £77 tickets, that again was too much, and people wanted to make a stand.

'The outrage over furloughing was clearly widespread, especially when you consider the idiotic "this means more" slogan. They [the club] can't ever be huffy about being held to a higher standard.'

However, Steven does acknowledge that there is often a double standard applied by some supporters in terms of the running of the club. While most of us feel Liverpool is different from the likes of Chelsea and Manchester City, which are run by oligarchs, all of us were excited when reports emerged of a Dubai takeover in the 2009/10 season.

'Liverpool fans castigated first [Roman] Abramovich, then [Sheikh] Mansour,' Steven told me. 'However, when we were linked with Dubai most only saw the chance of multimillion signings! It's hard not to be a hypocrite most of the time.'

These inherent contradictions are everywhere and are a function of how the game is run. There is a conflict at the heart of it, which is about the interests of the different parties concerned. The gap between what supporters want and how they view their clubs, and how owners feel on these issues is becoming increasingly visible.

Moore's assertions, that Liverpool is a club run on socialist principles always felt more like an attempt to align the club's marketing strategy and corporate image with that of the bulk of its followers. It was about capitalising on Liverpool's identity as a strong community with a collectivist soul, something that appeals on an emotional level and just happens to be a sponsor's dream. It was about masking the gap, and I have never bought it.

The *Daily Mirror*'s David Maddock agreed, sharing my scepticism about the club's new-found conversion to socialism and arguing, 'Liverpool FC is wholly owned by American venture capitalists, who bought the club because they felt it was under-priced, and therefore ripe to make an exaggerated profit on, that is a much greater profit than is usually possible in the market. That proved true, so their instinct was correct. The club is now worth at least ten times their total outlay in purchasing and financing it, quite probably more.

'I've always argued that the Premier League is almost a distillation of capitalism – kind of more capitalist than just about every other business model, because the rich exploit the poor to get richer on so many levels, and the only way to achieve success is to be as ruthless in that as possible.'

So, why the furious reaction by fans, writers and the media to Liverpool's decision? Were the club's critics being fair?

Maddock continued, 'Fans criticise the club for not exploiting its position to make more profit and it's true. If the club is going to be successful it must exploit every revenue stream ruthlessly. I think the Premier League, in a sense, is disaster capitalism writ large.

'When it comes to the furlough stuff, they clearly misread the public mood incredibly badly. In the middle of a global pandemic, when we are all being asked to pull together, they have extended that ruthless profit at all costs mentality to extreme lengths. And, in contrast, Everton announced immediately they would pay all staff full wages, even those who are employed on a casual basis on matchdays. Which shows it is possible. This has put Liverpool's decision into stark contrast.'

So did Maddock think that Everton had shown the way. Is it possible for a capitalist enterprise to behave ethically, or be socialist and succeed? He remains sceptical: 'Everton may be the people's club, but they cannot become the people's champions by being "ethical", whatever that means.

'It's a horrible situation. We all want football clubs to be successful, but many of us want our football clubs also to show principles, ideals, and ethics. These tend to be based on socialist philosophies. And of course are not possible in any way at the top of the game.'

For Maddock, so long as football clubs are run along these lines they will always 'behave badly' and misjudge the mood. Only when their behaviour threatens their profitability, will they adjust their approach. This has clearly been borne out by events. So why do we all believe Liverpool FC is a socialist club?

The arrival of Bill Shankly in 1959 is rightly judged to be a defining moment in the development of the club. His great unifying message and collectivist ideals were the launchpad for a period of unparalleled success. And that ethos has continued to both resonate and influence supporters of the club to this day. He was undeniably a socialist, declaring, 'The socialism I believe in isn't really politics, it's a way of life. I believe the only way to be successful is by collective effort. Everybody working hard for the same goal and sharing the rewards at the end of the day. It's the way I see football. It's the way I see life.'

The arrival of the Scotsman, while justifiably seen as pivotal in a football sense, also drew a clear defining line between the politics and ethos of the supporters, players and manger on the one side, and the administration of the club on the other. Another of Shankly's quotes is emblematic of this: 'At a football club there is a holy trinity. The supporters, the players, and the manager. The directors don't come into it. They just write the cheques. In fact, we write them. They just sign them.'

Therefore, it is possible to argue, even logical to do so, that Liverpool's 'socialism' does not and has never existed in the boardroom. It has been a vital driving force for the way the team plays, it's attitude and what we always referred to as the 'Liverpool Way'. It has galvanised our support and made us feel that we are part of the team on a matchday, that we can influence how the game is played, and even that we have a duty to do so. However, it has never guided the business side of the club, which has until very recently never professed to be concerned with such things.

You could argue that aligning your corporate identity with that of your supporters is a shrewd move. Maybe doing so could contribute to a virtuous circle where unity in the stands and on the pitch feeds a similar ethos off it. Perhaps it could lead to the evolution of a more egalitarian enterprise, a model for others to follow.

I believe the desire to see this happen is behind the revulsion and horror expressed by many people. Perhaps, in Liverpool, they saw something of an ideal. To see the club's ownership team seemingly betray that ideal appeared to have hurt them more deeply than Mike Ashley and Daniel Levy's use of the furlough scheme did.

Nobody likes a hypocrite. Somehow it hurts more and angers us more when someone or something behaves in a way that robs of us of our image of them. It reaffirms our deepest fear that deep down 'they're all the same' and it does not matter how high-minded their ideals may seem, money always talks.

So, if the response of the media and commentators seemed relatively easy to understand, what of the supporters? Are they simply naïve dupes, taken in by Peter Moore's clever marketing trick? Do they really believe that Liverpool Football Club as a corporate entity is motivated by different things than all the rest? I think it's more complicated than that.

To my generation, there is a deeply held feeling that our club is different. It is often mocked and referred to among other things as 'cloying Scouse exceptionalism'. However, it is a genuine mindset. I have never felt our perceived uniqueness owed anything to the institution of the club, but more to the people, the stories, the irreverence and contrariness of the Kop and its refusal to be generic. More to the attitude of the city itself than the boardroom. After all, they just sign the cheques.

That so many of us now see the behaviour of the club's administration as harming our self-image, our uniqueness and socialist identity is fascinating. We never felt that way before. Under the worst excesses of Hicks and Gillett, we could always dissociate. They're not our club, we would say. We are the club. That was at least in keeping with Shankly's ideal.

The early protest movements against that disastrous ownership model of Hicks and Gillett found expression in movements that had at their core the aim of wresting control of the club from the capitalists and handing it over to the supporters. Both Share Liverpool FC, a group that attempted to raise funds to buy the club from the Americans in 2010, and Spirit of Shankly, the Liverpool supporters' union, saw fan ownership as the way forward.

Their campaigns were about a 'dictatorship of the holy trinity' in the Marxist sense. The club would be run by and for the supporters, the players, and other employees. Various models of cooperative ownership of the club were discussed. However, without government intervention, the idea of supporters raising the necessary capital to take control of a club the size of Liverpool has become unthinkable.

For me, the protests that sprung up around the Hicks and Gillett takeover were a watershed in terms of the political consciousness of Liverpool supporters and to varying degrees the fans of other clubs too. From that moment on, fans were concerned about the governance arrangements at Anfield in a way they never had been before.

The politicisation of Reds followers can be traced back further, to the 1980s and the impact of Thatcherism on working-class areas like Merseyside. Support for the city council's fight against the Tory policy of 'managed decline' among the Liverpool and Everton faithful is well documented, in Tony Evans's excellent *Two Tribes*, for example.

The Hillsborough disaster, which occurred at the end of that decade, merely confirmed and solidified Scouse antipathy to the political right-wing and Thatcherism in particular. However, in each of these examples, the target was government, the state and the media.

Throughout all this the club was perceived to be an ally or at least not in the way. If it remained passive and neutral on the question of Tory cuts to local services, it was foursquare behind justice for the 96. After 2010, the image of the club changed significantly, at least as far as its supporters were concerned.

Hicks and Gillett faced a politicised fan base who were organised and could now focus their collective attention on the running of the club. Things would never be the same again. Liverpool's supporters were now sceptical of ownership, and willing to have their say in a way they never had before.

Today, it is not uncommon to hear supporters who had long since declared themselves 'Scouse not English' singing 'fuck the Tories', particularly on away trips around the country. The 'Scousers Hate Tories', 'Scouse Solidarnosk' – a homage to Polish

Trade Union Solidarity – and 'Unity is Strength' banners are also significant.

I believe this recipe of a politically left-leaning and highly politicised fan base, deeply sceptical of the establishment generally, and outside investors specifically, helps to explain the ferocity of reaction among Liverpool's supporters to the furlough issue, compared to those of Newcastle and Spurs. It may also go some way to explaining why the club backtracked so quickly.

However, to my mind there is a deeper question here than the issue of whether to furlough or not. The really important question for me is: whose game is this? In whose interests is it being run and how can we as supporters have more control over it?

There are those who would argue that it is perfectly reasonable and even desirable for football clubs to be run as businesses so long as they behave with a conscience and act in ways that are ethical and for the common good. This proposed accommodation between an enterprise with capitalist motives and socialist ideals – a mixed economy if you like – is problematic in my view.

The fundamental driving force of any capitalist enterprise is the maintenance of revenue, the reduction of cost and accrual of profit. That applies in the good times as well as during downturns when income streams are restricted. This is evidenced by our ownership seeking to monopolise revenue streams – trademarking Liverpool and seeking to negotiate European TV rights separately from the Premier League's collective agreement. It has also found expression in early attempts to hike ticket prices.

These are not examples of a capitalist enterprise behaving badly. This is exactly how one is supposed to behave. You may accept that as merely a reality of the modern world and something we must live with. However, if you do, don't be surprised when the club's actions frequently clash with your ideals, as Liverpool FC's have.

On each occasion, the club has apologised and corrected its 'mistake'. Some have argued that while this is commendable, it would be better served by avoiding these mistakes in the first place. My argument is that this is unrealistic. An acceptance of football as a business, in my view, means accepting that our clubs will continually come into conflict with the aspirations of their followers. Therefore, it will always be necessary for supporters to organise in order to have their voices heard and potentially force their club to change course.

It may sadly be that without meaningful supporter involvement at board level – or the holy grail of cooperative ownership of football – Liverpool's willingness to listen and correct their failings in response to protest, may be the best we can hope for.

Anfield's Final Hillsborough Memorial Postponed: Families and Survivors Continue Their 'Journey Without a Destination'

On 15 April 2020, Anfield should have once again been packed out. Not in celebration or joy, but in commemoration, remembrance and still, after more than 30 years, anger, hurt and a deep sense of injustice. This was to be the final memorial service to be held at the Reds' home, but like so many other aspects of life, it would be rightly sacrificed in the name of public health.

In its place, the city of Liverpool and supporters around the world found other ways to show their solidarity. Fans were encouraged to change social media profile pictures in honour of the anniversary, or place scarves, football shirts or pictures in the windows of their homes. Across the city, the flags at the town hall flew at half mast, and the club would lay a wreath at the memorial on 96 Avenue followed by a minute's silence.

In a statement, Margaret Aspinall, chairwoman of the Hillsborough Family Support Group, said, 'We wish to keep as many people safe as possible and we believe this is the right approach.' She, perhaps more than most, understood why safety must be paramount.

As has so often been the case over the previous three decades, the journey for peace and justice would go on. And those who had already borne more pain than they should, would do so with a sense that closure was as illusive as it ever had been. At least they would not journey alone.

Five months earlier, on 28 November 2019, the jury in the trial of David Duckenfield, match commander on the day of the disaster, returned a verdict of not guilty on 95 counts of gross negligence manslaughter. It would mean that, 30 years on from the tragedy, with the supporters exonerated, nobody would be held accountable for Britain's worst sporting disaster. It came as a hammer blow to the families of the deceased and all who had campaigned for justice and accountability.

Survivors, the families of those who lost their lives, and countless others had suffered three decades of needless torment. Meanwhile, energy that should have been spent rebuilding lives was instead devoted to fighting against an establishment that simply wanted to sweep the disaster under the carpet and move on.

Men, women, and children carrying the unbearable weight of grief and loss were forced to become campaigners, study legal texts and relive the disaster in minute detail in courtroom after courtroom. It should never have taken two public inquiries, civil and criminal proceedings, two coroners' inquests, an independent panel report and over 11,000 days to right the wrong that was done to these people and their community. However, despite all of that, the wrong has not been righted.

The not guilty verdict, delivered in a drab courtroom in the north-west of England, meant that the only man to face criminal charges for the deaths of all those people had been acquitted. It also meant that good people who had endured too much already had sat through days of testimony and evidence, much of which dredged up traumatic memories and rehashed long discredited theories and conspiracies.

The coroner's verdict in 2015 had exonerated the supporters. It had found that David Duckenfield's decision-making and actions on the day directly contributed to the deaths of 96 people. It concluded that those who died – many of whom could have been saved had expert help arrived sooner – were unlawfully killed.

After the verdict in Preston, families were left asking, 'If Duckenfield is not guilty, just who was it that unlawfully killed our loved ones?' The answers to that question will now have to wait.

The verdict would embolden those seeking to divert culpability to people whose names have long since been cleared – the supporters. Scores of internet trolls used the verdict to repeat lies and distortions that had long since been discredited.

In the aftermath of the tragedy, a healthy state would have wrapped its arms around the families and the survivors. Every service and all aid would have been placed at their disposal, justice would have been swift, and learning would have been profound.

In a healthy state, the survivors would have been cared for from day one. They would have been offered the support necessary to rebuild their lives. However, their journey suggests that the British state, in 2020, was far from a healthy one.

It is instead deeply pathological. In the face of catastrophe, its first instinct was to protect itself, the powerful and their institutions. Sadly, this was as true on 15 April 2020 as it was in 1989.

Consider the behaviour of the court in response to an anguished relative who, struggling to cope with the enormity of the verdict, yelled out, pleading with the judge to tell him who it was who unlawfully killed the 96. He was simply ignored, and the court was adjourned, with cold, callous formality.

Equally depressing was the fact that the disaster and the campaign has been seen by many as a 'Liverpool issue'. In most cases this has always been well meaning and welcome. However, in others, there has been an attempt to portray the campaign as another example of Liverpool's perceived contrariness or 'victim' mentality.

However, the ramifications of the disaster have been felt far beyond the confines of the city of Liverpool. Hillsborough is the country's tragedy – it is football's tragedy.

The idea that Hillsborough is purely a Liverpool issue has led to several unhelpful attitudes and behaviours over the years. At the time of the disaster it made it easier for some to shift responsibility on to a city that had already been cast in the role of England's 'troublesome child'.

Much later a column edited by Boris Johnson wrongly branded Liverpool as a 'self-pity city'. This deepened the hurt and made the campaign for truth and justice much harder to fight. In 2020, these ideas are still being parroted on the terraces of football grounds around the country.

Supporters of other English clubs still sing about Scousers who, they say, are 'always the victim'. In doing so they unwittingly participate in the sort of stereotyping that has exacerbated the pain and misery plaguing survivors and families. It is perhaps easier to do that, if you believe that this is just 'them over there, moaning again'. Or, 'It's been 30 years. Why don't they move on?'

It's much harder to say those things when you accept that the tragedy could just as easily have happened to you or the people you care about. This of course is true. Hillsborough could easily have happened to supporters of any English club.

The Hillsborough Independent Panel Report highlighted several incidents, prior to 1989, in which a similar disaster was narrowly averted. Equally, many of the victims of Hillsborough were not from Liverpool and have also suffered greatly in its aftermath.

Forty-one of the 96 who perished were from other parts of the UK. Their families are rightly just as angry and equally vocal.

Louise Brookes, the sister of Mark Brookes, who died in the Sheffield catastrophe, lays this out in a statement to a government report into the treatment of the Hillsborough families. The report is entitled 'The patronising disposition of unaccountable power', and it is authored by the Right Reverend James Jones.

It is a powerful and moving documentary of the experience provided by those caught up in the days and the weeks after the tragedy. In it, Louise points out that, in addition to the deceased, many of whom came from outside Liverpool: 'The survivors are also from all over the UK. Two of the lads who tried to save my brother were from Devon. Five out of the seven women who died were from London.

'When people refer to it only being a Liverpool disaster, it makes me feel like my brother is invisible.'

Invisible. How utterly debilitating and despairing must it feel to believe that your experience has been overlooked. How hard must it be to labour on for decades, fighting for truth and justice and to feel that you are invisible?

Many born and raised in Liverpool are immensely proud of the way their city came together in the aftermath of the tragedy. They could have fractured or succumbed to the many unnecessary challenges that came their way. But they did not, because they understood that, at its heart, Hillsborough was a human disaster.

However, there have also been bereaved families in London and other parts of the country who feel the pain and anger every bit as much as any Scouser. Survivors, many of whom fought to save the lives of the stricken and injured on the pitch that day, came from all over the land, not just from Liverpool.

More than ever, it is important to recognise that Hillsborough was a human catastrophe that touched not just one city but the world of football and beyond. Its lessons have meaning for all of us, regardless of which team we support or where we are from.

Sadly, we will never bring back those lost loved ones or restore the years of peace that have been stolen, certainly not with mere words. As James Jones wrote in his report: 'There can be no closure to love, nor should there be for someone you have loved and lost. Furthermore, grief is a journey without a destination. The bereaved travel through a landscape of memories and thoughts of what might have been.

'It is a journey marked by milestones, some you seek, some you stumble on. For the families and survivors of Hillsborough these milestones have included the search for truth, accountability and justice.'

Solidarity with those affected by the disaster, wherever they are from, remains important. The loss of an organised memorial at Anfield does not change that. With or without our support, the families and the survivors will continue their 'journey without a destination'.

They make it from every corner of Britain, not only Liverpool. And all of us have a role to play in making that journey more tolerable.

From Tainted Title to Null and Void, and the Asterisk Delusion

There is a perception about Liverpool Football Club and its supporters that has increasingly gained traction in recent years. It is largely manifested on social media and in the songs sung by rival supporters when they visit Anfield, when they don't visit Anfield, and whether they are playing Liverpool or not. These perceptions range from thinking we are deluded and that we think we are more special and better than all the rest to the more damaging and insulting claims that we have a 'victim mentality' and are thieves and scroungers.

There are also wild conspiracy theories, which claim that the Premier League, UEFA, VAR, and the sports media are all in cahoots to ensure that Liverpool win the title. This last notion has one glaring flaw in it of course. Because, if it's true, it must be the most incompetent conspiracy cabal ever, given that the Reds are closing out three decades without a league title.

These keyboard warriors and songsters even sought to undermine Liverpool's narrow near miss in the 2018/19 season, claiming they would be done for once VAR came into effect. Of course, all that flipped on its head when the Reds marched to the top of the table and stayed there, regardless of the introduction of technology.

So ubiquitous were these claims that it is easy for Reds fans to take them to heart, and even think that these views are representative of all supporters rather than being the deranged utterances of a very vocal minority. Writer Henry Jackson who scribes for This is Anfield, felt that the attitudes of rival fans particularly on social media had become something of a joke. He told me, 'The way some rival supporters have reacted has been tribalism at its worst. I'm all for it in football a lot of the time, but much of these responses have lacked class. Liverpool have blown away everyone this season and could win the title by the biggest margin in English football history, so it would be nice for other supporters to simply acknowledge that and move on.'

Jackson was keen to acknowledge the value of humour in football rivalry, saying, 'I have no issue with talk of an "asterisk title" being said in jest – I would probably do the same if Manchester United were in our position – but sadly too much of it is genuine, which is embarrassing. We were told all about how "unbearable" we would be when we eventually won the league again, but it's those who dislike Liverpool who are the unbearable ones.'

If Henry was able to laugh off much of the cries of Liverpool's detractors, he found the calls for the season to be null and void, because of the COVID-19 crisis, to be self-serving.

'The calls for a null and void season from some have been among the most selfish, narrow-minded arguments I've ever seen from football fans,' claimed Jackson. 'They have used this dreadful pandemic as an excuse to simply rob Liverpool of the Premier League title, caring far more about the Reds missing out than their own team restarting their season and achieving their goals.'

I have shared Henry's frustrations throughout the season. And I don't expect our rivals to celebrate our achievements. I don't even mind them trying to wind us up, that's part of the joy of the game. After all, I am more than capable of giving as good as I get. However, it was difficult at times not to feel like there was a concerted effort being made by supporters in general to undermine what was a historic league title.

Having said that, I couldn't shake the feeling that social media wasn't a true representation of the views of all football fans. There must be a silent and reasonable majority out there, mustn't there? So, with hope in my heart, I went looking for them And, as it turned out, I found plenty.

Jack Lusby, an assistant editor at This is Anfield, agreed with me. He suggested that behaviour on social media was symptomatic of a wider issue affecting all aspects of discourse in society.

'Personally, I haven't been concerned with other fans' views on the title, whether that be a deserved win, a "tainted title" or one that comes with an asterisk,' he told me. 'The wait has been so long and the gap between us and Manchester City so wide that little else matters other than finally getting it over the line.

'I think it speaks more of the tribalism of modern football, or simply tribalism in general – we see it in politics, too, for example, when what is "right" is not the primary concern, but whatever suits your chosen side best.'

Richard Dooler, a Southampton supporter, feels that social media itself contributes to a sense that there is conflict between supporters, when really there isn't. He argues that while natural rivalries do exist, sometimes they are manufactured and blown out of all proportion.

'The supposed "rivalry" between Saints and Liverpool fans because of the transfer dealings over the last few years has produced lots of banter and animosity,' he explained. 'I used to read a lot of the social media stuff between the rival fans but got fed up with the crap spouted by all sides.

'Some Liverpool fans do think they have a god-given right to win the league, while opposing fans often descend to petty goading. Of course, many rival fans will call it the "tainted title" but that's just jealousy. In 50 years, when this is long forgotten, it will simply say Liverpool, champions of England 2019/20.'

Derek King is a lifelong Spurs fan and echoed the views of Richard. He told me, 'My view on this season's league title is that it was obviously Liverpool's title to lose. Had the season been abandoned completely, I would have been fully supportive of awarding them the title. It would have been unacceptable in my view to null and void the season.

'Awarding the title with an asterisk would've been unfair and undeserved – this season's Liverpool team under Klopp has been one of the finest and most deserving of honours in recent years.'

Robert Daniels is a 59-year-old Everton supporter. He has supported the Blues his whole life. Despite the intense rivalry between the two Merseyside clubs, and while he had criticisms of 'Project Restart' overall, he could only sympathise with Liverpool's plight. Robert told me, 'As an Everton fan, I obviously only want to see Everton winning trophies. But bearing that in mind, I can honestly say Liverpool deserve the title. They have proven to be the best team over the course of the season. Plus, the last time they were in a position to win titles, it kick-started the blue half to win things as well.

'I also have one eye on Manchester. I'm always proud that this city has won more league titles than any other city, and I would like that to remain the case. I just need Everton to chip in next season.

'Football should be put on hold until it is safe to have fans back in the ground, and this season should be delayed and played to a finish when it's safe to do so. Fans spend all their lives going to support their team home and away for years.'

I even found sympathy among Manchester United supporters. Ian Pierce-Hayes and Chris Rule-Mullen, both lifelong United fans, gave very surprising responses when asked about Liverpool's surge to the title.

'As a United supporter there is a mixed feeling,' Ian told me. 'Firstly, Liverpool, whilst probably not playing as well as they have under Klopp, are untouchable at the top of the Premier League and their intensity and desire has impressed me. So, without doubt they are deserving champions by a distance. There's an old saying, "Your position in the league doesn't lie." I've always believed that.

'Obviously, the delay in seeing Liverpool lift the Premier League trophy has raised a smile, but I wouldn't wish a pandemic that has killed so many to derail their victory.'

Chris, who is a little younger than Ian, had similar views, and felt that while the rivalry between United and Liverpool is fierce and often crosses the line, those who take to their keyboards are not, in his view, representative of the whole. He told me, 'Ask a United fan which side they'd prefer to win the league – Liverpool or Manchester City – and to many of them it would present an impossible dilemma, akin to asking them to decide which of their two children they loved (or hated) most. Any answer would be a wrong answer.

'Liverpool have been operating at an incredibly high level in the last few seasons and will absolutely be deserving champions if and when they take the title. No asterisk needed – all teams agreed that it was safe enough to continue the season, and the playing field is as fair as it could be.

'Yes, the idea of the asterisk against the title win – or the initial rumour of the season being voided – was amusing, but the reality is that Liverpool deserve the chance to make history. They are the best team in the country and the record books should reflect that. So yeah, congratulations. Just don't get too comfy on that perch, eh?'

It seemed that everywhere I turned, whether it was ordinary supporters or football writers, the message was the same – we have no problem with accepting that Liverpool are champions. Aidan Williams, a Newcastle supporter and writer, told me, 'Firstly, when it comes to how the league will play out, my personal thoughts had always been along the lines of needing to complete the current season no matter what. If that meant the 2020/21 season start is delayed, or if the 2020/21 season becomes truncated as a result, that to me would always be preferable to trying to declare the current season over without completing it.'

Aidan also pointed out a key point that most of us miss, when complaining about the derisive voices on social media; most supporters of any club are more concerned with their own fortunes than they are with others.

He said, 'In a selfish way, a points per game ending, which could still happen if we have a rise in infections, would see Newcastle safe, whereas playing on exposes us to the risk of relegation even if our current tally is nudging us near to safety. But I would always prefer a completion over that.

'Points per game leads to all sorts of issues. Not in terms of the league title of course, but in Champions League qualification and relegation and prize money. So this is slightly separated from any discussion about Liverpool's title to me.

'I'm quite certain there are people who for whatever reason hate the prospect of Liverpool winning the league, but to try and lessen the achievement by claiming it's not as valid a title given this situation is ludicrous.'

Aidan is equally scathing of the null and void arguments put forward by not only football fans, but players and directors of other Premier League clubs, most notably those of West Ham United.

'The null and void argument is the realm of the paranoid and utterly blinkered,' he told me. 'I don't believe this was ever a consideration and nor should it be. Each club has its social media loons, and both Newcastle and Liverpool are no exception. For those in those bubbles it seems hard for them to accept that the opinions expressed there don't necessarily represent an entire fan base.

'All groups of fans think they are special and the "best" in some way or another. I think on occasion the claims of some Liverpool fans to be different from the rest grates with other teams' fans, as frankly we all feel just the same about our own clubs. Again though, I'm quite sure this isn't the view of a full set of supporters, but I do believe it is something that the blinkered fans latch on to as a reason to dislike Liverpool or its fans.

'But for any of that to diminish Liverpool's title is ridiculous. I don't think there is any justification for an asterisk against this season for Liverpool at all.'

Aidan's point about Liverpool supporters' claims to exceptionalism resonated with me. I must confess to being on something of a journey in that respect. Intellectually, of course I can concede that at a fundamental level we are just human beings and our allegiances shouldn't allow us or anyone else to feel superior to any other fan.

Having said that, old biases can be hard to shift. I grew up in the 1970s, in Liverpool, in the shadow of Shankly and the Beatles. The sense that Liverpool, the city, and the club, was special was all pervading. Of course, my football education coincided with the emergence of Bob Paisley's all-conquering team, and the attitude, colour and wit of the Kop has ingrained in me a deep sense that there is something special about us. Honestly, I don't think I'll ever completely shake that.

However, I am more than able to concede that other social and sporting stories will have welded the hearts of rival supporters to their clubs, and that they have just as much right to celebrate their uniqueness. Growing up is hard at times, and always filled with contradictions.

I'm forced to acknowledge that in believing that anything other than a subset of the supporters of other clubs are obsessed with Liverpool is perhaps the most revealing aspect of this, and probably more than a little self-indulgent.

Several fans I spoke to sympathised with Liverpool followers' annoyance that they were on the receiving end of a campaign to discredit their club's achievements. Alex Dutton, a fan of Manchester City, told me, 'I think Liverpool have been far and away the best side this season; for me they deserve to be crowned champions. I said to my Liverpool mates it's only because it was a short season or there will be an asterisk just to wind them up. I think because it has been such a long time since the last league win, there is that sense that Liverpool were close but still not there, yet [after the league was suspended].

'I can't imagine us being that far ahead only for a worldwide pandemic to take it away. It's the actual match-going regulars I feel most sorry for, watching every single game live in person with all the emotions that go along with it, only to have that taken away and watching it on TV like it's a soap. It must be painful.

'I've watched that "Agüero!" moment on TV many times since it happened, but nothing will ever match the feeling of being there at the time. It's probably the same for Liverpool fans. The thing with social media for me is that it's supposed to be an extension of people that share the same humours, etc., almost like a giant WhatsApp group if you like. Instead it seems to bring out the worst in people. I've been drawn into it, looked back and thought, "What am I doing?"'

Gary Thacker, a football writer and author who supports Chelsea, is also critical of those attempting to undermine Liverpool's achievements, telling me, 'Sometimes, you just have to take it on the chin and accept a bit of reality. Frankly, if my club doesn't win the league, I'm pretty much not bothered who does. I don't have that "hated rivalry" thing.

'For a certain phalanx of fans following some other clubs though, that isn't the case, and this season is causing them a whole lot of discomfort. The 2019/20 season is weird for so many reasons, not least, of course, because of the hiatus in the early months of 2020. The other reason, though, is that the top tier of English football was dominated by one club to an extent I cannot recall even being rivalled in my 60-odd years of watching football.

'Liverpool are some 25 points ahead of Manchester City. Sure, they've played a game more, but let's be honest here. Not even the staunchest City fan thinks that potential three points is going to make any difference. On paper, City are second but, in reality, it's fresh air that is second – and third for that matter!

'Liverpool are more than worthy champions. Rival fans should stop sucking lemons and chomping on sour grapes. Take it on the chin and acknowledge the reality. Liverpool are champions because they deserve to be. I've got no problem saying that as a Chelsea fan. Just wait until next season though!'

Will Sharp, another writer, and devoted Arsenal supporter, had this to say about project restart and Liverpool being on the brink of a 19th league title: 'Football's a huge part of my life, and the highlight of so many of my days, so I was overjoyed to have it back; to be able to escape into it again.'

His words as a devoted Gooner could just as easily have been uttered by the supporter of any club, and I guess that's significant. There is so much that unites us. He continued, 'On the topic of Liverpool's impending title, I do find it a shame that an otherwise absurdly dominant season will likely be remembered for other reasons. I've no real affection for Liverpool – and I have to admit I was ecstatic when Watford ended their unbeaten streak because, as an Arsenal fan, there's no denying it would hurt an awful lot to see a record so dear to me and my affection for my club being beaten – but, on a human level, there's something undeniably cruel about watching a decades long wait come to a screeching halt in such an unprecedented way.

'Nevertheless, there's no denying Liverpool's credentials and to even attempt to argue as to whether or not they're deserving of the title – or whether their title should be seen as being as legitimate as any that came before it – is ridiculous. If there's an asterisk, it'll be used to mark the season out as "the one that was interrupted by coronavirus".'

Of course, when the Premier League did decide on a return date, they left open the whole question of what to do if the season had to be curtailed by a second wave of the virus. Points per game had been kicked into the long grass, and Liverpool were to be given their chance to finish their season and claim that prized 19th league title. And it seemed a sizeable proportion of rival supporters were okay with that.

One man who has experience of marshalling rival fans as they debate live on air during radio phone-in shows is BBC Radio Merseyside Sport host Paul Salt. I asked him how he felt the season should be judged. If Liverpool were to win the league, should an asterisk accompany their achievement and how had the debate gone on the airwaves?

'This will go down as a season that will live long in the memory for two reasons,' he told me. Firstly, for the way this Liverpool team has conquered all before them in a way I've not seen since the brilliant 1987/88 of Barnes, Beardsley and Aldridge. Secondly, for the unprecedented circumstances in which they will have won it.

'When people say the title will be tainted, I'm not sure many Liverpool fans would go along with that. The supporters I've spoken to on the radio are just excited that the 30-year wait is nearly over. A whole generation of fans can't remember the last time we won it. I was only 13.'

But what about a season concluded on some mathematical formula? How did Paul think that would be remembered?

'I think had the title been won on a points per game formula, then the asterisk thing would have wound people up – despite the Reds being miles better than the rest. A Duckworth-Lewis style [two mathematicians who came up with a formula for calculating cricket scores] conclusion to the season would have felt unsatisfactory and incomplete. I've had visions of asterisk T-shirts being manufactured as a reminder of a brilliant but abandoned campaign – thankfully, it didn't come to that.

'These Liverpool players and Jürgen Klopp deserve all the acclaim coming their way regardless of the bizarre surroundings it's been concluded in. I think in years to come we'll be looking back on 2019/20 as a special season won in unique circumstances that nobody could ever have imagined.'

So, assuming those vital six points were secured, how might historians judge this league title? Early in June, I sought out Stephen Done, author, and curator of the Liverpool FC Museum at Anfield, and asked for his perspective on all this. Reluctant to count any chickens while the season was still up in the air, and clearly mindful of the irrelevance of football compared to the staggering loss of life due to the virus, Stephen nonetheless agreed to run through the various scenarios and consider how they may be viewed in the future. He told me, 'If Liverpool and the other Premier League teams can play out the remainder of their competitive games, lurching, limping their way in echoing empty stadia smelling of hand sanitiser, and in so doing, the Reds manage to garner those six vital points and thereby legitimately win the Premier League title, I see no issues. There would be no basis for complaint from anyone either, because even as it stands, Liverpool FC are so far ahead of City, and have until now played such extraordinarily dominant football, that they are clear winners elect.

'My sense is the Premier League want to see the top of the table concluded beyond challenge and debate. Whether the season then limps along in a series of games that increasingly become a "contractual obligation" for the top two or not, makes no difference to how history will record this.

'Liverpool FC will have won their 19th title and their first Premier League title, in one of the weirdest seasons ever, and in utterly convincing style. Memories for most are short. Within a year or two this will be a bizarre memory, and the stats will speak louder.

'I do really, really regret that I won't get to ride on the open-top bus, if we do get over the line. I've waited 30 years for it to come along. But let's not make light of everything. An open-top bus is no loss compared to the human loss paid, and we can all take it on the chin. Number 19 will still sound good, and I feel sure that Klopp and his team will push on to number 20 eventually.'

In truth, all Liverpool fans would identify with Stephen's words. Winning the league title, after such a long wait could never be diminished. Not by an asterisk, and not by the whinging of a gaggle of internet trolls either. Most football supporters, it seems, would also acknowledge the achievement. And we would all happily forgo that parade in the interests of public health.

Project Restart, Old Stereotypes, and a Rare Triumph for Common Sense

On 4 June 2020, with the UK government seemingly chomping at the bit to return the country to normal despite the continuing COVID-19 crisis and Britain having the second highest death rate in the world, the Premier League signalled that football would be back on 17 June, albeit behind closed doors. Clubs had already returned to contact training and there was a growing sense that it was now inevitable that the season would resume, although whether it would finish or not was a whole different question.

The growing feeling that Boris Johnson and Dominic Cummings had cooked up a policy of 'herd immunity' had already taken hold among many. Fuelled by an earlier TV appearance on the *Good Morning Britain* show, in which the prime minister discussed openly the prospect of the country 'taking it [the pandemic] on the chin, and allowing it to pass through the population', and the fact that many senior Downing Street journalists seemed to have been briefed on the importance of 'herd immunity', led many to conclude that we were governed by people who were either homicidal, incompetent or possibly both. Given all of that, it didn't seem too outlandish to suggest that they may also reprise their Brexit slogan and declare, 'Let's get the second wave done.'

All of us had mixed feelings about what became known as 'Project Restart', particularly with the death rate so high, and the rate of infection so varied around the country. Nevertheless, after the emptiness of lockdown and the pain of missing football, it was hard not to get excited about its return.

For others, though, it was still too soon. Even the plans to play behind closed doors couldn't assuage the sense among many that this was all a bit premature. The promise to test players twice a week, when the NHS was still struggling to test healthcare workers, seemed deeply problematic, and there were legitimate concerns raised by players of black, asian or minority ethnic (BAME) origin, who were seemingly twice as likely to die from the illness according to the data.

Watford's Troy Deeney was perhaps the most vocal among those raising the issue and indicated that he would not be prepared to train or play. To their credit, according to Deeney's team-mate Ben Foster, the striker enjoyed the full support of his club. Of course, that was entirely appropriate. All employees are entitled to refuse to work in an unsafe environment.

The whole issue was complicated and those genuinely arguing that football's return in the midst of such terrible human suffering was distasteful, unsafe or just wrong had a point. There were also suspicions, not without merit, that the whole agenda was motivated mainly by finance and that this was being given precedence over safety.

It's true that many clubs faced financial ruin, with their whole business predicated on playing football. Even the biggest clubs were facing staggering losses, discussing player wage deferrals, and furloughing staff.

Liverpool, meanwhile, perhaps motivated by a desire not to be seen as craving a restart for selfish reasons, had maintained a dignified silence throughout the process, at least publicly. Of course, behind the scenes their desire to get the season up and running as soon as it was safe to do so was clear.

The Premier League and clubs came in for a great deal of criticism during the period, with ex-Liverpool defender and Sky Sports pundit Jamie Carragher feeling that its public silence during the crisis, coupled with frequent 'off-the-record' briefings to media outlets, was leading to confusion and muddying the waters.

One club that perhaps could not be accused of this was Brighton and Hove Albion. Something of a lone voice, in terms of their public utterances, Brighton chose to hold regular weekly press conferences and frequent Zoom video meetings with supporters. And one issue they were particularly vocal about was the suggestion that if football was to return, then games should be played at neutral venues.

They were far from alone in raising concerns about this. Other clubs, notably those in relegation battles, had also voiced opposition to the plan. However, Brighton felt that claims they were trying to 'duck out of the season' or 'dodge relegation' were grossly unfair, and that they trusted their fans to respect lockdown rules.

At a press conference following a meeting of all 20 Premier League clubs, held on 14 May, Brighton CEO Paul Barber told journalists, 'One thing Monday's meeting proved was that it is not just my argument. A majority of clubs believed the same as us. Despite the speculation, the vast majority rallied around and certainly Richard Masters [Premier League chief executive] said all 20 clubs much prefer to stay in their own venues.

'I hope the government and police will support us on that. We've been very supportive all the way through this crisis, we've done whatever we can as a club to support the authorities, support the police and support the NHS.

'So I hope we would be trusted to put our own games on. I would trust our fans to listen to the messages and any individuals that didn't respond positively to requests to stay away would face whatever sanctions necessary.'

Furthermore, the club were adamant that in discussions with the rest of the Premier League, they had never asked for relegation to be taken off the table, nor had they ever asked for the season to be declared null and void, pointing out that their whole operational success is based on being able to play matches.

Some argued that should games be played behind closed doors the whole notion of home advantage would been rendered irrelevant. Others pointed to the German Bundesliga, where football had returned weeks earlier, and where home advantage appeared to have been almost completely wiped out.

However, for Brighton and perhaps other clubs who raised similar objections, reservations were not solely based on issues of competitiveness. Indeed, in discussions between Premier League clubs, those most vocal in opposing neutral venues cited issues concerning logistics, additional unnecessary travel, and argued that their local knowledge of safety infrastructure, healthcare and emergency services made it safer to play on a home and away basis.

There is of course a competitive argument for not playing at neutral venues. So much of a footballer's preparation for a game is mindset, routine, and familiarity. Perhaps that's one of the reasons why home advantage comes into play.

Taking players out of their comfort zone and placing them into unfamiliar surroundings, particularly when they are in a relegation dogfight or competing at the other end of the table, was understandably a concern for clubs. However, it clearly wasn't the only issue behind their reservations.

With debate and controversy raging in the background, football and Whitehall had decreed that they were going to attempt a restart of the Premier League on 17 June, kicking off with Aston Villa against Sheffield United followed by Manchester City versus Arsenal – both fixtures having been held over as a result of the League Cup Final. With those two games out of the way, all 20 teams in the Premier League would have played the same number of times.

Liverpool's first match back – with fixtures simply picking up where they left off – would be the Merseyside derby at Goodison Park. That of course raised the prospect of Liverpool securing their first league title in 30 years on the ground of their bitterest rivals.

It was a delicious prospect for Reds and a nightmare for Blues. If Manchester City lost to Arsenal on the reopening night, and Liverpool could beat Everton four days later, then the championship would be secured. It was all geared up to be a titanic encounter, and perhaps one of the most significant derbies in the history of the city.

It would be the kind of story supporters would talk about for years. It would either be a tale of how the Reds won the league on Everton soil, or how the Blues stopped their rivals wrapping up their crown. This is what makes football so appealing. These stories are part of the magic of the game. They are also a broadcaster's and sponsor's dream.

Nevertheless, the question of whether the game could be played at Goodison or not had yet to be resolved. There remained the prospect of the two Merseyside teams having to slug it out on the south coast, with an agreement in principle to move games to neutral locations if need be, and Southampton's St Mary's Stadium was potentially earmarked for the game.

Many Liverpool supporters found the whole issue distasteful and insulting. For others it was worrying and reminiscent of stereotypes built up and propagated in the 1980s.

The implication was obvious, that football supporters couldn't be trusted, and would risk their own safety and that of others to congregate outside their own stadia on matchdays. The fact that some people argued that football fans were so stupid they would ignore the chance to watch the game at home, with family and beer, choosing instead to stand outside an empty stadium in the street, following the game on their mobile phones, seemed ludicrous and lacking in evidence.

Throughout the whole debate, Liverpool, their players and their manager remained diplomatic. Jürgen Klopp insisted that it didn't matter where Liverpool won the title, only that they did it. It didn't matter to him if that was behind closed doors either.

'Of course,' he said, 'we only love this game, it is only the game it is because of the supporters and all that stuff. This is true. But this is the situation we are in, and we have to use it.'

Former players like Phil Thompson, John Aldridge and Terry McDermott all joined a chorus in stating that the only thing that mattered was the Reds getting their hands on that league title. Empty stadia or neutral venues, it didn't matter. McDermott declared, 'They could win it on the Moon for all I care. As long as they win it.'

Of course, all of this was true. It didn't stop the army of keyboard trolls from once again delving down deep into their repertoire and pulling out the 'tainted title' arguments though. 'It's not a real title for me' would be a frequent refrain on social media. 'Imagine having to win the league without your own fans there,' would be another.

Even players at other clubs and pundits joined in, suggesting that Liverpool's title had been 'spoilt'. Others pointed to the fact that Liverpool would even be denied a victory parade. As if any of that could diminish the joy of a first league championship in three decades.

To those who argued that the achievement had somehow been diminished by these things, Klopp had a very simple yet powerful response: 'We will decide what this title, if it happens, will mean. If we decide to have a parade in the middle of next season, if that's how long it takes, we will do it. And if people think we are crazy, we don't care.'

He was right and he had found the words necessary to lift his supporters and silence his detractors – at least for a little while – once again. But for many Liverpool fans the anger at the suggestion that they could not be trusted and that their team must travel to a neutral venue because of that was a source of great anger.

In fairness, it wasn't only Reds fans who objected. In a widely reported list of fixtures targeted for neutral venues, it was notable that all of them were in the north of England. The suggestion that fans in the north were less responsible than their southern counterparts was infuriating to some and confusing to others.

Mari Lewis, a Liverpool supporter, told me, 'I found the focus on northern clubs, in particular, as reminiscent of old stereotypes. Their choices seemed more about geography than match importance, as sides fighting relegation were not on the list.'

Unfortunately, as far back as April, the mayor of Liverpool, Joe Anderson, had helped to fuel these ideas by stating that the resumption of the Premier League was a 'non-starter' and that fans gathering outside grounds would create a 'farcical' situation. His comments were heavily criticised by Liverpool Football Club and supporters' groups, who argued that his comments, made publicly and without dialogue with stakeholders, were without evidence and undermined a previous commitment by all stakeholders to partnership and engagement.

Writing for This is Anfield, Aaron Cutler said, 'There is an insinuation our supporters cannot be trusted. It's a dangerous one.

'The muddled consensus seems to be that Liverpool fans will be unable to resist the urge to gather en masse as a long-awaited 19th title draws near. This is based on nothing but stereotyping.

'It's insulting to think, on the back of inevitable pleas from manager and players alike, that a sea of red will converge on Anfield in an attempt to recreate last summer's glorious homecoming parade.

'If you truly believe that, however, it's short-sighted in the extreme to downplay the club's following nationwide. Supporters' clubs operate as far south as Brighton.

'It may come as a shock to those in authority, but Liverpool supporters watch the news too. We're well aware of the devastating effect COVID-19 has had on this country and the fact we remain perilously close to triggering a second wave. Passion does not necessarily equate to stupidity.'

I spoke to the *Morning Star*'s James Nalton about what might lie behind these attitudes. James felt it was easy to draw a line linking the establishment's attitude to working-class footballers and the people who support them from the terraces. Their attitude towards both, he argued, is contemptuous.

'The government put the onus on Premier League players to help them provide public services that should already be provided by the state,' James told me. 'It's not a footballer's job to fund the NHS and social care through charities, they are already funding these things through their taxes. The government didn't put pressure on their mates in the city to contribute, just working-class footballers, who have also been constantly targeted by the increasingly right-wing media over the years. The fans are an extension of this.

'The government have almost encouraged public gatherings during lockdown through the half-hearted, mixed and muddled messages from Boris Johnson and his cabinet. Football fans are being judged by different standards to the rest of the country, whose gatherings on beaches and in parks were celebrated by the right-wing media almost like bonus bank holidays for the Brits.'

For many of us, football supporters were being prejudged and condemned without evidence, and before a ball had even been kicked. Nalton agreed and sensed a troubling double standard was at work.

He said, 'Football fans were being criticised for gathering outside football grounds even before any games had taken place. That's not to say football fans won't gather outside grounds, but there's no precedent to say they will as these are unprecedented times. There seemed to be one narrative for certain sections of society, and another narrative for others, driven and reinforced by an increasingly right-wing and monopolistic media.'

For others in Liverpool, the suggestion that football fans could not be trusted, and in particular that Reds fans were irresponsible, cut deep. The city has a now long history of fighting such prejudices and its people are acutely aware of the damage these views can do, especially when uttered by people in high office.

I spoke to Dan Kay, a journalist and live sport content editor at the *Liverpool Echo*, about this. His experiences and the way in which they have shaped his views on this subject will doubtless resonate with all Liverpool fans, perhaps fans of football in general too.

He said, 'Growing up and falling in love with football in the 1980s, it was very clear to me even as a child that being a football supporter carried a certain stigma. Back then, it was very much the game of the working classes with the cost of attending matches being within the reach of most ordinary folk and the culture of support being passed down from generation to generation like a family heirloom.

'Although I would have been too young to understand it at the time, the game and everything surrounding it is and always has been a microcosm of life, and mirrors much of the society it is part of. So as the landscape of Britain changed in the '70s and '80s with deindustrialisation leading to whole sectors of the country and workforces being left to go by the wayside, football grounds inevitably became a vehicle (although not the only one) for the pain and frustration many felt at those who had allowed that to happen.

'The outbreaks of hooliganism were of course grist to the mill for establishment forces who wished to reinforce this societal divide, painting it as a justification for why "these people" should be left to rot, which only served to polarise matters further. Positions and suspicions became entrenched with ultimately tragic consequences at Hillsborough, which obviously changed the game in this country beyond all recognition.'

Things undoubtedly changed after Hillsborough, in terms of infrastructure. Football stadia became safer and the supporter experience is undoubtedly a more comfortable one today than it was in the 1980s. Why then have attitudes towards supporters not evolved? For Dan, it is impossible to unwind the politics of class from the whole question, and for him and many others, because of that, we are simply seeing old patterns repeating themselves.

'Football became fashionable and gentrified, which is what some of the power-brokers had been wanting for some time,' he continued. 'Talk of a "Super League" had emerged in the mid-'80s – even if they initially had no idea how to do it. Hillsborough gave them that opportunity to rebrand and, as Adrian Tempany points out in his excellent – and I would say definitive – book, *And the Sun Shines Now*, wrestle or perhaps more accurately steal the game away from the working classes.

'He wrote, "It had seemed towards the end of the last decade of the 20th century, notably in the wave of hope and optimism following the Tories' deposal in 1997, that while 'new football' and the Premier League was already establishing a new status quo with the most commercially robust clubs like Manchester United rising to the top, the kind of demonising of the working classes which had scarred so much of the previous two decades was perhaps on the way out.

"But as 'New Labour' lost its way and ultimately its seat in power, the Tory establishment has struck back. So, when working-class football supporters and players are demonised these days it is only a reflection of what we are seeing in wider society and, essentially, history repeating itself."'

The man said to be behind the whole move towards Premier League teams having to play their remaining matches at neutral venues was South Yorkshire Police's Deputy Chief Constable Mark Roberts, the head of the United Kingdom Football Policing Unit (UKPFU). For many Liverpool supporters, the mention of South Yorkshire Police evokes mistrust and suspicion.

I spoke to him about the decision-making process during Project Restart. DCC Roberts was keen to emphasise that concerns were solely focused on keeping people safe and minimising the demand on forces at a time when they were expected to be busier than normal, and emphasised that he believed that supporters' behaviour would reflect that of the wider public. His concerns were with 'a minority'. He told me, 'As has already been seen with the curtailment of League One, some supporters gathered in groups to celebrate. So there is a realistic concern, but what is difficult to gauge is how big a problem it may be.'

The Deputy Chief Constable's comments about supporters celebrating the curtailment of League One, and presumably the promotion of Coventry City and Rotherham United, interested me. If he was right, then maybe there was a justification for concerns. My research did indeed yield a number of stories about a group of a few hundred Coventry supporters gathering to celebrate, and tales of confrontation with the police and some damage to property.

However, reports in the *Coventry Telegraph* and *Birmingham Mail* state that these events took place away from the stadium at St Andrew's, which Coventry share with Birmingham City, and instead occurred in Broadgate Square, which is located in Coventry city centre. It is therefore difficult to see how playing a game that might potentially lead to promotion would have prevented these supporters from gathering in their local town square to celebrate.

As foolhardy as the celebrations, in the midst of a pandemic, undoubtedly were, the numbers involved represent a tiny proportion of Coventry's overall match-going support and were dealt with by the local police. There were only two arrests and one youth went to hospital after falling under the influence of alcohol.

Coventry's highest attendance in the 2019/20 season was 21,193 for a cup match against local rivals Birmingham. Their average attendance in the previous season, involving games at the Ricoh Arena, was 12,363. Therefore, the presence of a few hundred in the local town square after their team had been promoted has to be judged against the fact that the numbers were relatively small, fans gathered away from the stadium and were dealt with by the authorities.

I could find no evidence of similar disturbances or gatherings among Rotherham United supporters. That doesn't mean they didn't happen, but coupled with the experiences above, it does cast doubt on the argument for moving matches to neutral venues.

Perhaps an examination of Scottish football, where Celtic were awarded a record-equalling ninth league title in a row, may be more relevant in terms of gauging how supporters in Liverpool may react to a Premier League victory. Glasgow's supporters are every bit as passionate as those on Merseyside and it is often said that the people of the two cities are similar in social characteristics.

A quick search did elicit a story about Celtic supporters gathering outside their stadium to celebrate, but the pictures printed in the local media suggest the numbers were limited to about a dozen people. Given the ground regularly holds 60,000 people, these numbers can hardly be considered significant. Nor do they justify the neutral venue argument.

So, what evidence could DCC Roberts point to, that supports fears of supporters congregating at grounds? He responded by saying, 'This is a genuinely unique circumstance so there is no definitive experience to draw upon. The final game in Germany before the suspension of the league was behind closed doors and there were issues with supporters congregating at the stadium. This has been seen in other countries also. Would anyone state with absolute confidence that there will be no issues, and would it be prudent to gamble on that given the public health threat? This needs to be viewed in the context of the number of deaths the country has suffered.'

Of course, football supporters, as much as anyone else are acutely aware of the public health threat posed by COVID-19. They are certainly not immune to it. We would all agree that it is impossible to predict the future, but perhaps reasonable projections can be made based on the experiences of other leagues.

I spoke to Chris Williams, a Bundesliga journalist with expertise in German football, and asked him about the experiences there, before and after lockdown. He told me, 'Anyone citing previous problems with fans gathering outside German stadiums as their reasoning for Premier League games being played in neutral venues, under Project Restart, is conveniently ignoring the facts to hand.

'The only match to have any sort of large gatherings outside while stadiums were closed was the Borussia Mönchengaldbach vs FC Köln fixture, played on 11 March 2020.

'This date was before any restrictions where put in place on the German population, so while the game was played behind closed doors people were free to meet in large groups and travel as they wished.

'On 13 March, Germany ordered schools and nurseries to close and postponed the academic calendar. Two days later, the borders to five neighbouring countries were closed; only on 22 March did the German government announce a national curfew.

'Football fans did congregate outside a stadium, legally, and not in contravention of any lockdown rules. Since the Bundesliga returned fans haven't turned up en masse, even with restrictions lifted and to a far greater degree than in the UK.'

So, even if we were to accept the argument that 'it's better to be safe than sorry', at the time that suggestions were made about games being played at neutral venues, there was little evidence in English, Scottish or German football to support that argument. But what of the even more contentious claim that only games involving northern clubs had been singled out for neutral venues. DCC Roberts denied claims that he had identified these games and clubs for consideration, stating, 'To be clear, neither I, nor the UKFPU, have identified which fixtures may be suitable to consider for a neutral venue. They were initially identified by the local forces, so that we could consider suitable contingencies.'

The suggestion that fixtures were originally earmarked by local police forces was somewhat confusing. Merseyside Police had indicated as early as May that it had no objections in terms of law and order about the Merseyside derby or any of Liverpool's or Everton's games being played on home soil. The force was, it said, happy to leave decisions on public health to the local Safety Advisory Groups.

A journalist I spoke to, who was party to off-the-record briefings during the process, agreed, suggesting that there may well have been some 'passing of the buck' going on. Referring to DCC Roberts's assertion that the games identified for neutral venues were singled out by local forces, he told me, 'That doesn't seem accurate from the information I received. I spoke to Merseyside Police early on when all games were being considered for neutral venues. They first said they had "concerns", but within about two weeks said they were happy to take the national police lead on the subject and would follow that. That implies the national lead was creating the policy, not the local lead.'

I contacted Assistant Chief Constable Rob Carden of Merseyside Police for comment.

'The derby game and Premier League title-deciding games had initially been highlighted as potential higher risk games due to the significance of the events,' he told me. 'We did not feel it was the role of the police to make decisions based on public health, as this was a matter for public health [Public Health England] and the government. We would have been supportive of neutral grounds for these games if the government had advised in favour of this though. In the absence of any such requirement or advice, we are obviously supportive of the games being played at home.'

My media source suggested that, in truth, discussions about neutral venues were indeed motivated by mistrust of supporters by many inside and outside the game, saying, 'The reality was that the police, the Premier League and even some of the clubs themselves didn't trust fans. But Liverpool and Everton were saying, "What evidence do you have for these fears, where's the research, where's the documented evidence?" It felt like this is to do with the demonising of fans all over again.'

So why then did those fears subside. Why the change of heart? The feeling was that the argument – football fans as a group on their own couldn't be trusted – was unsustainable once it became clear that huge sections of the general public were breaching lockdown regulations, without much criticism in the media or from politicians.

'I do think the fact that thousands of people flocked to the beaches as soon as lockdown was eased probably helped in a way,' the source continued. 'Because it's hard to say fans congregating is a problem, when there were far more on the beaches, without any police intervention. And, when even the prime minister's chief advisor flouted lockdown rules of course.'

This was a reference to Dominic Cummings, who infamously drove 200 miles, while symptomatic of COVID-19, and with his wife and child in the car, in order to, among other things, 'test his eyesight'. His behaviour caused anger and a degree of hilarity, but it also made a mockery of the assertion that football supporters should be singled out for criticism and that they alone could not be trusted to act responsibly.

Of course, we now know that no supporters gathered outside Anfield and Goodison before or after the games between Liverpool and Everton or the one against Crystal Palace. We also know that following the confirmation of Liverpool's first league title in 30 years, many supporters turned up outside Anfield, in an incident that passed off without any trouble. Indeed, supporters even stayed behind through the night to clean up the rubbish that had been left behind.

Sadly, scenes at the Pier Head on 27 June were different and shameful, although once again the reaction of the overwhelming majority of supporters was to condemn the behaviour of a minority and some even volunteered to clean up afterwards. This too will be covered in more detail later. However, what remains clear is that neither of these incidents would have been prevented by playing games at neutral venues.

The decision to allow games to go ahead on a home and away basis, was eventually taken on Wednesday, 10 June, and it was a unanimous one. It was met with relief by the club and the supporters also. And, it seemed, the mayor of Liverpool, Joe Anderson, had also been convinced it was safe to do so. He told The Athletic, 'We are in a better place than we were four weeks ago. We've been able to convey why it's so important nobody congregates outside or near grounds.

'We have had the opportunity since then to speak to fans and the clubs have done their part and got the message across that the supporters need to stay away. Both clubs have made it clear. Jürgen Klopp has made it clear. So I would have no objection to the games being played at our clubs' home grounds – both the derby at Goodison and Liverpool's games at Anfield.'

Critically, the city council's Ground Safety Advisory Group had argued that there was 'no evidence' to support suggestions that supporters would congregate outside stadia. It's chair, councillor and deputy mayor Wendy Simon, told the BBC that both Everton and Liverpool could play their remaining home fixtures 'safely and securely' behind closed doors at their stadiums. She went on to say that there was 'no evidence' fans would congregate.

She said, 'We are confident the measures in place will allow the matches to be held behind closed doors without any detrimental impact to all concerned and recommend to the city council that the safety certificates for both grounds be amended to allow this to happen.

'I'm sure fans of both teams will welcome this recommendation and, subject to ratification, we look forward to watching the first of these matches – the Merseyside derby on 21 June – which will be broadcast live on free-to-air TV for the first time since the Premier League began.'

It felt like a rare outbreak of common sense in a period where that commodity had seemed in short supply. I asked DCC Roberts for his views now that the local authorities had deemed the games could safely be played at Anfield and Goodison. His response was that he was glad to see the season could be recommenced but held out a warning that neutral venues may not be completely off the table.

'I'm pleased that the season can recommence,' he said. 'And if the games can safely be facilitated at their original venues then that's a good outcome for everyone.'

The decision was also welcomed in a joint statement issued by Liverpool and Everton supporters' groups, Spirit of Shankly and Blue Union. Both groups would call on all fans to adhere to social distancing rules.

'Spirit of Shankly and the Blue Union welcome the news that games are to be played on Merseyside,' the statement began. 'Building on the community work both sets of fans continue to do throughout this pandemic, we are confident supporters will respect safety advice and avoid visiting stadia where games are taking place.

'We fully understand the importance of lockdown as a measure to control COVID-19 and encourage all fans to stay away from any stadium and avoid congregating in numbers.'

Liverpool FC also welcomed the move and highlighted the role supporters had played in discussions.

The club said, 'Liverpool Football Club welcomes the decision by the local Ground Safety Advisory Group (GSAG) to support football matches being played behind closed doors on Merseyside.

'Following already positive discussions with key partners including Liverpool City Council, Merseyside Police, Spirit of Shankly, Everton Football Club and Blue Union we have committed to working together to restart the season safely with the overriding aim of ensuring these games are completed by prioritising public health so the return to football is a success for Merseyside. These discussions are very much part of our normal matchday planning and arrangements.'

It seemed clear that dialogue and engagement was always the way to ensure a sensible decision could be reached with all parties feeling listened to and valued. Given that, it is remarkable that some voices appeared to jump the gun and prejudge the whole process.

Whether that was the UKFPU, DCC Mark Roberts or more local voices is probably irrelevant. What remains clear, however, is that despite the tremendous work of football supporters during the COVID-19 crisis, there are still, depressingly, voices who would prejudge them and devalue them.

Thankfully, on this occasion, those voices were ignored. Football was back, and Anfield and Goodison would be at the heart of the 2019/20 season finale.

RETURN OF THE KINGS

Liverpool FC: June–July 2020

Not Quite the End of a Storm: Football's Return to a World in Turmoil

Premier League football returned in the week of 15 June 2020, and to a world in turmoil. In America, George Floyd, a 46-year-old black man, husband and father, died at the hands of the Minneapolis Police Department. In an incident that was filmed by the public, a white officer, Derek Chauvin, knelt on George's neck for almost nine minutes, despite him pleading for his life and telling the officer that he could not breathe. George died because of the incident, which sparked a wave of protest all over the world.

Black Lives Matter demonstrations took place across the UK, and in Bristol a statue of slave trader William Edward Colston was torn down by demonstrators and dumped in the river. In London monuments to Churchill and others were encased to protect them from a similar fate.

This led to counter-protests by seemingly drunken far-right neo-Nazis, who had vowed to protect the country's statues and defend the police, by urinating on the former and throwing steel barricades at the latter. The whole debacle would end in embarrassment for the so-called 'patriots' with one of their number having to be carried to safety over the shoulder of a Black Lives Matter protestor. The iconic image was captured by photojournalists and relayed around the world.

Liverpool supporters and those of other clubs reacted with revulsion at the behaviour of a right-wing mob, masquerading as patriots spewing their racist bile on our streets, while being referred to as 'football supporters' by many in the media. The attempt to associate them with football felt particularly insulting to people like Jay McKenna, regional secretary of the North West Trades Union Congress. Sharing a tweet from Fans Supporting Foodbanks he tweeted, 'There seems to be a characterisation of those in London [far-right protestors] as "football fans". They aren't like me and the football fans I know. The football fans

I know watch football, celebrate difference and look out for each other.'

Footballers threw their weight behind the movement for racial equality and demands for an end to institutional racism, and Liverpool Football Club were among those leading the call. In a show of solidarity, the first-team squad were pictured, in an image that went viral on social media, 'taking a knee' around the centre circle at Anfield.

Sadly, one supporter tweeted the CEO, demanding the withdrawal of support for the Black Lives Matter movement, threatening to give up her season ticket if the club continued to 'surrender to thugs'. Liverpool FC responded by offering the so-called fan education, while saying it was happy to take her ticket back. Its support for the campaign, it said, was 'unequivocal'. The overwhelming response of Reds was supportive of the decision, with many demanding a ban of the fan in question.

With the public taking to the streets and football clubs showing solidarity, the prime minister, Boris Johnson, appeared to feel that silence was golden. When he did eventually emerge to promise that he would stamp out racism, he added that attitudes will take time to change. Well, I suppose he should know. After all, his own attitudes on race appear to have barely evolved since his days in the Bullingdon Club.

His government did, however, spend a fair bit of time lecturing protestors that the virus thrives at mass gatherings, which kind of made a mockery of their decision to allow 5,000 Spaniards to enter Liverpool from the COVID-19 hotspot of Madrid in March. A study by COVID-19 Genomics UK Consortium, and published in the *Liverpool Echo*, appeared to demonstrate that as many as 34 per cent of Britain's virus cases came from Spain.

Meanwhile, in another example of just how tone-deaf cabinet ministers had become, health secretary Matt Hancock lectured footballers on the need to take a pay cut to help the nation, ignoring the hoarding of billions of pounds by his party's donors. Manchester United forward Marcus Rashford, whose charity work had already helped provide millions of meals for children living in poverty in the UK, rammed those words right back down the minister's throat, penning an emotional letter to the government appealing to them to reverse a decision to cancel food vouchers during the summer holidays.

Of course, the PM initially declined the opportunity to stand on the right side of history before U-turning in the face of public outrage. Hancock later thanked Rashford for his work, but in a glorious illustration of just how out of touch he was he referred to the footballer as 'Daniel' during a TV interview.

The UK's 'recovery' from the COVID-19 pandemic was slow, and there was a great deal of anger at news that the death toll could have been halved had the lockdown started a week earlier. However, in the Premier League, bi-weekly testing protocols were producing an extremely low number of positive tests.

This meant that despite progress against the disease appearing to be comparatively poor, football was well on course for a return. The first games were to take place on Wednesday, 17 June with Manchester City hosting Arsenal, and Sheffield United travelling to Aston Villa.

Most of us welcomed the distraction and the chance to escape once more into the beautiful game. All games were scheduled to be broadcast live, and it promised to be a festival of football, albeit watched from our armchairs. Games would be played behind closed doors, as they had been across Europe.

With no football in the UK for months, many Reds had taken to watching games from the Bundesliga. But it wasn't the same for many. Mari Lewis was one of them.

She said, 'I've been watching loads of the Bundesliga, but I have no team – or any properly strong feelings about most of the others – so I'm not attached to it in the same way. I find myself more distracted with the Bundesliga on TV. I'm more likely to be on my phone, reading or doing something else.'

So the return to the Premier League would be very welcome to all of us. And it wouldn't be complete, certainly not at Anfield, without a transfer saga or two. For Liverpool, that took the form of the much-vaunted chase for the signature of RB Leipzig's Timo Werner. There were also persistent rumours linking Philippe Coutinho with a return to L4. While no one really believed the latter, there was genuine hope that the former would be wearing a Liver Bird on his chest in the next season.

The player himself had been talking up a move to the Premier League and his admiration of Jürgen Klopp. It seemed the feelings were mutual. Werner had a well-publicised buy-out clause, and securing his signature seemed almost a formality. Put simply, if Liverpool wanted him, he was theirs.

However, in the week before the resumption of the English game, news broke that the player would be joining Frank Lampard's Chelsea instead. Liverpool had baulked at paying the clause in his contract. There was understandable disappointment at the loss of a clearly talented player who would certainly enhance the squad. However, for some, the temptation to go completely overboard and declare that all is lost, is overwhelming.

The long-forgotten FSG Out campaign was revived for one night only, in an astonishing return gig on Twitter, with some alleged supporters either declaring that Klopp had been sold out, or that they had never rated the player anyway. It's a heady mix and all good fun of course.

More sensible heads pointed out that with the club's balance sheet taking a huge hit due the suspension of football, Liverpool's position might actually make sense, and Chelsea's apparent lack of concern about the implications of Financial Fair Play rules may not. Klopp was calm and clear: how could the club explain that it was asking players to agree to wage deferrals on the one hand, while splashing out £50m on a new player on the other?

The Reds, it seemed, were focused on keeping hold of the stars they already had. Rumours began to circulate that Virgil van Dijk was about to become their highest-paid player and that they were also confident of tying down Gini Wijnaldum. Meanwhile, Adam Lallana, a man who would probably have already left were it not for the suspension of football, received a contract extension allowing him to remain at Anfield long enough to finish the campaign.

Liverpool, along with all Premier League clubs, had returned to full contact training and had even warmed up for the restart with a 6-0 hammering of Blackburn Rovers behind closed doors and away from the cameras. Footage would eventually emerge, showing the Reds looking hungry and sharp. In particular, Naby Keïta and Takumi Minamino impressed, with both getting on the scoresheet.

It seemed everything was in place and Liverpool were set to hit the ground running. Skipper Jordan Henderson talked of the players desire and intensity in training and their determination to honour a campaign that had promised so much, only to be placed into enforced hibernation. Klopp spoke of not just wanting to win two games, but of setting a new benchmark, and Pep Guardiola talked of his willingness to form a guard of honour for Liverpool at the Etihad.

It seemed like the stage was set. *The Independent* ran a 16-page pull-out at the start of a week that had the potential to be a truly momentous one for the club. On its front page were photographs of Liverpool's last championship-winning side, from 1990, alongside Klopp's men. Across those images, the words 'History Delayed, Not History Denied' were emblazoned.

The only fly in the ointment appeared to be an article in the *Daily Mirror* that reported on how 'conspiracy theorists' suggested that the 'Mayan prophesies' had been misinterpreted. They had not predicted the apocalypse in 2012. Instead, the end of the world was actually due the week the Premier League was to return. It seemed Liverpool FC just could not catch a break.

Portacabin Reds Inch One Point Closer to Their Dream and Jürgen Sets a New Derby Record

If the week had started with great expectations and a sense of portent, it would end – on Sunday, 21 June – not with a bang, but with a whimper. And there could not have been a greater metaphor for the return of Premier League football to Merseyside than the sight of Liverpool players changing before the game in a portacabin in the car park at Goodison.

I always wake on the morning of the derby with butterflies in my stomach. They flutter gently there throughout breakfast but reach a crescendo by the time kick-off arrives. It remains, for me, the most eagerly awaited and nerve-twisting game of the season. Irrespective of league position or form, this is a match that Liverpool simply cannot lose, in my eyes.

A defeat to Everton – though I must say I'm beginning to forget what that's like – hurts more than any other. The historical aspect of the rivalry coupled with the geographical proximity to Blues makes defeat simply unbearable for either side. When most of us work or even live with our rivals, there is literally no hiding place.

So, as I rose from my pit, looked out the window at the gathering clouds and saw the rain pounding the ground outside, my gut lurched. It was back. After 106 days, football was back, and it had returned with the derby, of all games. If we win, I thought, we are three points from heaven. Lose, on the other hand, and doubt will seep in through the cracks and the pressure will mount. It will be unbearable. I should point out that I also get ridiculously dramatic on derby day.

Everton fans were unusually quiet in the run-up to the match. My phone hadn't pinged with the usual abuse and promises that 'this time, in this game, the Blues were going to do this, that and the other to Liverpool'. There was nothing, no banter and in that sense, this was certainly the strangest derby I had ever experienced.

Talking to This is Anfield broadcaster Matt Jones and The Blue Room's Dave Downie didn't hold out much hope for their team's prospects. Both suggested that Liverpool would have too much for Everton and pointed to the hosts' depleted squad and the visitors' quality as reasons for them to be fearful.

There was at least one crumb of comfort for Blues. Manchester City had already ensured that Liverpool could not clinch the league title at the home of their nearest neighbours and historic rivals by winning 3-0 against Arsenal in midweek.

That meant, assuming Klopp's men triumphed at Goodison, they could potentially be crowned champions against Crystal Palace at Anfield the following Wednesday. There was also the slightly less satisfying prospect of them winning the holy grail without kicking a ball should City fail to beat Burnley on the Monday evening.

In the end, neither outcome would be possible as a result of a tortuous stalemate in which, it is fair to say, Everton could easily have won. Maybe it shouldn't have surprised us. Both teams had only had three weeks of training, Liverpool had played only one friendly against Blackburn, and Everton's squad was threadbare. The game was always destined to be a tight affair with neither side tearing up any trees – and that is exactly what it was.

In the days beforehand, Klopp had appealed to fans not to gather outside the ground. In truth, supporters' groups like Spirit of Shankly and the Blue Union had already made strong statements to that effect and nobody expected that the masses would turn up and embarrass themselves. Well, apart from whoever decided to fly an aeroplane at low altitude over the ground just in time for kick-off that is.

Merseyside Police later tweeted their praise for Everton and Liverpool fans, and pointed out that they had collectively proved their doubters wrong. 'The eyes of the country and the world were on Merseyside this afternoon. You have proven what fantastic supporters we have and for that we can not thank you enough,' the post read.

Jürgen had been in great form for his pre-match press conference. With restrictions still in effect, the press call took place via video link and taking one look at the assembled journalists, the boss joked that he could tell that barbershops and hairdressers were still closed.

Then it was on to more important matters, with Klopp taking the government to task over its handling of coronavirus and claiming that Boris Johnson was on another planet – a sentiment many people in Liverpool would sympathise with. He also spoke of his incredulity that in 2020 people were still suffering from racism; something he declared was 'unbelievably dumb'. Once more, the boss was perfectly in sync with the city of Liverpool.

However, it was his frank comments about his fears that the season might have been declared null and void that captured the imagination of supporters and journalists alike. His confession that he had entertained thoughts that his team could be robbed of such a tremendous achievement were perhaps more surprising than they should have been.

He had dismissed the notion when asked before the suspension of football came into effect. But, with hindsight, it seems ridiculous to suggest that he wouldn't have harboured the same fears as the rest of us. On the question of whether any potential league title should come with an asterisk attached to it, he was typically brilliant.

After first claiming he thought asterisk was a cartoon on television (presumably he was referring to the French cartoon, *Asterix the Gaul*) he then utterly owned the idea. 'Yes, do it,' he declared. 'Give us an asterisk, because winning this league is the most difficult of all.'

With that single sentence, the boss had buried three months of jibes and taunts. For all their attempts to cancel the Reds' incredible season, and then, when that failed, to undermine it and claim it was devalued, Liverpool's rivals were now powerless in the face of history. The Reds would be given their chance to win the title their performances so richly deserved, and nothing Everton could do at Goodison could stop them. Liverpool were 22 points clear of their nearest rivals and Klopp had our destiny firmly in his hands.

He was also chasing another chance to make history and surpass even the record of the great Bob Paisley. In the 1970s, Bob's Liverpool went ten games without defeat to Everton, a record that Jürgen had already matched. Avoid defeat in this match, and he would set a new benchmark.

The game got under way with players on both sides taking the knee in support of the Black Lives Matter campaign, and their names on the back of their shirts had been replaced with that slogan also. Trent Alexander-Arnold had spoken passionately before the game about how he wanted to be remembered for making a positive change in the world, more than for the trophies he had won, indicating both what a great lad he is and also how deeply affected he was by the tragic death of George Floyd in the United States.

There was also a minute's silence for the victims of COVID-19. The badge of the NHS appeared on the front of players' shirts. This was no ordinary match and it was played in extraordinary times. Football would not feel ordinary for a long time.

Klopp chose to leave Mo Salah on the bench. All week there had been speculation that the Egyptian was injured, but the boss had insisted that 'nobody was ruled out'. In his place was Takumi Minamino. There was also a start for Naby Keïta.

Everton's main threat came from Dominic Calvert-Lewin and Richarlison up front. The latter had attempted to wind up the Reds in the build-up by effectively claiming that Virgil van Dijk was over-rated, although his boast that he had once dribbled past the Dutchman probably wouldn't cut much ice with the European and world champion.

The Reds dominated possession for the entirety of the game but failed to create anything significant in the final third. They lost James Milner to injury in the first half and Joël Matip in the second. In the case of the former, Joe Gomez was a more than able substitute. However, for the latter, Dejan Lovren was not. It is no coincidence that with the introduction of the Croatian, coupled with the substitution of Keïta, Liverpool dropped off.

Lovren's error allowed Richarlison to glide past him on the wing and almost led to a goal. Jamie Carragher, working alongside Martin Tyler and Gary Neville on commentary, could just about be heard describing the defender as 'useless' over the noise of the computer-generated crowd sounds.

He was more diplomatic on the mic, saying that the defender was 'too emotional', suggesting that Everton could target him as a point of weakness. Many Reds would agree with Carragher's assessment, both on and off the air.

For all Liverpool's dominance, the best chances fell to Everton, with Tom Davies hitting the post after Alisson could only palm away a corner late on. The fact that Liverpool's goalkeeper was singled out for praise by the commentary team, and by Klopp after the game was over, was telling.

Alisson had virtually nothing to do for 80 minutes, but when called upon he pulled off a series of significant saves. His contribution to the Reds' title charge has been immeasurable.

In the end, Everton earned their draw, and probably felt they could have nicked all three points. For the Reds it was another small step to the title, that important first game was firmly under their belts, and Klopp's record in the derby had now surpassed that of Paisley.

We would all look forward to facing Crystal Palace the following Wednesday and hoped that Burnley could pull off a shock and make that game a title decider. But for now, Liverpool were five points from heaven.

Liverpool 4 Crystal Palace 0: Stunning Reds on the Brink of Greatness

Ever since the final whistle at Goodison, I'd had this uneasy feeling in the pit of my stomach. Sure, it was a derby, it was at their place, and yes, those games don't always produce barnstorming battles. Think the last-minute Mané winner, after Sturridge had struck the posts, and you'll conjure up memories of a dull encounter. There have been so many of them in the derby that I shouldn't have read too much into it. But I was.

Liverpool hadn't looked like scoring, while Everton could have had a couple if they were any good. Luckily, they're not. Meanwhile our closest title rivals, Manchester City – who were still miles behind us in a very distant second – were scoring for fun. Pep and his backroom team had briefed the media that their players weren't ready, that they were short of fitness, but with victories over Arsenal and Burnley they had scored eight goals without reply, and the gap had been cut from 25 points to 20.

Liverpool still only needed five points from their remaining eight games to secure the title, and logically there was no way they wouldn't do it. But logic and football fanaticism have never been the best of mates, and they haven't been talking to each other for years.

The world of punditry, desperate to keep alive the suspense in a season that was hurtling towards the final scene, spoke of a title party that was 'dragging on' and talkSPORT had waded into Liverpool's performance against the Blues, prompting former Reds goalkeeper Chris Kirkland to post on social media about his dissatisfaction with the radio station's treatment of Liverpool.

Inevitably the question was posed. Could City catch Liverpool? Of course, with hindsight, it was all just hot air. But in those days following the resumption of football, I allowed myself to ponder the unthinkable. Could the Reds really blow it, now? To be honest, given the crazy nature of 2020, was it really all that outlandish? Well, yes, obviously. But it wasn't obvious to me as I rose from my pit on Wednesday, 24 June.

The background to everything remained one of chaos and seeming madness on the political and world stage. Protests demanding racial equality continued across America and the world, and instead of seeing this as a defining point in our history, a time to step back and address the issues of inequality and social injustice, our leaders seemed bogged down in debates about statues, slogans and street names. Of course, that's what they preferred; why talk about the substance when you can build straw men to distract the angry and the righteous.

While all this was going on, the UK government was busy stripping back its COVID-19 restrictions, and the health secretary was boasting about a death count that was 'only' in double digits on one particular day, despite it being regularly in triple digits since March.

Though the sense that all this was moving far too quickly was at times all consuming, the need for normality was too. It was a strange mix. Wanting, on the one hand to retreat into a cave and wait for all this blow over, and on the other desperately wanting to meet the lads in the pub, feel the excitement as we contemplate the game and collectively muse about when and where the title will be sealed.

I had missed football so much. At times, it was like a hunger pain, so strong that it makes you feel sick. That feeling nagged at me all day, and by the time the match arrived, televised in an empty, sterile stadium, I felt like someone had offered me a stick of celery instead of the banquet I craved.

Klopp had done his best to tell us that he would make sure the players felt our presence, that we had given them so much, but now it was time to support the team from home. He was right of course, but I longed to be in the ground, screaming and shouting and feeling that buzz. I couldn't though. None of us could, at least not in body.

In spirit, well that was a different story. Most clubs had done their best to create something that could come close to replacing the presence of supporters on matchday. Some had draped giant, commercially printed wraps over seats, bearing slogans or images of fans, while some had gone for cardboard cutouts of supporters. Others had erected giant screens with video links to fans at home celebrating the action, though time lags made for some hilarious moments with supporters appearing to be woefully behind the action.

At Liverpool, we chose to do it a different way. And, as the kick-off approached the Kop would once more be resplendent in banners, if not song. Thanks to the work of supporters group Spion Kop 1906, an army of volunteers and the legendary Peter Carney, huge swathes of the old terrace were draped in all manner of flags, bearing words that are poetic, inspiring and hilarious. Reminders of former battles and past glory were everywhere and the message to the players was simple: we may be far away, but we are here with you in spirit.

Peter Carney is an artist who for decades has used the mighty Kop as his canvas. His banners and flags have been exhibited across the Continent, and he debuted some new ones at Anfield in readiness for the game against Palace. And for him, one banner in particular held special significance, and was there to represent all supporters.

'The seed of the idea for putting banners on the Kop in an empty ground can be seen flowering in the red-and-yellow-striped banner in the middle of Block 104,' Peter told me. 'Them stripes are the back of the original Hillsborough memorial banner.

'The front of the original banner was displayed in the space between the Kop and the skies on 15 April, to mark the 31st anniversary of the Hillsborough disaster. It symbolises the social distance we were all living, suffering.

'The back of the banner was first seen, attached to the bottom, for the Arsenal match on 29 May 1989. It represented people who were not there, then. I felt it was apt to display it this time to represent people who were not there, again. We never won it in '89, but the banner was there when we last won it in 1990. Hopefully, people will feel that though they couldn't be there themselves, they were represented by the Hillsborough memorial banner.'

The banners had a huge impact on the players, with Klopp mentioning them in his post-match comments. However, one in particular resonated with the family of a Liverpool legend who was no longer with us. Tommy Lawrence's name adorned the Kop, in front of which he had earned the affection of countless Reds in days gone by.

The family of the former goalkeeper were deeply moved by the gesture. Tommy's son, Stephen, told me, 'It's a great honour for myself and my sisters Tracey and Jayne to have Dad's flag displayed in Anfield for the game tonight. There are so many fans of this great club – it would take me too long to mention them all, but they know who they are – that have supported us since our father's passing. We are so grateful to them.'

Klopp had done his all to rally the supporters. Faced with questions about City's imperious displays against Arsenal and Burnley, he denied he had thought about the narrowing gap. Instead, he mused on how great his side must be to have gone 20 points clear of that Guardiola team. It was trademark Jürgen, flipping the question on its head and taking the sting out of it.

If he'd been wearing a grey suit and tie, and had spoken in a Scottish accent, we'd have all been transported back to Anfield of the 1960s and early '70s. But while Klopp may be cut from similar cloth to a legendary Liverpool manager, he may be doing a similar job in terms of waking a sleeping giant and placing it back where it belongs, he is weaving his own story.

So, as the game approached, the streets around Anfield were reassuringly quiet. No supporters had gathered. The same had been the case at Goodison.

For stadium announcer George Sephton, Project Restart had brought with it a new worry. He told me, 'I didn't know if I was going to be involved initially. Surely, they wouldn't need an announcer to talk to an empty ground. And in any case – VAR was going to be in use and there was no room for me alongside the VAR operatives to socially distance.

'When the Bundesliga started up again in Germany I watched like a hawk. My counterparts over there were being used. Their idea was to create an atmosphere which was as close to normal as was physically possible.

'In the end I got the call from Anfield. A plan was in place. I was in! We had several rehearsals and a full-blown friendly match against Blackburn. We were ready.'

As well as working for the club for almost five decades, George is a supporter, and was as keen to see the action resume as any of us. He was sure the title would be won but hadn't envisaged it being sealed against Crystal Palace.

'First game back for Liverpool was the derby game against Everton. People were predicting a win over there to take Liverpool to the brink. Personally, I was fully expecting a 0-0 draw,' George said. 'Both teams were rusty, and Everton were now being managed by a world-class, successful and very experienced Italian manager, who had three solid months to prepare for this game. It was always going to be another 0-0.'

The Reds may have looked listless against the Blues, lacking a cutting edge and appearing almost lethargic at times, but they were relentless against Palace. It seemed the hunger was back, and so too were Andy Robertson, Gini Wijnaldum and Mohammed Salah. The team had balance, and this was undoubtedly Klopp's strongest possible line-up.

Liverpool were at the Londoners from the off, and I could sense they'd stepped up a gear. It was like the derby had been a curer after the hangover of lockdown. Now their synapses were firing, and sinews were aching for action. If they felt the weight of expectation on their shoulders, they hid it well, or maybe they used it to drive them to victory. Either way, Klopp's men looked far from inhibited. They were loving it.

Roy Hodgson, the Palace manager, wasn't helped by an injury to his most dangerous player – Wilfried Zaha. Clearly struggling from the start, Zaha pulled up in the 15th minute. His loss meant Trent Alexander-Arnold would be given free rein down the right. And with Robertson marauding down the left, the omens were not good for the visitors.

The Reds' first came from an act of impudent class. Liverpool won a free kick some 20 yards from goal, and a trio of players stood over the ball. Among them was Klopp's West Derby-born prodigy.

Though they made a good attempt at swing doubt in the minds of the Palace defence, there was no question that young Trent would take the set-piece.

The ball flew over the wall, curled and dipped at precisely the right moments before rippling the back of the net. The was no roar of the Kop or dancing in the stands, but on sofas across the world, there was joy and relief in equal measure.

Liverpool's second was in every way an equal to their first. A stunning pass down the middle by Fabinho found the chest of Salah. The Egyptian controlled the ball brilliantly, gave Hennessey in the Palace goal the eye, and slotted it into the net with ease. The Reds were 2-0 up now and coasting.

At home I still felt tense, but in truth there was no need to worry. Opta's heat map would later show that for the first time since records began in 2008, a team had not managed a single touch in the opposition penalty area. Liverpool had declared their own lockdown and Alisson could have gone home to play guitar if he'd liked.

The second half was more of the same, with Klopp's men imperious in every department. It's worth noting also that this was a Crystal Palace team that had won their previous four games. They were no match for Liverpool in this mood though.

As if to drive home the point, Fabinho, who had been peerless in the middle of the park, accepted a short pass from Robertson and fired a stunning shot from fully 30 yards into the Kop goal. It was a strike worthy of a crowd, deserving of that thunderous cry we have become so used to down the years. It would have to content itself with our admiration from afar, but our appreciation was not diminished by distance.

Three stupendous goals from a trio of scorers but the Reds weren't finished yet. They had arguably saved their best for last. This time their attacking triad combined to carve open Palace and seal three points for Liverpool and leave them just two points from the title we all craved.

Mané picked up the ball in the centre of the pitch, quickly switched it to Firmino and immediately raced forward in anticipation of what was to come. The Brazilian fed Salah, who spotted the run of his Senegalese strike partner and fed him with a delightful slide-rule pass. Mané took the ball on and, opening up his body, stroked his shot into the far corner and past the outstretched hand of Hennessey.

Sadio had started the move and finished it in a move that underlined the brilliance of Liverpool's front three, Individually, they are simply incredible, but put them together and the resultant alchemy produces something akin to magic. It will take some player to break up that partnership, and it is little wonder Klopp and Liverpool blinked in the pursuit of Timo Werner.

With the game now over, we could all now relax. Whether we would win the title hadn't really been in question since January, though world events had intervened to cloud minds, well my mind at least. Most Reds had been utterly convinced of the championship since the moment that Salah raced on to an Alisson clearance and grabbed Liverpool's second against United, under that crimson sky.

However, the null and void arguments of the intervening months had left people like me wondering if the fates had other ideas. Would our hubris on that day back at the dawning of the year cause us to stumble once more? However, after the Palace win, I'm certain that, had I been standing in Block 109 during this game, even the most cautious and superstitious among us would have been singing 'we're going to win the league'.

The only question now was when and not if, and by how many points would they win it. The gauntlet had been thrown down in front of City, who faced Chelsea at Stamford Bridge the following night. How would they respond? Could they delay Liverpool's title party for another week?

As has so often been the case during the 2019/20 season, Pep Guardiola's men proved incapable of rising to any of Jürgen Klopp's challenges.

Reds in Heaven as City Crumble at the Bridge: Liverpool Become Champions Under Lockdown

Following Liverpool's complete destruction of Crystal Palace on 24 June, all the tension evaporated. After the derby draw on the Sunday, deep down in the darkest recesses of my soul, I had entertained the fear that we would stumble on for the remaining games and barely limp over the line. Oh, let's be honest, it was worse than that. I worried we'd fall apart and throw it all away. There, I've said it.

I wasn't the only one either. The *Irish Examiner*'s Steven Kelly tweeting in reference to Liverpool's inhibited display as contrasted with City's exuberant and free-flowing style, said this: 'Team playing without fear v team that is probably shitting itself and carrying crippling loads of expectation.

'Shouldn't make 20 points difference by game 38, but it won't be 20 by the end that's for sure.'

It might have chimed perfectly with what my dark psyche was telling me, but it was the last thing I wanted to read as I scrolled through my timeline. So the victory that put us just two points from heaven also removed a huge great millstone from around my neck. We could win the title now, without kicking a ball, if City failed to defeat Chelsea on 25 June. Or, if not, we could secure number 19 at the Etihad the following week, and even if that didn't happen there would still be six games left to grab those precious points.

As Anfield fell into darkness, and the players left for home, a discussion broke out in the Sky Sports studio between Graeme Souness and Jamie Redknapp about what the ideal title-winning scenario would be, and I found myself siding with Harry's lad.

Souness, not surprisingly given how he played the game, wanted the Reds to win it 'on the pitch'. It was about going to their place and planting a marker for next season, he suggested. Souness does like to plant his flags in opposition pitches to be fair.

That's exactly the spirit you want in a midfield general and given Redknapp and I have never been described in those terms, we both disagreed with Graeme. 'Listen, it's been 30 years. I joined after they won the last one, so I blame myself,' joked Jamie. 'I just want it done and out of the way.'

Winning the league while you're not even playing may not be ideal, but it was fine by me. It would mean we could sit back and relax as we dined at the top table while everybody squabbled and scrambled around for the crumbs. It would mean the celebrations could start early.

Chelsea were chasing a top-four finish and with Manchester United breathing down their necks, they had no choice but to take the game seriously. City, meanwhile, had a fixture pile-up in the offing and the FA Cup to think of. Pep Guardiola suggested he may rest his key players, and Jürgen Klopp joked that he had a promising career playing poker, should things not work out in football.

In the end, Pep fielded a team that should have been capable of winning the game. They didn't of course, and Liverpool supporters would break down the gates of heaven as a mixture of relief and ecstasy engulfed us all.

Not being prepared to risk bankruptcy by adding a BT Sport subscription to my Sky Sports one, I was forced to follow the game via a mix of Twitter, the Premier League app on my phone and the various shouts and screams from my neighbours' gardens. I may have splashed the cash for a title decider involving the Reds to be fair.

Chelsea had gone one up in the first half, and it became difficult to avoid the idea that it was actually going to happen. Though as the minutes ticked by, I became obsessed with the idea that even thinking City were going to drop points may cause the universe to intervene. Football brings out my insanely irrational side in a way nothing else can.

Then, in a moment of second-half weakness, I turned on Sky Sports only to see Matt Le Tissier – who was watching the game on a screen I couldn't see because of broadcasting contracts – confirm my worst fears by informing viewers that Kevin De Bruyne had equalised with a stunning free kick. I could only conclude that I had jinxed it, and went back to pacing around the garden, while frantically checking my phone utterly convinced that Pep's men would go on and win the game.

As if to rub it in, a text from a mate informed me that Sterling had hit the post and my heart sank. It's only a matter of time before they're in front, I thought. Then a roar went up from a neighbour's garden. I checked the Premier League's app, but it was still showing the game was 1-1. By now I had also convinced myself Twitter was cursed, so I couldn't look at that for an update.

It all hinged on whether the roar from distant gardens had come from a family of Evertonians or Reds, because something had definitely just happened. I frantically refreshed the screen to no avail, then a message from a friend said 'Penalty!' I relented and looked at Twitter, to see that there was a VAR check, then saw a post from Gary Lineker declaring that 'Fernandinho had surely handed Liverpool the title'. Then, the people behind the fences confirmed it with a huge primal scream.

More pacing followed along with an agony of waiting. My watch said the game must be over, but a text message said there were six minutes of injury time. Six! 'Where did they get that from,' I moaned, apparently oblivious to the fact that I wasn't watching the game and had no idea if that was a reasonable amount of time or not. This was becoming unbearable.

Eventually, I went inside and watched as a smiling Le Tissier told us all that the referee was about to blow the whistle and Liverpool would be crowned Premier League champions. It was all a surreal dream and it felt like it was happening to someone else. After everything we had gone through, after three decades, it came down to this. A referee's whistle in a stadium 200 miles away, in a game we weren't even involved in would deliver the holy grail.

How do I describe my feelings at that moment? Where do I even begin? I wrote about it on This is Anfield the following day, and I'm not sure I could better those words here, so I will repeat them: 'Where do I begin? I could talk about the fact that my granddad, George Maguire, after returning from the war, stood on the Kop throughout the 1946/1947 season as Liverpool marched to their first league title in 24 years.

'Or how he would start a family around the same time, and my mum would soon enter the world. She'd grow up in the same tradition, but she would wait 17 years to see the Reds win their next league crown. Three years later she married a Red called William, my dad, and I was born later that same year, in 1967.

'I'd wait just six years before the Reds clinched another title. I'd witness another ten of them in my spoilt (in the footballing sense) upbringing. In 1990, as I stood on the same terrace that my mother, father and my grandfather had stood on, I would watch the Reds clinch their 18th and my 11th First Division title. I had become part of a tradition that now stretched back more than 40 years, a birthright almost.

'Five years later my son was born. If you had approached me as I celebrated that night and told me that I would become a dad before the decade was out, I'd have laughed in your face. At 22, I felt barely mature enough to take care of myself, never mind anyone else.

'If you had said that my son would wait 25 years before witnessing the Reds become champions of England, I'd have turned the air blue.

'His has been the longest wait. I think of all the things that have happened in that time, the fall and rise of nations, the transformation of the city in which we live and the near destruction of the club we both love, at the hands of two hucksters from across the Atlantic.

'Then, eventually, miraculously our paths would collide with Jürgen Klopp and Liverpool could once more reclaim its place at the very top. It hardly seems real and it swamps me in a wave of emotion.

'So as the clock ticked down on the game between Chelsea and City, with the Londoners leading 2-1, I'm not sure I will ever be able to describe my emotions. But what would eventually become this piece of writing was careering around my head.

'I thought of my mum and my grandad, who are no longer here, of the best mate I said goodbye to years ago. And I thought of my son. When the final whistle sounded at Stamford Bridge, I sank to my knees and screamed.

'All around the house fireworks lit the sky, and the thunderclaps filled my ears. In the streets outside car horns sounded and neighbours cried out in joy. I reached for the phone and called him, but I could barely speak.

'"We did it, lad. We did it at last," I somehow said, through choking tears.

'"I know, Dad. I can't believe it."

'"Believe it, son."'

The Reds had won the title with seven games to spare, and though 24 June would go down as the latest a title had ever been won by calendar date, it was the earliest ever in terms of competition round. The gap to our nearest rivals was 23 points and should it stay that way, it would surpass the 19-point gap set by City. There was also the possibility of achieving a record-breaking 107 points if they could win their remaining seven games. Liverpool were also now the only team to simultaneously hold Premier League, Champions League, FIFA Club World Cup and UEFA Super Cup titles.

This was certainly an incredible manager and team, one for the ages. More importantly though, they had delivered what we had craved for decades. The Reds had reclaimed their place at the summit of English football and in doing so would silence an army of critics.

A tearful Jürgen Klopp would bow out of an interview live on air that night, as he was overcome with emotion. The magnitude of the achievement overwhelmed him. He later said that the triumph was forged in the spirit and soul of Kenny Dalglish and built on the legs of Steven Gerrard. The credit, according to Klopp, belonged everywhere but at his door.

The German's modesty aside, this was his achievement. Sure, it had been fired by an incredible bond between manager, players and supporters. The famed 'Holy Trinity' had never been stronger, and Anfield and the travelling Kop had pushed the Reds over the line many times. It's true also that Liverpool's glorious past has inspired us, but it was Jürgen who reminded us that we needed to create new stories and make our own history.

It was Klopp who put the fractured trinity back together, it was he who turned doubters into believers, and merely great players into world beaters, and it was he who assembled one of the best backroom teams in modern football history. An old saying, often quoted in management and leadership seminars, states that 'a wise man surrounds himself with people who can do and know things he doesn't'. If that's true, and I think it is, then Klopp was the wisest man in football.

Danke Jürgen.

The Damn Bursts: The Mindless Few and the Perils of Tribalism

On Thursday, 24 June, after three months of a lockdown that was already being eased by Parliament, and after supporters had heeded calls to stay away from stadia when the season restarted, they could hold back no more. In a great wave of euphoria, a sea of Liverpool supporters descended upon the streets of Anfield. They had come to their holy place, to be together and to celebrate a first league title in 30 years.

Decades of pent-up emotion collided with months of social isolation and powered by sheer relief and joy exploded in a celebration of colour, songs and banners. The police were there, they stood back and allowed it to happen. Their light-touch approach is to be applauded. While from a public health point of view it was risky, this was not criminal activity.

Cars streamed past the Paisley Gates, sounding their horns as they went, and supporters clambered on railings, lit flares and serenaded their heroes. In the skies above what seemed like a thousand tonnes of ordinance exploded and the smell of gunpowder was all around. This was a celebration, decades in the making. Thirty years had ended and there was no holding back the red tide for many.

Sixty-one-year-old Marie Eakins was there, outside Anfield, and told me how she had seen nothing like it in her life. Summing up the joyous carnival atmosphere, she said, 'I've been a red for as long as I can remember. I've been through the highs and the lows as well as the most emotional times with this club, but Anfield last night was an entirely unique atmosphere. I wouldn't have missed it for the world.'

Many rival supporters, particularly those of a Blue persuasion saw their chance and took to social media to complain about the noise, while others moralised about the behaviour of people who merely wanted to celebrate something joyous after three months of feeling cut off from the world, their families and their team. As disingenuous as that was, they did have a point about the risks of thousands congregating at close quarters.

The pandemic had not gone away, and Liverpool as a city was still disproportionately affected. The risk of a second wave was real and present. Spirit of Shankly, Liverpool Football Club, the council and the police had all appealed to supporters to celebrate at home. Those who gathered around the stadium were taking a huge risk, and that has to be acknowledged.

However, their behaviour has to be judged in the context of a fog of mixed messages from Parliament, scenes of crowded beaches in Bournemouth, people doing congas in the streets to celebrate VE Day and being lauded for it, coupled with clear evidence that the prime minister's own senior advisor, Dominic Cummings, had breached lockdown and got away with it.

To many, an impression had already been created of a lockdown ended, of a return to business as usual. Eager to get the economy back to normal, the PM was urging people back to work, and a Tory MP in Parliament had called on people to 'do their patriotic duty and go to the pub' as soon as they were open in early July. The two-metre rule, previously enforced in order to reduce the risk of infection, was now downgraded to 'one metre plus' – if other mitigations were in place.

I make no attempts to justify or excuse, that's not for me to do. However, in judging the spontaneous celebrations outside Anfield, I'd encourage all to consider the context. Consider also that many of those who did, stayed late into the night in order to clear the rubbish left behind from the streets.

A report in the *Liverpool Echo* showed how, despite their hangovers and tiredness many chose to stay behind and clear up.

'The streets surrounding Anfield were left strewn with beer cans and bottles after fans came out last night to celebrate the club's first Premier League win in 30 years,' it said. 'Today, Sky News north of England correspondent Tom Parmenter tweeted, "Just watching some Liverpool fans helping tidy up some of the bottles and cans left strewn around Anfield after the celebrations last night. They haven't been to bed yet."'

Attempts to join bandwagons and to label and stereotype supporters are often undermined by reality. In any large group of people, you will find those who behave irresponsibly as well as those whose social conscience is an example to all. That's the case whether you are a football supporter, a sunbather or a government advisor. To selectively single out football supporters in general, or as was the case in the aftermath of Liverpool's league title triumph, fans of one particular club, is wrong and unfair.

That criticism reached new heights two days later after a celebration at the city's Pier Head ended in chaotic scenes, with one man filmed launching a firework at the Liver Building. The act of sheer stupidity caused a small fire, which was extinguished. He was later arrested on suspicion of arson.

In the absence of a focal point for celebration due to continued COVID-19 restrictions, thousands had gathered at the Liverpool landmark with the knowledge of the police and many expressed their incredulity that the event had been allowed to go ahead in the first place. The atmosphere earlier in the day had been carnival-like and though many felt the gathering was a mistake, or that it should have been dispersed, there was initially a general feeling that people were simply finding an outlet for their pent-up emotion.

As is often the case, as the day wore on and bellies filled with beer, the behaviour of a minority brought shame on the whole. And it gave ammunition to people who, despite their pious utterances, have deeply ulterior motives, and who are all too happy to invoke old stereotypes and slurs.

Instead of basking in the glorious afterglow of a title win, many of us were fending off the often selective and usually faux outrage of rival supporters. Worse still, by the following day 'Hillsborough' was trending on Twitter as hundreds of trolls attempted to link scenes at the Pier Head to the tragedy, while suggesting Liverpool supporters had caused the disaster themselves. Heysel was also dredged up and, in doing so, those who sought to score points because of petty tribalism were helping to bring not just Liverpool supporters but all football supporters into disrepute.

The actions of a mindless few were being used to suggest that Liverpool fans were somehow different to the rest, naturally lawless and dangerous. In their attempts to detract and demean, they were playing into the hands of those who would like to portray all supporters in a similar light.

Among Liverpool supporters there was outrage at the behaviour of some who claimed to support the club. The Liver Building is a potent historical symbol of the city and loved by all. To have casually launched a missile at it, while others apparently celebrated was disgusting. The overwhelming majority of Reds in the city were appalled and condemned the behaviour. However, that was not the narrative on social media.

Many attempted to portray this as 'typical' of Reds, and accused the media of ignoring it because of some concocted theory about bias towards Liverpool. These were claims discredited by the widespread attention given by the media to the events, both locally and nationally. They also ignore the public condemnation of the acts by Reds on social media, Spirit of Shankly, the city council, police and Liverpool Football Club itself.

In a joint statement, the club, the council and the police said, 'Throughout the last week, Liverpool Football Club, Merseyside Police, Liverpool City Council and Spirit of Shankly have worked together to consistently remind people that the region is still disproportionately affected by the COVID-19 pandemic and ask people to celebrate LFC's Premier League title win safely.

'Several thousand people turned up at the Pier Head on Friday, 26 June and some chose to ignore the social distancing guidance and risk public safety.

'Our city is still in a public health crisis and this behaviour is wholly unacceptable.

'The potential danger of a second peak of COVID-19 still exists and we need to work together to make sure we don't undo everything that has been achieved as a region during lockdown.

'When it is safe to do so, we will all work together to arrange a victory parade when everyone can come together to celebrate. Until that time, the safety of our city and our people continues to be our number one priority.'

This is clear evidence that supporters and officials had been working together to maintain public safety, and that the actions of a minority had undermined their efforts. This flies in the face of claims that the behaviour is somehow a 'natural trait' of those who happen to follow a particular football club.

Another Liverpool-supporting journalist, Kristian Walsh, tweeted the following: 'What happened last night was disgraceful. The people involved should be ashamed. Their actions don't represent an entire fanbase. Not even a real percentage of it. If you give dickheads a chance to be dickheads, they'll be dickheads. Tribalism is grim. That's pretty much it.'

Meanwhile, Jay McKenna, another Liverpool supporter and activist, tweeted about the damage such tribalism does not just to Reds, but all supporters: 'The tribal football bias people have applied and the way some have characterised it – with Heysel, victim or other comments – demeans their arguments. And is grim. I hope they're reflecting on that like they demand of others.

'What they don't realise, or don't care about, is the damage it does – to each other, the city and the image of supporters. It makes it harder next time anyone on our behalf says to give supporters the benefit of the doubt.'

At around midnight, a local man, Mark Cowall, who runs a mental health support group, helped to organise a posse of 25 volunteers who supported council workers with the clean-up. He told the *Liverpool Echo*, 'I was there last night with my kids and the atmosphere was electric, I enjoyed every minute of it. You can't blame the city for going out and celebrating, I think any city in the whole world would have done the same.

'The city is full of passionate people. Yes, go out and have a party, celebrate, but I would say take your rubbish away with you.'

Peter Furmedge, the co-founder of City of Liverpool Football Club, praised the actions of volunteers in a tweet, saying, 'Credit to the volunteer crew of young lads and girls who've turned up to help clean up the Pier Head. The staff from the Port of Liverpool Building gave them a round of applause. The fireworks dickheads, getting all the attention, will still be scratching their arses in bed.'

There was clearly great disdain for those who had brought shame on Liverpool supporters and the city as a whole. David Usher, writer and editor of the The Liverpool Way fan site, said, 'Not too bothered about the spontaneous gathering at Anfield (still wish it hadn't happened tho) [sic]. Disgusted at the selfishness (and in some cases behaviour) of those who went to the Pier Head though. Loads of us hammered Joe Anderson but this proved him right. Well done, pricks.

'Klopp asked you all to stay at home and do the right thing, but you couldn't even do it for him. Instead you've made us all look bad and will now spread the virus to who knows how many people who – unlike you – had stayed in and done the right thing.'

Dave's views gave an indication of how most of us felt that those who had got out of control at the Pier Head would make it difficult for us to call for supporters to be treated with respect in the future.

George Sephton, the stadium announcer at Anfield for almost 50 years, is a man who has seen many celebrations down the years. Perhaps nobody understands the psyche of Liverpool supporters better than George.

'I absolutely understand the passion, the joy and the euphoria that drew people to Anfield on Thursday night,' he told me. 'If I hadn't been on live TV at the time, I might well have gone down there myself. It was a moment in the club's history.

'On the other hand, I have no time for the mob who gathered at the Pier Head on Friday night. From what I saw there were very few red shirts to be seen, and whoever those people were have just given ammunition to those who hate Scousers. I think they were nothing more than a bunch of morons who suddenly had an excuse to go out and get drunk on a Friday night like they used to do before lockdown.'

In an open letter to the *Liverpool Echo*, published on 29 June, Jürgen Klopp praised the supporters of the club and all the people of the city, but drew attention to the events at the Pier Head and their potential impact on public health. In a long letter, he had the following to say: 'What I did not love – and I have to say this – was the scenes that took place at the Pier Head on Friday. I am a human being and your passion is also my passion but right now the most important thing is that we do not have these kind of public gatherings. We owe it to the most vulnerable in our community, to the health workers who have given so much and whom we have applauded and to the police and local authorities who help us as a club not to do this. Please – celebrate – but celebrate in a safe way and in private settings, whereby we do not risk spreading this awful disease further in our community.'

It is a great shame that someone like Jürgen should have had to place these words in the middle of such a wonderful letter that said so much about him and the city we love. Devoting so many words here to this appalling incident is also regrettable. It would be better writing about how wonderful the atmosphere in the city was in the aftermath of our triumph, not about how a minority soured the celebrations.

However, the issue had to be covered. It is after all now part of our Red Odyssey, and in describing our journey I have never sought to gloss over the darker moments. It is important, though, that these events are understood in their context, and that it is clear that the behaviour of a mindless few did not represent the majority. That their behaviour was utterly condemned by Liverpool supporters across the board.

One group refusing to see all supporters tarnished with the same brush was the inspirational Fans Supporting Foodbanks. Often lauded for their work feeding the hungry and collecting PPE for NHS workers, these devoted Reds and Blues have shown the world that unity is strength and reject tribalism in all its forms. In a statement it said, 'Reports in the media have shocked all decent people. We have no intention of getting dragged into the mire. Let's start the fightback, let's shout from the rooftops about the good things supporters in this city do.'

Dave Kelly, an Everton supporter and the group's co-founder, added, 'I'm absolutely appalled by the negativity surrounding the events that unfolded over the past 48 hours down at the Pier Head. Unfortunately, football gets the blame for it. A small minority of mindless thugs has tarred the tens of thousands of good Blues and Reds.

'Personally, I would much rather concentrate on the good things that good fans have done. Real fans can see the good things we all do. Don't let the mindless minority set the narrative.'

So I will end this chapter with the words of a great Evertonian. I could not have said it better myself.

Jürgen and His Men Toast a Team for the Ages and Media Drink in the Glory

As the seconds ticked away at Stamford Bridge, in a hotel in the Formby area of Merseyside, Jürgen Klopp and his players were gathered in a garden patio outside, watching the game on a television screen. The decision had been made after the victory over Crystal Palace the night before that the whole squad would gather just in case their rivals, Manchester City, stumbled. Klopp had made the event compulsory.

The manager watched as the night wore on. Chelsea had gone in front before Kevin De Bruyne had drawn them level with a stunning goal. The Reds just needed the Londoners to hold on for a point and the title would be theirs. Frank Lampard's men would do so much more. Fernandinho conceded a penalty and Willian put Chelsea 2-1 up. Liverpool were in dreamland and the championship was coming home, finally.

As his players watched intently, waiting for the moment they would join a pantheon of Anfield greats and take their place in the most glorious hall of fame in English football, Jürgen chatted on the phone with his family in Germany. Then, as he sensed his date with history approaching, he told them to simply listen because 'something special was about to happen'. With that, he placed the device on a table and joined his men.

The countdown of the final few moments echoed across social media as the players, captured for all eternity on video, marked each second with glee. Then a huge roar went up as they danced and hugged in celebration. The scenes were mirrored across the globe as supporters' emotions erupted. Fireworks were unleashed and car horns sounded from Anfield to Australia and Bootle to Beijing. This was a league title celebrated all over the world, a sleeping giant had awoken, and its roar was felt by hundreds of millions.

The sight of Klopp dancing in the after party at Formby Hall, was nothing compared to the delirium in homes and gardens and around Anfield, as all of us became one. Thirty years of hurt had ended, and Liverpool were champions of everything; England, Europe and the Earth. If there's a tournament on Mars, I believed we'd win that too.

Liverpool's owner, John W. Henry, took to Twitter to declare that this was a season for the ages, and who could argue. His tweet received almost 14,000 shares. He wrote, 'This was a season for the ages and for the faithful of Liverpool Football Club. It has been an incredible year of magnificent achievement culminating tonight in capturing the Premier League title.'

The football media were unanimous that this was a team for the ages, and Liverpool had staked their claim to not only be the greatest in the club's history, but possibly the best in the history of the Premier League. As tributes and congratulations flooded in from rival clubs and managers, journalists eulogised about the attributes of Klopp's incredible team.

Chris Bascombe, in a series of articles for *The Telegraph*, pointed to Liverpool getting it right on and off the pitch as one of the key factors in the Reds finally clinching number 19. After 30 years of bad decisions and false dawns, Liverpool were finally in a place to compete at the very top of the game. He also felt that Klopp's connection with supporters was crucial.

Journalists took to social media to laud the Reds' achievement. Melissa Reddy of *The Independent* tweeted, 'Liverpool are champions of England. After a painful 30-year wait, the "will never happen", the worst of times and the near misses – number 18 becomes 19. By a massive margin. By mentality monsters. By Jürgen Klopp's design.'

The Athletic's James Pearce posted a picture of a red rosette that held special significance for him. Above a picture of the memento, he tweeted, 'My dad bought me this in 1990. Finally, it's true again. What an achievement by Jürgen Klopp and his players. They have been sensational. The 30-year wait is over.'

Paul Joyce, writing in *The Times*, captured just how formidable Klopp's Liverpool had become. Citing comments from another Premier League manager, he reveals a picture of a team that had become virtually invincible.

He said, 'Liverpool's squad is not without egos, but they do not detract from the overall aim. Sometimes the majesty with which they have performed is best described by their opponent. "You can focus on stopping Firmino dropping deep and picking up the ball," one Premier League manager said, "but then there are the full-backs to stop. So you look at that and then there are the rotations in midfield from the likes of Henderson and [Alex] Oxlade-Chamberlain.

'"They have so many ways of attacking, it is just hard to stop them. No one wants to just defend but if you try and go at them they'll pick you off. And, don't forget, all that's before you try and work out how you are going to get past Van Dijk and Alisson to score yourself."'

The team had been immense, for more than two years they had been relentless. For fans who had dreamed of this moment for decades, the need to honour them and celebrate became overwhelming.

Dominic King, writing in the *Daily Mail*, captured the moment of history, when Liverpool supporters realised their team were finally champions again: 'You could hear the rumbling two miles away, over the incessant tooting of horns. It had just gone 10pm and the moment they had been waiting 30 years for had finally arrived. Now was the time to mark this momentous occasion.

'Cars zoomed down Queens Drive, speeding in the direction of where multi-coloured flashes were illuminating the night sky. It felt like the entire city was trying to get there, racing from their homes to be outside the famous old stadium.

'The final whistle had barely sounded at Stamford Bridge but, at the bottom of Utting Avenue, the road block had started to form. Cars were ditched, passengers jumped out and they began to sprint across Stanley Park, ready to join the cacophony and be part of history.'

For *Times* football writer Henry Winter, the title win was the result of a marriage made in heaven between Jürgen Klopp and Liverpool. The manager, he said, 'imbued Liverpool'.

He added, 'Klopp's personality imbues Liverpool. That energy and positivity, appetite for work and resilience in adversity. That connection with fans. That love of the game and passion for winning underpinned by sports science and meticulous preparation. And he's fun.'

The Athletic's Simon Hughes spoke for a generation when he tweeted emotionally:

'I was six the last time this happened. Can't remember it. I can remember everything from 1991 onwards, though, from which point 1990 seemed like an eternity before. All these years later, Liverpool have finally done it.'

Ben Webb, a writer for Copa 90, described his feelings in the aftermath of Liverpool being confirmed as champions to me. It was clearly an incredibly emotional moment for him.

'I sat there, all alone and in a state of pure euphoria,' he told me. 'My senses were all on sporadic hyperdrive – in tears watching Jürgen encapsulate his emotions one minute, then back to hysterically bouncing around my living room the next. Liverpool FC were champions! I wasn't expecting the title to be clinched on that night and it caught me off guard, to be honest.

'I didn't sleep a wink, how could I? It was almost surreal trying to comprehend the fact that after everything that had gone before, this was it, this was the moment nothing can spoil. It was inevitable given the monumental points lead, yet this moment still felt so unexpected and pure. King Kenny, welling up, arms in the air celebrating. The current players deservingly going ballistic together. The scenes of red smoke and jubilation outside Anfield. The significance of the occasion gradually began to sink in.

'It meant more than I could have ever imagined. All of the false dawns, all of the nearly moments that weren't meant to be, all of the constant reminders being used as a stick to beat us with by rivals and the media – gone. Thirty years of weight and expectations upon the shoulders of the players, legends and fans – finally alleviated. The champions of England, once more.

'Legends immortalised for putting us back on our perch. The champions of everything. Honestly, the relief is indescribable. It's everything – and more. Danke, Jürgen. Danke.'

This had been a coronation many of us thought we would never see. Some of us wondered if our children would ever see it. After years of being also-rans, Liverpool were now worthy champions again. Let history show that, despite earlier talk of tainted titles, journalists and supporters were united in their praise for Klopp's heroes.

Elation and Relief as Reds Become Champions of Everything

The aftershocks of Liverpool's 19th top-flight title rumbled across the globe. From Anfield to Adelaide, the Dingle to Delhi, Old Swan to Sweden and Garston to Greece. L4 may have been the epicentre, but supporters would feel the earth shift beneath their feet in every corner of the world.

For all supporters, young and old, this was a title of huge significance, particularly for those of us who had lived through the glory years of the 1970s and '80s, before enduring a three-decades-long drought. John Pearman, editor of the popular Liverpool FC fanzine *Red All Over the Land,* found it difficult to find the right words to describe the impact of the triumph.

'What does this title mean to me? Putting my feelings into words isn't easy,' he told me. 'But this team, this manager and it has to be said, this club and all involved with it, have done so much for so many; it will surely go down as one of the greatest titles ever.'

For supporters who had spent years watching from afar, it felt like a reward for their dedication. Fan Andy 'Toggsy' James, who is also an Australian broadcaster, told me, 'Seeing the Reds crowned champs will make the nights riding a scooter in Bali to bars at midnight to watch games, or standing in back alleyways in Singapore at 2am surrounded by Indian cab drivers and being accosted by transsexual escorts, while all of us watched a small TV perched on top of milk crates, or trying not to wake friends in LA while watching games at six in the morning worthwhile.'

David King, a Red from Dublin in the Republic of Ireland, told me of the historic links between Liverpool and Ireland, his heroes John Barnes and Ronnie Whelan, a fellow Dublin boy. This was a title that meant so much to him.

He said, 'So many times we have come close only to fall short. So many times we have had to watch and listen to our rivals laugh and joke at our expense as they lifted the title aloft. Jürgen brought with him a tidal wave of belief, it was infectious and so is the football that his amazing side play each week. To be honest, it hasn't fully sunk in yet.

'My own daughter is now eight and has seen Liverpool lift our first league title in her lifetime. For the first time in a long time I am confident she won't have to wait as long as I did to see them lift another.'

Dermot Nolan and his 21-year-old son Fionn, from Enniskillen, Northern Ireland, are also lifelong supporters and the significance of them both having seen the Reds win the league was huge.

'This title win means everything to me,' said Dermot. 'I was a young boy in 1973 and '76 and those are my earliest recollections of title wins, along with the success of the '80s. I was at Stamford Bridge in '86 when Kenny scored and at Anfield in '90 when we beat QPR. So, to go 30 years of not winning it has been tough, more so since we came so close on a few occasions.

'I feel utter relief that it's finally won, but so proud of the players and Jürgen Klopp. It's not lost on me that the title was won in the 96th minute. That's a fitting tribute to honour those lost supporting the Reds.'

Fionn felt he now had his own stories to pass on, capable of stacking up with the best of his father's.

'As a younger Liverpool fan, this is something I've waited for my whole life,' Fionn told me. 'I've listened to my dad speak about the great teams of the '80s. But finally, me and other fans of my age have something we can celebrate and remember. We now have our own memories of great games we can pass on to younger generations.'

Matthieu Pierre, a Liverpool supporter in France, didn't believe that Chelsea would do the Reds a favour. He described to me how his night unfolded.

He added, 'I did watch the game against Palace, but not the City versus Chelsea game because I honestly didn't think that Chelsea would cause any harm to the Citizens. Nor did I follow the live score. But the notifications and messages began before 11pm and then I knew.

'To be honest, my first feeling was a bittersweet one. The title was so clearly evident that the joy was a bit restrained. I had wished for a last-minute winning goal against City in front of a roaring crowd, like Agüero's. That could have happened last year and I'm quite sure the explosion of joy and relief would have been even bigger.

'It amazes me how much the way this title was won fits to every single bit of the lyrics of "You'll Never Walk Alone". I think it's beautiful and couldn't and shouldn't have been any other way.'

Rick Olivares, a journalist based in Manila, in the Philippines, felt reborn by Liverpool's championship win. For him, it was the culmination of a lifelong dream.

'As the final whistle blew on the Chelsea-Man City game that formalised the title in Liverpool's expectant hands, I began to cry,' said Rick. 'Hot tears of joy and relief began to stream down my face. My wife asked me why I was crying.

'Well, this Premier League title and what it means? I think I have died and gone to football heaven and back. The Reds are reborn. And so am I.'

Amanda Ellem, a Red from New South Wales in Australia, told of the journey fans in Oz have been on, and how this has made up for the agony of the 2018/19 season finale.

'I keep going back to the last game of last season. To a packed-out Cheers Bar here in Sydney and the title going either way, well their way. Everyone was so deflated, but we had fun at stupid o'clock celebrating this team of Reds. How does a team come back from that?

'Throw into that the heartbreak of Kiev, the joy of Madrid and it's been a journey. We were meant to be having the party our lives, but we didn't due to [COVID-19] restrictions. We all know, here in Oz, that we are lucky in these terrible times. But we love the Reds, these Reds.'

For Andy Beijer, of the Liverpool FC Swedish Branch in Enköping, the title victory took some time to sink in. He told me, 'After it was clear we'd won number 19, I felt a bit empty. It wasn't until after a good night's sleep that the emotions came flooding in. I hugged my wife, Asa, and the kids who are all massive Reds. It became clear that we were league champions after 30 years of hurt and coming so close a few times.

'Now I have a feeling of pride and joy and I'm so happy for all fellow reds all over the world. This club has fans everywhere, which I could see when I was fortunate to attend Madrid, Istanbul and Qatar triumphs. Winning these titles and being European, world and now English champions is a dream come true for any football supporter anywhere. And that our team did it. Wow!'

Dhriti Bania, from Delhi in India, was over the moon that she had finally seen Liverpool clinch number 19 and spoke glowingly of Jürgen Klopp. Dhriti poetically told me of her love for the city of Liverpool and its team, and how following the Reds was 'like a cornerstone that pins you to sanity'.

She said, 'We've won everything under the sun – Champions League, Super Cup, Club World Cup and the English Premier League. It was sheer heart and hard work of our lads that delivered all of this. Out there on the pitch they almost give up their soul for us every time. My team makes my heart burst with pride.

'I have just one word to sum up what I'm feeling now that my beloved club has become the champions of England and that is "Petrichor", the unique comforting smell of rain hitting scorched earth, the ethereal fluid said to flow like blood through the veins of the gods. The euphoria of our win has simply intoxicated and filled my veins with freshness and my soul with contentment. Thank you Jürgen Klopp, I simply utterly love you to bits.'

Fahd Basheer, another supporter from India, told me of his sheer joy at seeing his beloved Reds finally crowned champions. Born in 1993, he had missed the last time Liverpool were kings of England.

'I've been a fan since 2003, when I was just ten. This title means pretty much everything to me and my family, for all the obvious reasons. I've been through 17 years of the 30-year hurt. I'd like to think marrying my wife in 2017 changed all of our fortunes really,' he laughed.

'The Kiev final, my first Anfield visit in 2018, the second in 2019, Champions League winners and now Premier League winners. If any coach could pick any team up after the disappointment of a 97-point second-place finish , then downplay a Champions League title in the same season and push these players on to do what they have done this season, only Jürgen Klopp could do that. I'm extremely happy for the entire Liverpool FC family.'

Moushumi Bora, a lifelong fan and senior sports editor based in Delhi, felt that 2019/20 was a remarkable journey for supporters in India: 'It was a lifetime in a season! This season was not about hoping but knowing. Part of it was about struggling to stay in the moment, not getting ahead of ourselves – Klopp is unbelievable, his boys so special.

'So many times we had suffered after finishing second in the season before. But it was a perfect symphony this time round and we sang along merrily. My most vivid memory is Alisson's stride and slide tribute to Salah's bare-chested glory in the United game. Back to front, we have been remarkable. It isn't raining but pouring ecstasy now. It's all for one and one for all. Klopp and his musketeers have all of us in a huddle.'

Nassos Siotropos, a passionate Red from Greece, told me how lucky he felt we all were to have Klopp. A keen historian of the club, Nassos felt this championship would be remembered for a long time.

'Liverpool winning the league will no doubt be remembered as a fantastic achievement,' Nassos told me. 'Jürgen Klopp's arrival at Anfield has been the main reason for the Reds' success. After we had been crowned European champions, European Super Cup winners World Club [Cup] champions, and now winning the most difficult league in the world, this must be the ice on the cake. We are very lucky to have Klopp as our boss.'

Across the Atlantic, in Austin Texas, Steven Wilson is the president of the official Liverpool FC supporters' group. He also produces and cohosts the Liverpool Connection podcast. He told me that seeing the Reds finally win the Premier League felt like a reward for the remarkable lengths many had gone to, to follow Liverpool in the 80s and 90s.

'It's like finding the last Infinity Stone,' Steven told me. 'It's the elusive title to make our US experience complete. The last title was won before the total access to Liverpool, so we did not have the experience of being English champions. This completes our bond with those from the past. All Liverpool fans, far and wide, can now say that we were there when Liverpool was crowned the best team in the land.'

Two men there at the very beginning of the Bill Shankly revolution were George Scott and Victor Gill. George was a former reserve player at the club in the 1960s, while Victor, who trained at Melwood, would eventually join the Shankly family, becoming the great man's son-in-law. George would leave the club after five years for a career in Aberdeen and then South African football. However, he sensed there was something of his old boss in the way Jürgen had masterminded this achievement.

'This season has topped it all. Jürgen's boys have demolished all the competition and here we are right back up on our perch at the pinnacle of the game after such a long wait,' he told me.

'What a party it was. When I do reach the top of that elevator to join Shanks and the boys in the heavenly five-a-sides, I can go with a smile of satisfaction on my face, having at last seen the boys win that Premier League. I was beginning to doubt I would ever live to see it and now it is real.'

Victor agreed, arguing that Klopp's use of psychology reminded him of his old boss. He told me, 'For obvious reasons, the Boss [Bill Shankly] has always been my favourite. But then along comes Klopp and the methods he uses are very much like Shanks. I knew Shanks very well, but I don't know Klopp at all, except for his methods of using psychology as well as fitness to win trophies. But just like Shanks he is a very lovable man.'

Victor's daughter, Karen Elizabeth Gill, is the author of *The Real Bill Shankly*. Karen told me that the work Jürgen Klopp was doing was every bit as significant as that of her grandfather.

She said, 'It's absolutely incredible what the team and Jürgen Klopp have achieved this season. I'm so looking forward to the new chapter that Jürgen is writing in our club's history. I know that my granddad would be proud that the story he started is to be continued and his legacy is being kept alive with such a great manager at the helm.'

Another family for whom this title had great significance were the Wadsworths. Walter Wadsworth was a Bootle-born centre-back who played in one of the greatest Liverpool teams of all time, in the 1920s. His son Bill spoke to me and felt his dad would have been proud of Klopp's charges.

'Dad would certainly have raised a Guinness or two to celebrate,' Bill told me. 'He may even have brought out his "swan dance". What this was I'll never know, but apparently it caused great amusement at the local pub!'

Walter's grandchildren Jacqueline, Susan and David were full of praise for the current crop of players and the style in which they reached their goal.

'It's the teamwork that shines so brightly for me,' said Jacqueline. 'Every player played their part, committed to the cause, with Jürgen at the helm leading with energy, charisma and above all belief. Let's push on now and make it the double next year to match the Untouchables' back-to-back feat of 100 years ago.'

For David it was the humble nature of the manager and players that stood out most. He told me, 'It's not just winning the title, it's the way we won. The whole ethos of the club has been professional, composed and never getting ahead of themselves. I'm very proud.'

Susan and Walter's great-grandchildren, Catherine Dunn, Jamie and Ty Wadsworth were all ecstatic. For Ty, Klopp's men had served up the best football he had ever seen.

'It's so refreshing to see a squad where there are no egos,' said Ty. 'With everyone putting the team first whilst also playing the best and most exciting football I've seen during my life as a Liverpool fan – Klopp truly has turned doubters into believers.'

Christopher Wood is a Red from Gloucester who has attended 1,039 matches between 1966 and 2020, and who has devoted his life to studying the history of Liverpool FC. He felt Klopp's was the best Liverpool team he had ever seen. That's quite a statement, given the truly great teams he had witnessed over the years.

'Supporting Liverpool has dominated my life as both man and boy,' said Christopher. 'I have been truly blessed to see so many things that supporters of other clubs can only dream about. I say without hesitation that this 2020 triumph means more to me than anything they have previously achieved. I say that because we have waited so long and wanted it so much.

'They suffered such final-day heartbreak a year ago, but just rolled up their sleeves and went again. They led from start to finish in a quite extraordinary campaign. It wasn't just the best Liverpool team I have ever seen; it was the best Liverpool team anyone has ever seen.'

Liverpudlian Louise Lacey told me of a lifelong wait for the Reds to become kings of England, and her gratitude to Jürgen and the players.

'I started supporting Liverpool in 1992 and I never imagined that I would have to wait 28 years for us to lift the league title,' said Louise. 'Winning the Premier League and becoming champions of England is always special but doing so during a pandemic adds extra meaning to our title run, especially when there were concerns that the league couldn't be completed safely.

'Jürgen Klopp has brought such an energy to our club, he made us believe again when all hope seemed lost. Our manager is the perfect fit for our great club, and I hope Klopp and our team remain together at Anfield for many years to come.'

Fellow Scouser Phil Roberts agreed with Louise. He also told me how he looked forward to a day when he could properly mark the occasion along with family and friends. 'I'm in my early 30s and I have no recollection of the 1989/90 season. So, it feels as though I've waited a lifetime to see the Reds win the league. For us to push on and get over the line this time is a dream come true for me. Despite the current lockdown, I know a time will come where I can properly celebrate Liverpool becoming champions of England with my friends and family, and what a party it's going to be!'

Another locally based fan, Ray Carrick, a retired ambulance worker from Merseyside, felt a gap had been filled in Liverpool's trophy collection and that a monkey was finally off our back. He sensed there was more to come.

'This was the missing prize in the pack,' Ray said. 'Liverpool are not used to a drought like this. From 1963 to 1990 we used to win the league title every two or three years. And while we have won at least 17 other trophies since 1990 the league title kept eluding us. Now we have it back and we want more. Roll on number 20.'

Keith Salmon, an author and Liverpudlian who now lives in the Isle of Man, told me, 'If you told me in May 1990 that it would be 30 years before we'd win the league again, I would have asked you what you were smoking. Roll it forward to 2019, and we missed out by just one point and 12mm. I thought we were destined not to win it. This season, the Reds have been magnificent.

'I didn't need Chelsea to beat City, we were champions from Boxing Day onwards. I will remember 2020, sharing it with my lad who got to see his first league win, for the rest of my life.'

Val Westbury-Birchall, from Liverpool, reserved special praise for the Liverpool boss. She told me how he had helped Liverpool fans to be patient during lockdown.

'I admire Klopp so much for showing such common sense telling the fans to be patient when the games were delayed due to the virus,' she told me. 'He's such a role model and the best thing to happen to our club.'

Cal Maloney, the niece of former Reds full-back Chris Lawler, told me of the joy of celebrating number 19 with her son. She had been so overcome with emotion that she had taken to the streets of Anfield in her car.

'To be with my sons the night we finally got our reward, Premier League champions 2020, was totally overwhelming,' said Cal. 'Especially because they hadn't witnessed a league title win before. A drive around the streets of Anfield with them that night to soak in the atmosphere of the gridlocked roads is a special surreal memory of a day. It's one I'll never forget.'

Tracey Murray, the daughter of the late Tommy Lawrence, Liverpool's legendary goalkeeper during the Shankly era, felt great emotion and believes this will galvanise the children of other Reds legends to come together and celebrate in the future.

She said, 'Seeing my dad's banner, as well as those of his other team-mates who have also sadly passed, out there in the stands, proudly on display alongside other iconic flags, I just had a feeling there was more than luck or even skill with us last Wednesday. This last year has seen myself my brother and the children of some of my dad's team-mates become friends for the first time ever.

'We hadn't known each other growing up. We should have all met but due to lockdown it never happened. We never made it to the supporters' club for one of the last games as planned, but this victory feels like a catharsis of everything finally coming together and at exactly the right time. I just can't wait for us all to get together and celebrate for our dads.'

Lee Tracy is the grandson of Tom Bromilow, a Liverpool club captain in the 1920s. He told me that Klopp's Liverpool had been like a well-oiled machine: 'I've been trying to think what this team has done and come up with a parallel. I decided it is similar to a Formula 1 racing car. On race day everything has to come together. Every cog, every wheel has to be masterminded to fall into place and every element has to be at 100 per cent performance. This is the Liverpool team this season.'

Kevin Cowdall, poet, and author of *Paper Gods and Iron Men*, recalled a lifetime following Liverpool and felt Red fans could feel justifiably satisfied.

'I'm old enough to remember the last time Liverpool won the league title,' Kevin told me. 'The 18th, and just the latest in an ongoing procession of success and glory – or so we all thought.

'This may be the end of the long, painful journey to regain the title, but it's also the start of a bright new one. Now we can rejoice, brag, wallow, and enjoy the moment (even under lockdown) for all its worth.'

Helen Littlejohn, a lifelong Red from Fazakerley, felt this team's march to the title had convinced her that the glory days were back again.

'I was 22 the last time Liverpool won the league and if you had told me then it would be 30 years before we won it again, I'd have laughed at you,' said Helen. 'I think Jürgen Klopp and these players have made me believe again. I believe Anfield is a fortress again, I believe we can beat any team and I believe we are back on our bloody perch.'

Sean MacGregor, at 25, had never seen the Reds lift the title. He told me how much it meant for his generation to have a championship-winning team to celebrate: 'It means a great deal after having gone my whole life not knowing what it feels like. I've been lucky because we had won everything else. Though this was the one we craved most. At times it felt like it may not happen though.

'But this manager has galvanised the support like no one else since Shankly, and the most exciting thing for me is that I think it could be the start of a dynasty. It has been an emotional journey with these players, who I think will go down as one of the greatest-ever sides in club football.'

Justin Shanahan, a registered nurse and a part-time steward at Anfield, spoke of the tinge of sadness that had accompanied the joy of a first league title in 30 years.

'Being the champions is amazing and long overdue. I'm not sure it's actually sunk in yet,' said Justin. 'Despite the high, it feels a little disappointing with the lockdown. Having waited 30 years, I've been buzzing all season; now we've won it and I can't really celebrate. It feels a little flat. It may be because I still can't believe it, it may be because of lockdown and no fans being at the game, it may be that it doesn't feel part of the same season or it may be that we've really known we've won it for a few months now, and have just been waiting for it to be mathematically impossible for us to be caught.

'Whatever the reason, I am so looking forward to the team being able to show the trophy off to the fans on an open-top tour of the city. Or seeing it on display at Anfield; that's when it will really sink in.'

George Sephton's voice has been the soundtrack to my match-going life as the stadium announcer at Anfield. I would hear him in childhood, throughout my adolescence and into adulthood. Now my son hears him too when he stands on the Kop. Yet for all the glory George's eyes have seen, this title victory has left him deeply emotional.

He said, 'The final whistle in the game between Chelsea and City was one of the great moments of my adult life. It was like all my Christmases had come at once. After all those years I really thought we'd never be champions again – especially after the near-misses of recent seasons.'

Ruth Rule-Mullen, a solicitor from Liverpool, saw a coincidental symmetry in her journey as a Red and her daughter's first steps on the road to fandom. She told me, 'The last time Liverpool won the title I was only a teenager having become a fan at the age of eight. It's so surreal 30 years later to have won again when my own daughter is eight and just learning about football. It has been a rollercoaster of mixed emotions, of will we/won't we, due to the strangest of times during the pandemic.'

John Whitehead, a lifelong Liverpool supporter from the Midlands, told me of his journey as a Red. This was a league title of huge significance for him.

He said, 'I'm 49 and a Liverpool supporter since I was six. Not a Scouser so I guess you could say on the back of Keegan playing for Liverpool at the time that I'm a "glory hunter". I've no memory of winning a league title. I do remember watching the 2-0 Friday night defeat to Arsenal on the TV that decided the title [in 1989].

'I've been standing on the Kop now for just over 28 years, a season ticket holder for 24 years. For me, the league has always meant everything. The near-misses, all of them, have been utterly painful and Istanbul and Madrid, although beautiful, were only consolations.

'When that whistle went in London, I held my head in my hands and had a quiet little weep to myself. Immense. Thank you Jürgen.'

Another fan, Chet Murarji, originally of Croydon but now living in Leicester, had been following the Reds since 1978, and he told me of his sheer exhilaration as the title was confirmed.

'Finally, on the evening of Thursday, 25 June 2020, we reached the promised land,' he said. 'The league title was confirmed. The first thing I did was jump up and down and shout at the top of my voice and then I cracked open a can of lager to celebrate.

'A tear flowed when King Kenny was being interviewed [on Sky Sports] and again when Jürgen was overcome with emotion. My thoughts turned to melancholy for the 96, Bill, Bob and Joe. I eventually went to bed about four in the morning on the Friday.'

Kieran Smith, who runs the Liverpool Historical Group, told me that Jürgen's men compared favourably with the great teams of the past. He felt they had now written their own history.

'Finally, after many years, we have truly rediscovered our swagger,' said Kieran. 'We have gone into games expecting to win. Our attack has been sublime, with some fabulous goals to boot. The midfield, led by a captain that has faced criticism and ridicule, can determine the pace of an entire match. The defence wouldn't look out of place alongside those featuring Yeats, Thompson, Smith or Hansen.

'Liverpool have a proud history of great goalkeepers; with Alisson Becker we undoubtedly have the world's best. Jürgen Klopp has an aura all of his own yet is akin to Bill Shankly and his 1960s revolution. This Premier League title has been as much a relief as it is an awesome celebration of greatness. Now my own children will be able to speak of the great Liverpool side of this generation. For that alone, I am thankful to be a Red.'

David Goulding, a diehard fan from Liverpool who lived through the Paisley years and the glory days under Dalglish, also felt this was about a baton being passed from one generation to another. David said, 'It's my son's birthright. It's me passing the baton to him, the same baton that my dad passed to me. He held it through the Shankly years and passed it to me and my brother during the Paisley years. We all enjoyed the Dalglish years together.

'Since the last victory in 1990, my dad died. He didn't get to see the Klopp years. My brother and I have enjoyed them with our four sons. My lad's first game at Anfield was the Dortmund 4-3. A night none of us will forget. Then we shared the disappointment of Kiev, and the glory of Madrid.

'Now, at long last, my brother and I can properly pass the baton to our sons. Liverpool – thanks to Jürgen Norbert Klopp – finally back on our perch at the top of the English game.'

However, for some, like Ian Salmon, a Liverpool playwright and author, there was only quiet satisfaction. Ian told me of how he had long believed that this title had been won months ago. He described how he felt the moment he knew the rest of the world realised it too.

'I was calm,' he said, describing the moment the referee signalled the end of the Chelsea versus Manchester City game and in doing so confirmed the Reds as league winners. 'The actual moment that we won it didn't unleash any great outpouring of joy. No delirium.

'The league was won by Mo's second goal against United – all the celebration came in the instant singing of "we're going to win the league". It was obvious. Everything else was a formality. I never thought we'd see a side better than that of 1987/88. Last season gave us that; gave us a side that could chalk up the fourth-highest points total in history but only came second.'

I asked Ian what he thought of attempts to detract from Liverpool's achievements, the asterisk debate and why he felt this side was the greatest of his lifetime. His answer was emphatic.

'I hope this season goes down in the record books with the asterisk that so many opposition fans crave,' he declared. 'And I hope that asterisk says: greatest start to a league season in any league across Europe in the history if the game, greatest number of wins in a season, greatest number of points in the history of the game, a goalkeeper that gained the Golden Glove award for number of clean sheets despite missing a quarter of the season, the Golden Boot for the third season running and simply the greatest team you're ever likely to see.'

Amen to that.

The Klopp Factor: Transformational Leadership – Generational Impact

'I will not stop. We will not stop. That's it.' With those words, Jürgen Klopp warned the rest of football that Liverpool's desire to dominate English and European football was undimmed by their Premier League win. They were words that would resonate with fans of an older vintage, and spark comparisons with the legends of the past.

In the aftermath of Liverpool's 19th title win, the shackles were off. Those who had shied away from comparing him to the greats of the past, most notably Bill Shankly, threw caution to the wind and were happy to point to the seemingly unavoidable comparisons.

Some had been doing it all season. However, so totemic is Shankly's name, so heavy is his legend and so priceless is his legacy, many of us approached the question with caution. Klopp of course would downplay comparisons with the legendary managers of Liverpool's past, pouring scorn on calls for a statue to be erected in his honour.

When I look at the task that faced Shankly upon his arrival at Anfield in 1959, there are both similarities and differences with the job Klopp inherited.

While Bill would have to drag the club out of the second tier of English football, begging and pleading for the money to enable him to do it, Jürgen's job was also to rebuild, but from a much higher base.

When Jürgen arrived, his stock in football couldn't have been higher, just like his illustrious predecessor. The club had wanted him earlier, just as the Liverpool board had courted Shankly long before his signature was eventually secured. And the German coach would find a club punching well below its weight, but with all the ingredients for success already in place. All that was required was a signing here, a clear-out there and a sprinkling of faith, and the place was ready to lift off.

Both men took four years to lift major honours; Shankly won the First Division in 1963, Klopp the Champions League in 2019. Each man delivered a holy grail; Shankly the club's first FA Cup and Klopp the first league title in 30 years and Liverpool's first of the Premier League era.

Of course, if you go looking hard enough it's possible to find patterns everywhere. Liverpool supporters perhaps more than most value the bond with their manager, and in truth we have all been waiting for another messianic figure to lead us to the promised land for a long time. Gérard Houllier and Rafa Benitez had both attracted similar favourable comparisons in the early days of their reigns. However, neither possessed the charisma of Shankly or Klopp and, of course, the football played under these men bore no resemblance to that played in glory days.

All these men understood the power of the supporters and sought to mobilise that to full effect. However, no manager in the last 30 years has come closer to a communion with the Kop than Klopp has. From the moment he arrived, Klopp seemed to get the problem gripping the club. It was riddled with self-doubt and suffering an inferiority complex. He would set about solving those issues and when he spoke the supporters listened.

After a defeat to Crystal Palace in what feels like a long time ago in a galaxy far away, he chided those who left early, leaving him alone. The response was instantaneous and the effect overwhelmingly positive. I can think of no manager in my lifetime who could have taken us to task and not only got away with it, but have us agree with him.

Too often the relationship between supporters and the man in the dugout has been one of mutual appreciation, with the boss preferring to keep the people in the terraces on side. Not so with Jürgen. Watch him remonstrating with supporters in the Main Stand, when he perceives they are moaning too much, and you see a picture of a man supremely confident in his ideas, his players and so ensconced in the culture of the club that he can tell us off and we'll just say, 'You know what, he's got a point.'

We love Jürgen because he feels like a kindred spirit. Cross any Scouser and they'll soon let you know about it. But the same people will walk a mile to help you out if you need lifting up.

The boss is cut from the same cloth. Infinitely generous and fiercely committed to the cause. If you slacken off for even a second, he'll be on your back straight away. I can think of nothing more Scouse.

Shankly would tell his charges that they were playing for the supporters, it was their job to make the people happy. Jürgen has said the same, but he has always been willing to call on us to lend a hand when the players needed our help. The holy trinity of players, supporters and manager has never felt stronger in my lifetime.

In winning the Premier League, Jürgen elevated himself above the role of Liverpool manager. His opinions were frequently sought on Brexit, COVID-19 and of course the question of racism in football and society. His answers would reveal a man of deep principles. He is more than a grinning cheerleader, as one mate put it at the start of his reign.

He spoke of being on the left, of his desire to see everyone doing well and of his abhorrence at social injustice and division. 'We are better when we are all together,' he said, pointing to the dressing room as a template for multicultural and multiracial success.

These words are modern day equivalents to Shankly's socialism, which was about everybody working together and sharing in the rewards. However, just as Shanks had lectured on how working as a collective could yield individual rewards, Jürgen told LFCTV that while he agreed that the 'team was the star', the individuals were important, and had to understand what they contributed to the whole.

By restoring the Reds to the pinnacle of English, European and world football, Klopp had now become not just a leader of a club but someone who carried the hopes and dreams of most of the city. Unlike Shanks though, his sphere of influence stretched across the Mersey to the entire globe.

His open letter to the people of Liverpool, written in the *Liverpool Echo* in the days after the Premier League triumph, was rightly praised for its unifying message, and for his obvious understanding of the culture of the place he now called home. There was also a rebuke once again for supporters who had transgressed at the Pier Head. However, it is this passage that stood out for me: 'I have the great privilege of being manager of Liverpool Football Club. It is a privilege that I carry with me every single day because I know that I am working for you. I knew that Liverpool was a special place before I came here almost five years ago but it is only when you get to know the people that you feel the city's heartbeat and then you are able to realise just how special it is.

'This does not only apply to Liverpool fans either. I am obviously biased because Liverpool is my club but I am not so biased that I cannot see that Everton fans are the other side of the same coin and that the rivalry that exists is so important to the city's identity.'

These are the words of a leader. A man who has found a connection with the people, and who understands them sometimes more than they understand themselves. He has earned our respect, and I would suggest there are more than a few Blues who grudgingly like the man. This was of course the case with the great Scotsman who transformed the place 60 years ago.

Both men were transformational leaders. They took something that was broken and hurting, and they healed it and elevated it beyond its station. Shankly's legacy was a generational one. The fire he lit in 1959 burned fiercely until 1990. As Liverpool stare down on the rest of the league in 2020, there is more than a little hope in our hearts that Klopp's flame will become an inferno.

I asked my son, Joe, about his evaluation of Klopp's impact, and what the boss meant to him. He told me that he felt that what

Jürgen had done had transcended football and connected with supporters and people in a way no manager in his lifetime had.

'To my mind, what Jürgen Klopp and this team of players have been able to do over the last four years has been about so much more than simply winning football matches,' he said. 'They have provided moments and memories that will live in folklore forever. They have brought friends and families closer and reconnected many with the club. They have gilded the experience of escapism sought by every football fan and have done so whilst staying true to their principles and their commitment to each other.

'They have made a famously nervy crowd believe again, they have given Kopites the confidence to loudly proclaim "we're gonna win the league", and they are not going anywhere. The cyclical nature of modern football may make dynasties like those enjoyed by Messrs Ferguson and Wenger a thing of the past, but what Jürgen Klopp and this team have laid down is a foundation for a future legacy of success.'

I am certain that if you're reading my 25-year-old son's words as a veteran of the Shankly era, they will sound eerily familiar. It may not be time to build a statue of Jürgen just yet. However, Klopp's legacy is now assured. His leadership, like Shankly's, is transformative. We can only hope and believe it will also have a generational impact.

The Sweet Silver Song of a Lark

ON 22 July 2020, with the skies over Anfield already filled with the aroma of gunpowder, Jordan Henderson shook off the injury that had robbed him of a place in the team, shuffled his feet, spun around to face the cameras and thrust the Premier League trophy aloft. Pyrotechnics exploded, a light show erupted into life and in homes, on streets and in gardens across the globe Reds drank it all in. Thirty years of waiting were over, Liverpool had been officially crowned champions of England.

In defeating Chelsea 5-3 in the final home game of the campaign, they had stretched their invincibility on home soil to three seasons. During their epic march to the 2019/20 title, Liverpool had won 18 and drawn one of their 19 home games. They had become a fearsome side, unbeatable and Anfield was now an impregnable fortress.

The Reds were once more champions. But it wasn't how we wanted it to happen. In the 30 years since we last won the league title, while optimism turned to hope before succumbing to longing and ultimately collapsing in doubt, I had dreamed of standing on the Kop, watching our captain hoist the trophy in the air and allowing the waves of noise and emotion to wash over me. I'd imagined the laughter and tears of joy as I hugged those around me and roared my delight. Instead I would have to experience it all from afar. The Kop, that great community that transcends the concrete steps and plastic seats would be fragmented and dispersed across the city, the country and the world. Being a Kopite has long been a state of mind anyway, about a sense of belonging, kinship and song. So, though we were far apart, we were all still together in spirit.

Long after the final whistle and with the ticker tape still falling from the skies, the players mounted a pitch invasion from the steps of the terrace where I had stood for over four decades. I imagined myself, a 52-year-old casting aside the years and running with joyous abandon on to the lush green grass, perhaps draping a scarf around the shoulder of one of my heroes before falling to my knees overcome with emotion. We'd have surely poured on to the pitch at the end of the game, swarming the turf like ants and swallowing up the players in a wave of ecstasy. We will do one day, but for now this would do.

There was symbolism everywhere. The trophy had finally been lifted with the Reds on 96 points at the top of the table. The significance of that number was not lost on any of us. Kenny Dalglish, the man who had led the city out of the heartbreak of Hillsborough and who had walked by our side for 30 years, the last man to secure that glorious piece of silverware, would be the one to hand it over to a new generation.

And what a generation this was. From back to front the team had been immense throughout the whole season, smashing all manner of records and securing the title in record time. Liverpool's nearest rivals, Manchester City, barely a hair's breadth ahead of the Reds in the previous campaign, were now an eye watering 18 points behind. So relentless were Jürgen Klopp's men, nobody, not even a team assembled at a cost of billions could compete.

However, for all of their current domination, the seeds of future glory were sprinkled amongst the current crop. Nineteen-year-olds Neco Williams and Curtis Jones would feature enough times in the season to qualify for a winners' medal, meanwhile 17-year-old Harvey Elliott would share the winners' platform on the Kop with them. Though he had fallen short of the regulation five games needed to secure a medal, he had earned the admiration of his manager and the respect of his team-mates.

On the pitch, Liverpool had paraded the best pair of full-backs in the world all season, and surely in Trent Alexander-Arnold and Andy Robertson they have a supply line of goals and assists that will last for a decade to come. Trent would underscore the point, curling in a spectacular free kick and doubling Liverpool's lead in the first half, after Naby Keita, another player who sparked into life during Project Restart and who promises much in the coming season, had put the Reds in front with a stunning blast from the edge of the box.

As the half headed into three minutes of stoppage time, Liverpool were 3-0 in front and seemingly cruising, when Olivier Giroud gave Chelsea hope and probably changed his manager's half-time team talk in the process. It was frustrating but following the resumption of the Premier League we had grown used to this version of the Reds. The intensity and brilliance remain, but perhaps understandably the mind-bending levels of concentration may have caught the last train to the beach.

This miniscule and entirely understandable slackening off once the title was secured probably robbed this Liverpool team of claiming an all-time points record. A defeat to Manchester City and a draw to Burnley at Anfield meant that surpassing City's 100-point total would no longer be possible. It mattered little though.

I asked Jamie Carragher whether, as a player, it would have hurt him to come so close to the record but to have missed out. He told me that in years to come nobody would care about that.

'I'd have wanted it.' He told me. 'But I wouldn't have been too bothered to miss out. These players are legends forever.'

The second half delivered the kind of thrills and spills a title crowning event deserves, and there was even a first Anfield league goal of the season for Roberto Firmino, who headed home a glorious cross from Trent Alexander-Arnold at the Kop end. Surely that would be it, the Reds were home and hosed we thought. Frank Lampard had other ideas.

The Chelsea boss, mindful of his side's need to secure qualification for European football in the season to come, threw on the ace up his sleeve. Christian Pulisic gave a cameo performance that made a mockery of his manager's decision to start him on the bench, giving the Liverpool back line a torrid time, scoring one and setting up another and dragging his team back to 4-3.

Lampard's frustration on the touchline was evident throughout, and he would even clash with Reds boss Klopp. He would later accuse Jürgen of a touch of arrogance, while Klopp would say he hadn't expected to be angry during the game, but he had enjoyed 'fighting with Frank Lampard'.

As the game neared its conclusion, with Chelsea straining to get that one goal and one point that would secure Champions League football with a game to spare, and Liverpool desperate to lift the trophy on the back of a win, Andy Robertson would turn defence into attack and create the goal that sealed the game.

In the 83rd minute, and with the sound of fireworks clearly audible over the words of the commentary team, Chelsea launched a free kick into the Liverpool box. Outside in the streets of Anfield, supporters were already partying.

But Curtis Jones, on as a substitute and now guaranteed a Premier League winners' medal, wasn't about to surrender the points. He cleared the ball out wide to Sadio Mané, before racing headlong into the Chelsea box. Robertson immediately spotted the gaping hole in the Chelsea midfield and raced into it just as Mané threaded the ball to him. The Scotsman outmuscled Jorginho and raced for the 18-yard area before whipping in a perfect cross.

Jones, who had raced the length of the pitch, passed up his opportunity to write his name in lights and stepped over the ball, allowing the onrushing Oxlade-Chamberlain to smash it into the roof of the net. It was 5-3 and game over. Liverpool would be crowned champions and remain unbeaten on home soil.

The result and the performance had an air of role reversal about it. Chelsea once a benchmark, at least on the pitch, had now become the plucky underdogs. They had been full of endeavour and spirit and had fought hard, but they had fallen short to a Liverpool side full of class and quality. They had taken on the role so expertly played by Liverpool during the last 30 years.

I was reminded of that incredible Champions League quarter-final encounter at Stamford Bridge in 2009. When Rafa's Reds had rocked the Londoners, fighting their way to a 4-4 draw that was full of grit and heart, but just nowhere near enough. We had taken pride in that heroic failure because that's all we could do. Not now. Not anymore.

Liverpool were no longer the nearly-men of English football. They were the best team in the land, on the continent and in the world. We now had both pride and glory. A point emphasised by Liverpool CEO, Peter Moore, who tweeted that '30 years of "so close" are behind us [...].'

Jürgen was less poetic but equally in touch with the mood. As he stood on the pitch, shouting into a TV camera, he yelled out to an audience of hundreds of millions, 'We should celebrate at home, drink what you want, prepare for a party when this bullshit virus is over.' I love drunk Jürgen. We all do.

In just four full seasons our German coach had dragged the club from mid-table mediocrity, from its status as the near-miss kings and elevated it to the pinnacle of world football. He had built a team we could both love and trust and in doing so he had made all our dreams come true. He never promised we would conquer the bloody world, but that's exactly what we had done.

But what of our captain. Klopp would say Jordan Henderson took on the hardest job in football when he stepped into the shoes of a living legend. No player could replace Steven Gerrard, but Jordan redefined the role and led his team in a different way. In doing so he had earned his place amongst the pantheon of Liverpool captains who have lifted the league title aloft. No man since Alan Hansen in 1990 had tasted such joy and no one in the 128-year history of this club is more deserving.

As I bring down the curtain on this volume, I am mindful of the words of our famous anthem. We walked through a storm with our heads held high. We deserve this golden sky and can rightly revel in the sweet silver song of that lark. Our team has journeyed from flatterers to deceivers to a bastion of invincibility. We have all abandoned doubt and embraced belief and we have all earned our rewards.

Drink it in Reds. We go again tomorrow.

You'll never walk alone.

Coming Soon from Pitch Publishing

The Lost Shankly Boy: George Scott's Anfield Journey by George Scott with Jeff Goulding

The Lost Shankly Boy is an enthralling tale of triumph over adversity and hope amid despair. It tells the story of George Scott, a young boy from Aberdeen, who dreamed of a career in football and ended up rubbing shoulders with one of the game's managerial greats, Bill Shankly. Shankly would assemble a team to rival the famous 'Busby Babes' – his very own 'Shankly Boys'. With Tommy Smith and Chris Lawler already at the club, he would add Gordon Wallace, Bobby Graham and a 15-year-old George Scott – 'the lost Shankly Boy'. Scott provides a fascinating insight into modern Liverpool's formative years and Shankly's Anfield. His is an untold story of a dream crushed and of a career rebuilt in Scottish football and taken to new heights in the South African Premier League. *The Lost Shankly Boy* speaks to every kid who dreams of football glory. It is a never-say-die tale of passion, commitment and hard work that will resonate with anyone who has ever tasted the pain of rejection – only to rise again and grow stronger.

Praise for *The Lost Shankly Boy: George Scott's Anfield Journey*

'A gripping story of a young man's quest to become a professional footballer, his fightback from a series of challenges – including a hair-raising brush with death in South Africa – and ultimately of a bond between player and manager that has spanned a lifetime. All of it told with an easy-going style that at times takes you closer to the history of the Shankly era than ever before.'

Dave Usher, The Liverpool Way

'An honest tale of the beginnings of the Shankly era at Liverpool, seen through the eyes of a talented yet humble boy. A brilliantly told story, with a stellar cast, yet the real star is George Scott and the impact that his short career at Liverpool had on the rest of his life. Jeff Goulding manages to encapsulate this incredible story and transport you so vividly into the fabled boot room, that you can smell the dubbin on the boots.'

Stuart Horsfield, These Football Times

'Parts of his book will make you howl with laughter while others will have you reaching for a box of tissues to mop up the tears. We can only be thankful that the "Lost Shankly Boy" was eventually found and encouraged to tell us all about his amazing journey.'

Christopher Wood, LFC History

'George Scott was a Liverpool player for five years, but his extraordinary story shows how Bill Shankly managed his entire career.'

Chris McLoughlin, senior writer, Reach Sport

'George's book captures every emotion. You will laugh and you will cry as his story, so brilliantly written, takes you from humble beginnings to the heart of Liverpool's rise to world fame, both culturally and on the football field. It is a pleasure to read as George's inspirational story unfolds. Bill Shankly insisted on working with people of good character. This book illustrates why George Scott was part of Shanks's Red revolution.'

Kieran Smith, Liverpool FC Historical Group

'The George Scott story fills in the gap between what life was like for the men who became legends and those who didn't quite make it. It illuminates what the life of reserve players was like and how they had to cope with life after Liverpool.'

John Pearman, *Red All Over the Land*